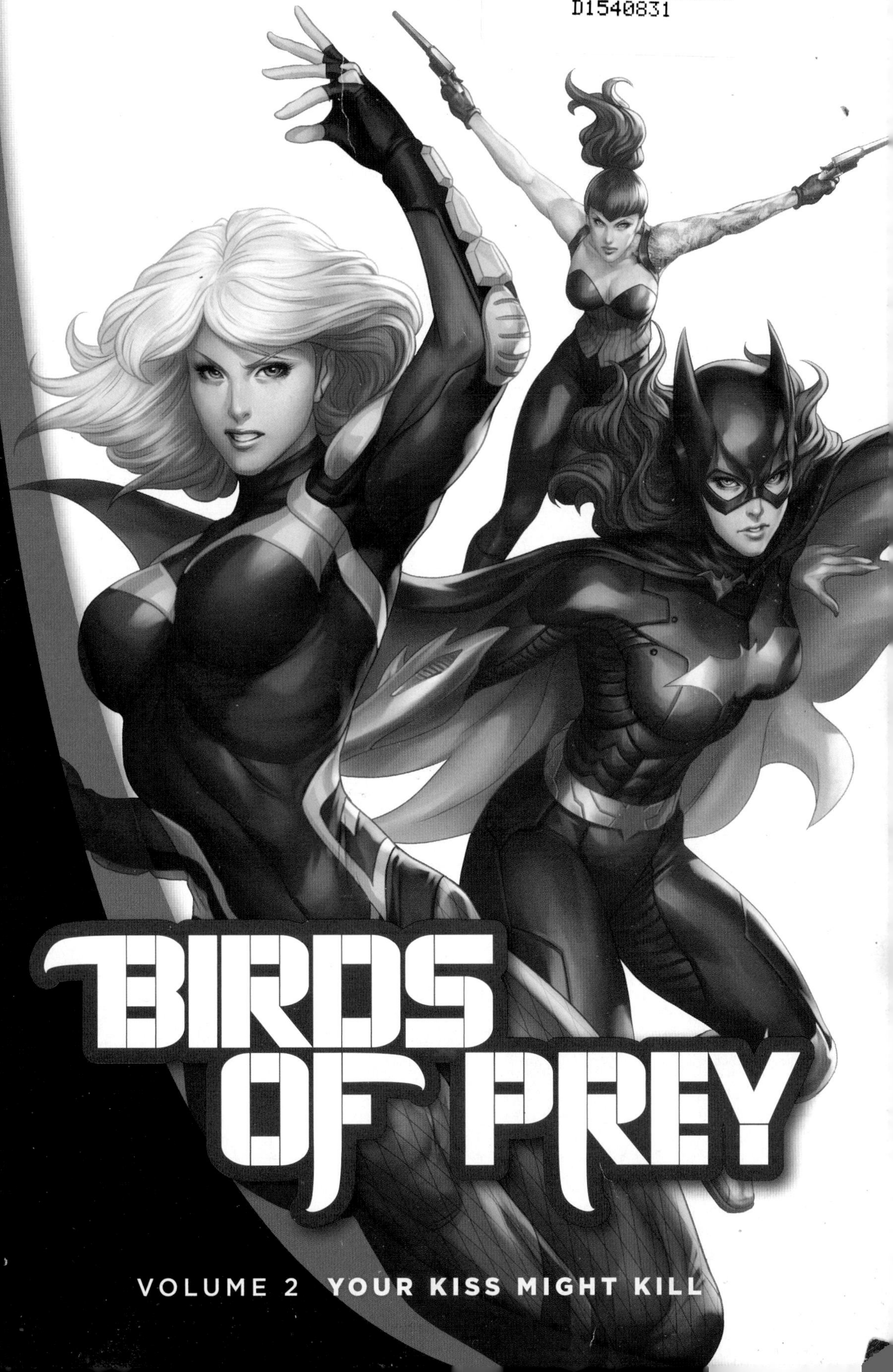

BIRDS OF PREY

VOLUME 2 **YOUR KISS MIGHT KILL**

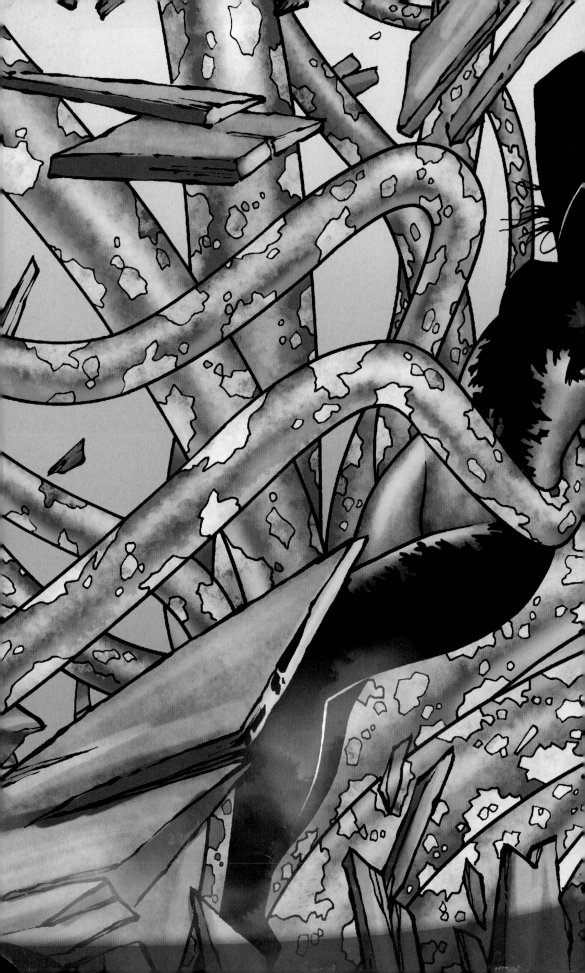

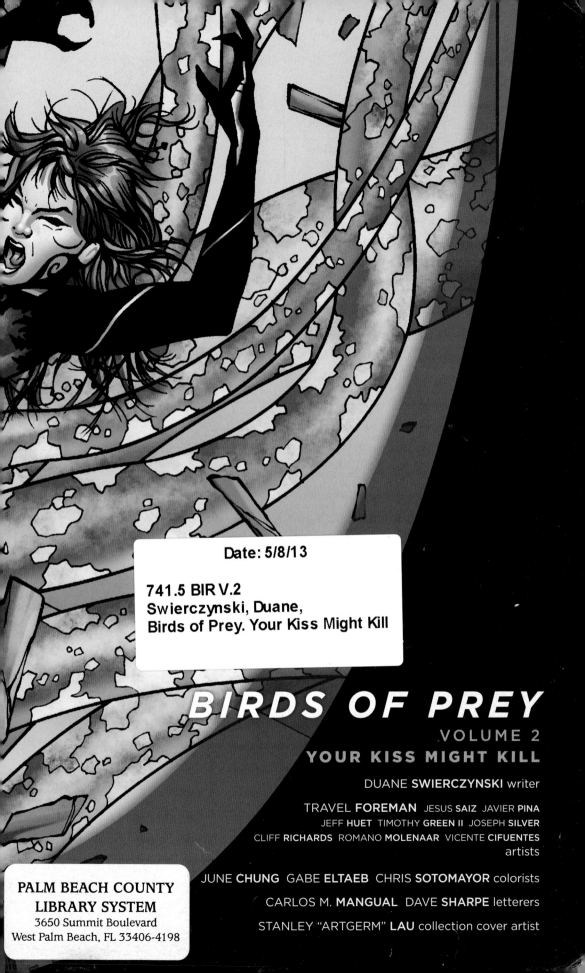

BIRDS OF PREY
VOLUME 2
YOUR KISS MIGHT KILL

DUANE **SWIERCZYNSKI** writer

TRAVEL **FOREMAN** JESUS **SAIZ** JAVIER **PINA**
JEFF **HUET** TIMOTHY **GREEN II** JOSEPH **SILVER**
CLIFF **RICHARDS** ROMANO **MOLENAAR** VICENTE **CIFUENTES**
artists

JUNE **CHUNG** GABE **ELTAEB** CHRIS **SOTOMAYOR** colorists

CARLOS M. **MANGUAL** DAVE **SHARPE** letterers

STANLEY "ARTGERM" **LAU** collection cover artist

BOBBIE CHASE RACHEL GLUCKSTERN Editors – Original Series KATIE KUBERT RICKEY PURDIN Assistant Editors – Original Series
ROWENA YOW Editor ROBBIN BROSTERMAN Design Director – Books ROBBIE BIEDERMAN Publication Design

BOB HARRAS VP – Editor-in-Chief

DIANE NELSON President DAN DIDIO and JIM LEE Co-Publishers
GEOFF JOHNS Chief Creative Officer
JOHN ROOD Executive VP – Sales, Marketing and Business Development
AMY GENKINS Senior VP – Business and Legal Affairs NAIRI GARDINER Senior VP – Finance
JEFF BOISON VP – Publishing Operations MARK CHIARELLO VP – Art Direction and Design
JOHN CUNNINGHAM VP – Marketing TERRI CUNNINGHAM VP – Talent Relations and Services
ALISON GILL Senior VP – Manufacturing and Operations HANK KANALZ Senior VP – Digital
JAY KOGAN VP – Business and Legal Affairs, Publishing JACK MAHAN VP – Business Affairs, Talent
NICK NAPOLITANO VP – Manufacturing Administration SUE POHJA VP – Book Sales
COURTNEY SIMMONS Senior VP – Publicity BOB WAYNE Senior VP – Sales

BIRDS OF PREY VOLUME 2: YOUR KISS MIGHT KILL

DC Comics, 1700 Broadway, New York, NY 10019
A Warner Bros. Entertainment Company.
Printed by RR Donnelley, Salem, VA, USA. 3/15/13. First Printing.

ISBN: 978-1-4012-3813-1

SUSTAINABLE
FORESTRY
INITIATIVE

Certified Chain of Custody
At Least 20% Certified Forest Content
www.sfiprogram.org
SFI-01042
APPLIES TO TEXT STOCK ONLY

Library of Congress Cataloging-in-Publication Data

Swierczynski, Duane, author.
Birds of Prey. Volume 2, Your Kiss Might Kill / Duane Swierczynski, Travel Foreman.
pages cm
"Originally published in single magazine form in Birds of Prey 8-12, 0."
ISBN 978-1-4012-3813-1
1. Graphic novels. I. Foreman, Travel, illustrator. II. Title. III. Title: Your Kiss Might Kill.
PN6728.B497S94 2013
741.5'973–dc23

2012046016

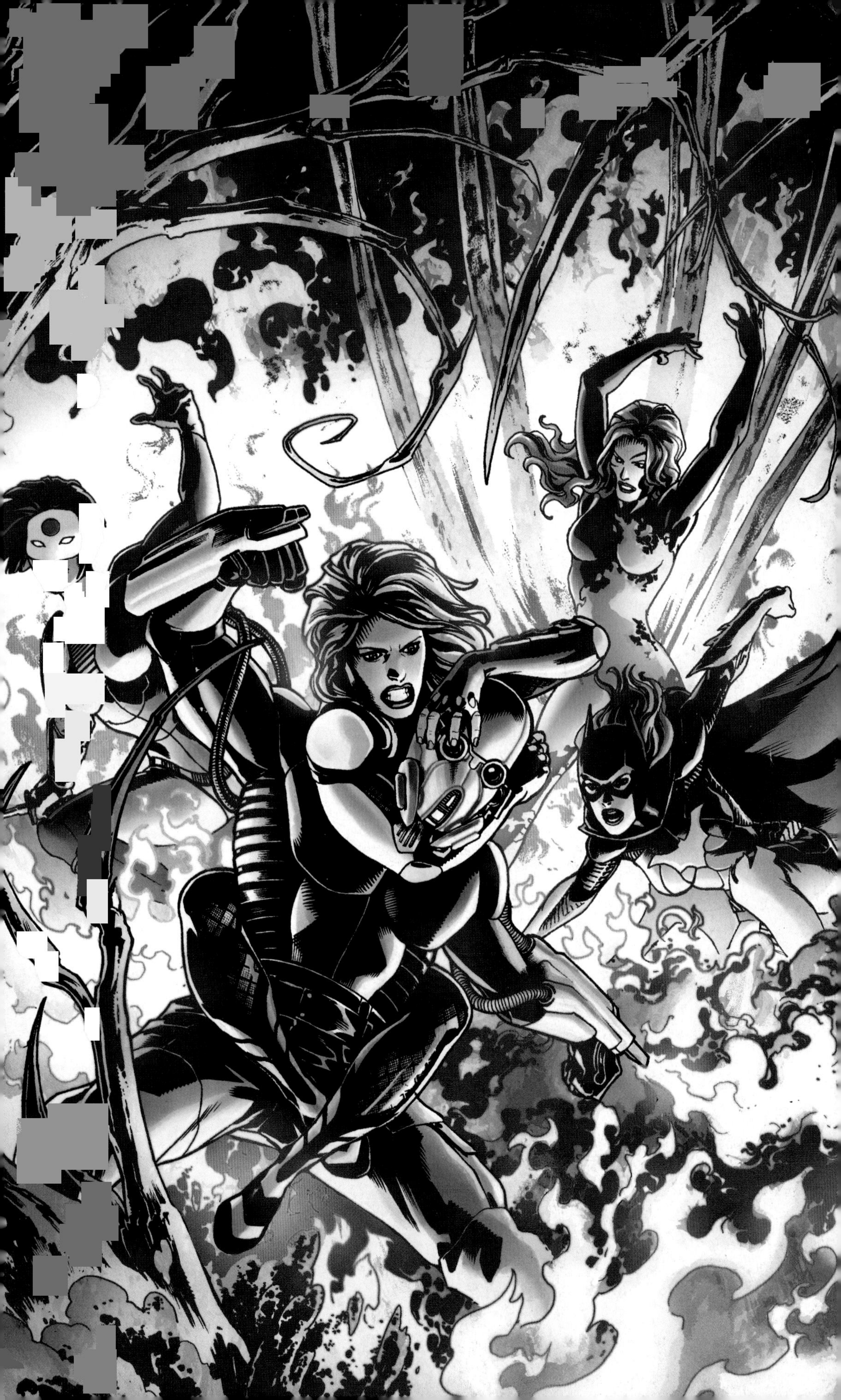

A FAR CRY

DUANE SWIERCZYNSKI writer JESUS SAIZ penciller JAVIER PINA finishes cover art by JESUS SAIZ & SANTIAGO ARCAS

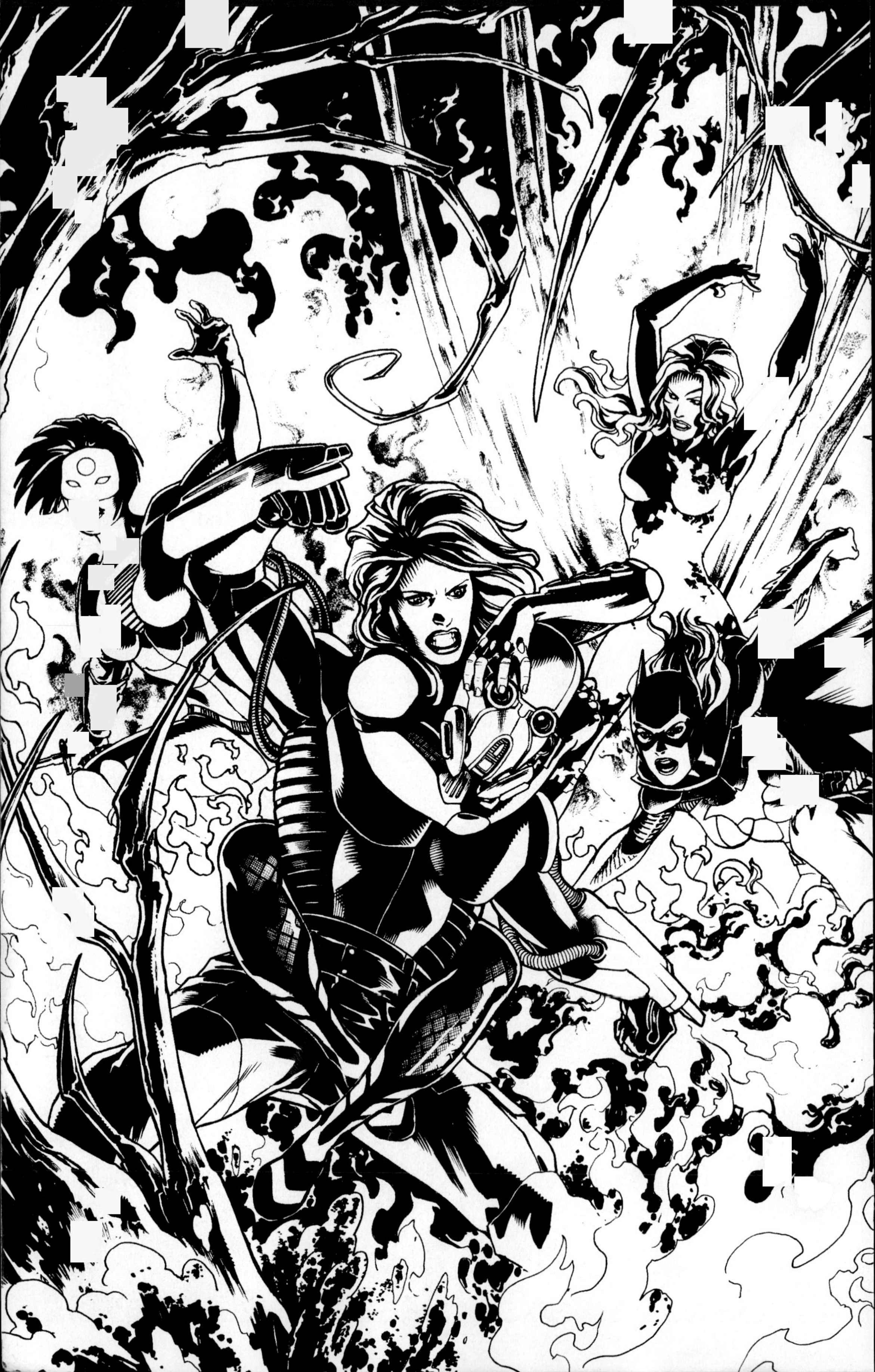

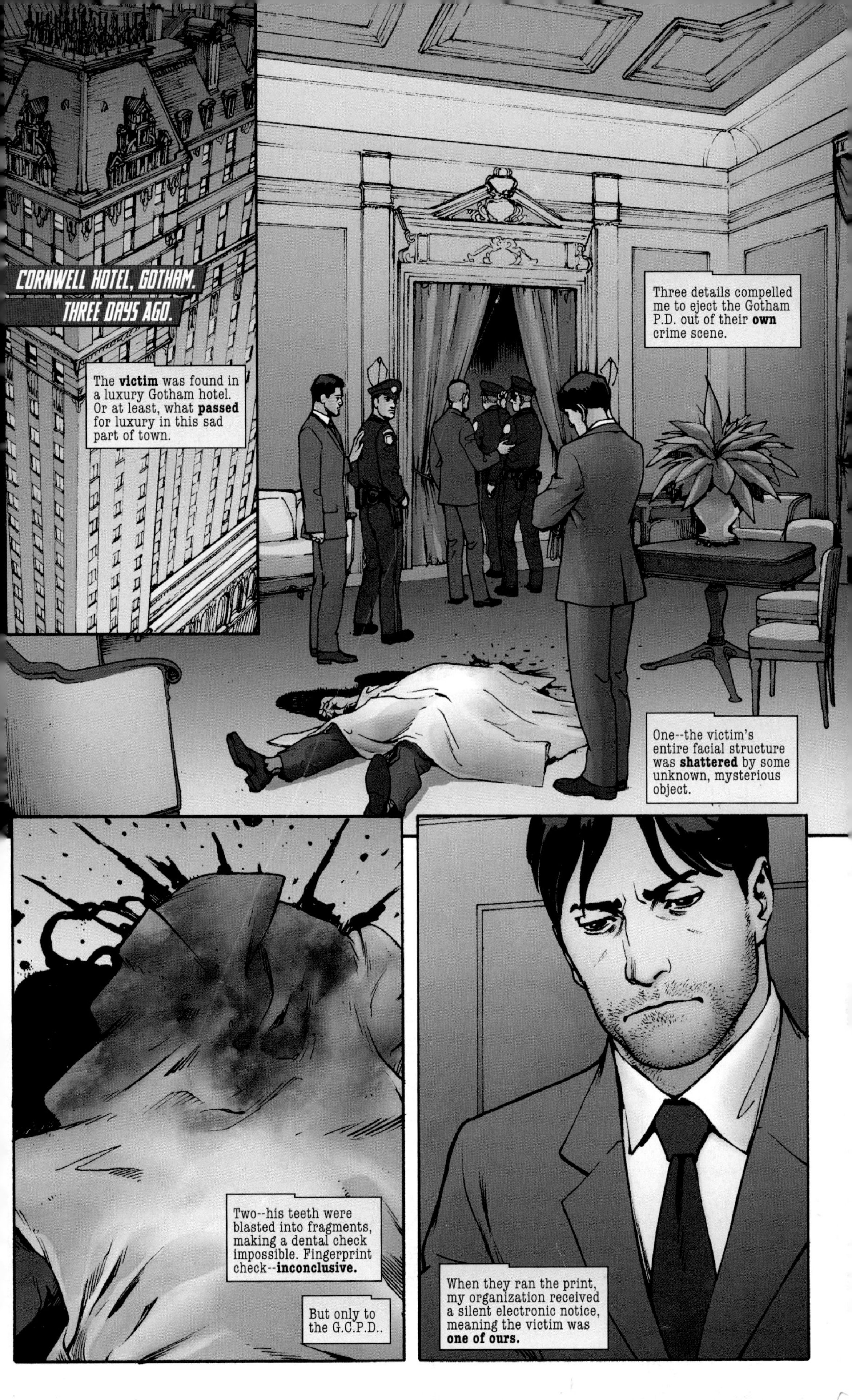
CORNWELL HOTEL, GOTHAM.
THREE DAYS AGO.
The victim was found in a luxury Gotham hotel. Or at least, what passed for luxury in this sad part of town.
Three details compelled me to eject the Gotham P.D. out of their own crime scene.
One--the victim's entire facial structure was shattered by some unknown, mysterious object.
Two--his teeth were blasted into fragments, making a dental check impossible. Fingerprint check--inconclusive.
But only to the G.C.P.D..
When they ran the print, my organization received a silent electronic notice, meaning the victim was one of ours.

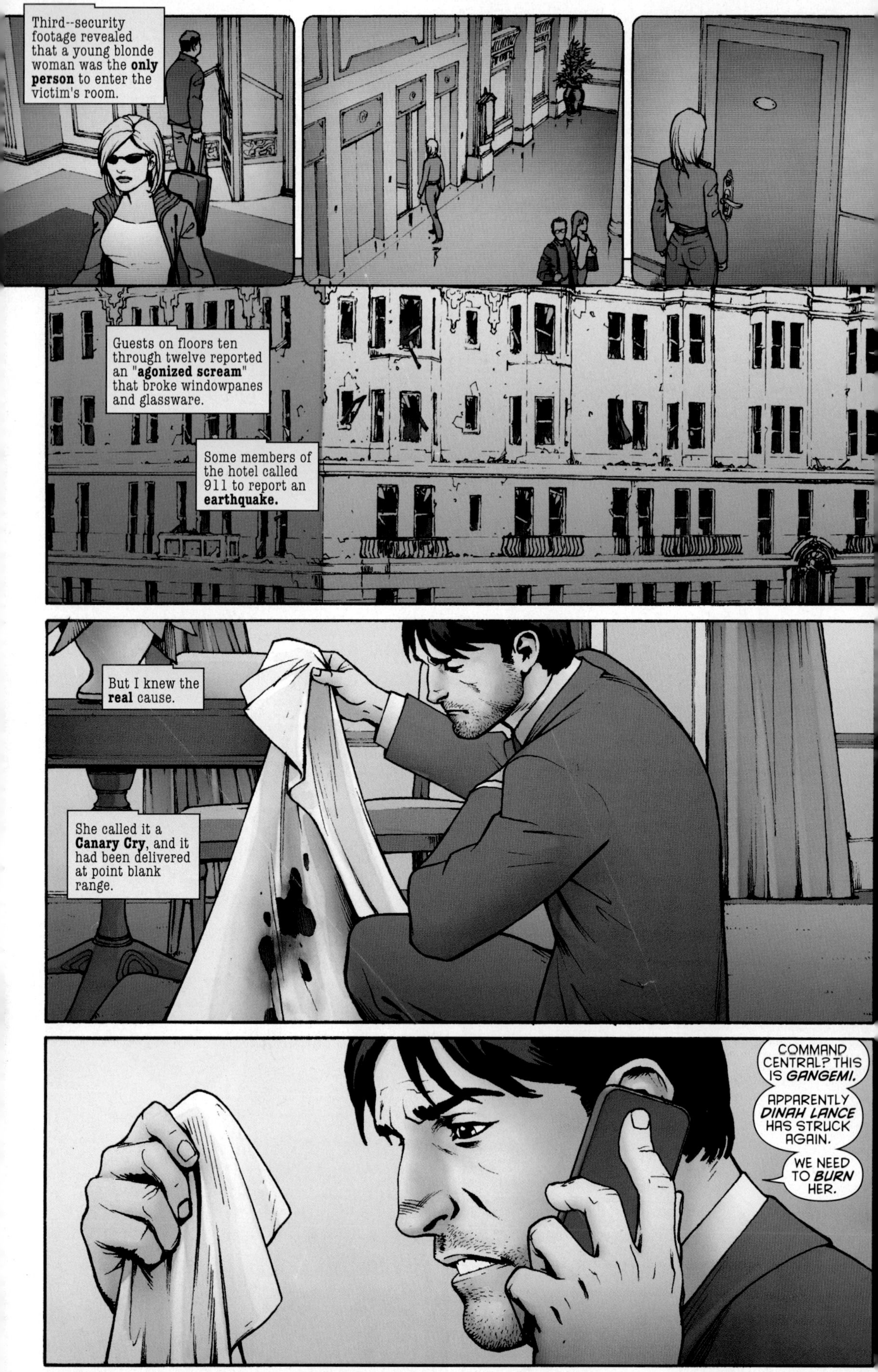

Third--security footage revealed that a young blonde woman was the **only person** to enter the victim's room.
Guests on floors ten through twelve reported an "**agonized scream**" that broke windowpanes and glassware.
Some members of the hotel called 911 to report an **earthquake.**
But I knew the **real** cause.
She called it a **Canary Cry**, and it had been delivered at point blank range.
COMMAND CENTRAL? THIS IS *GANGEMI.*
APPARENTLY *DINAH LANCE* HAS STRUCK AGAIN.
WE NEED TO *BURN* HER.

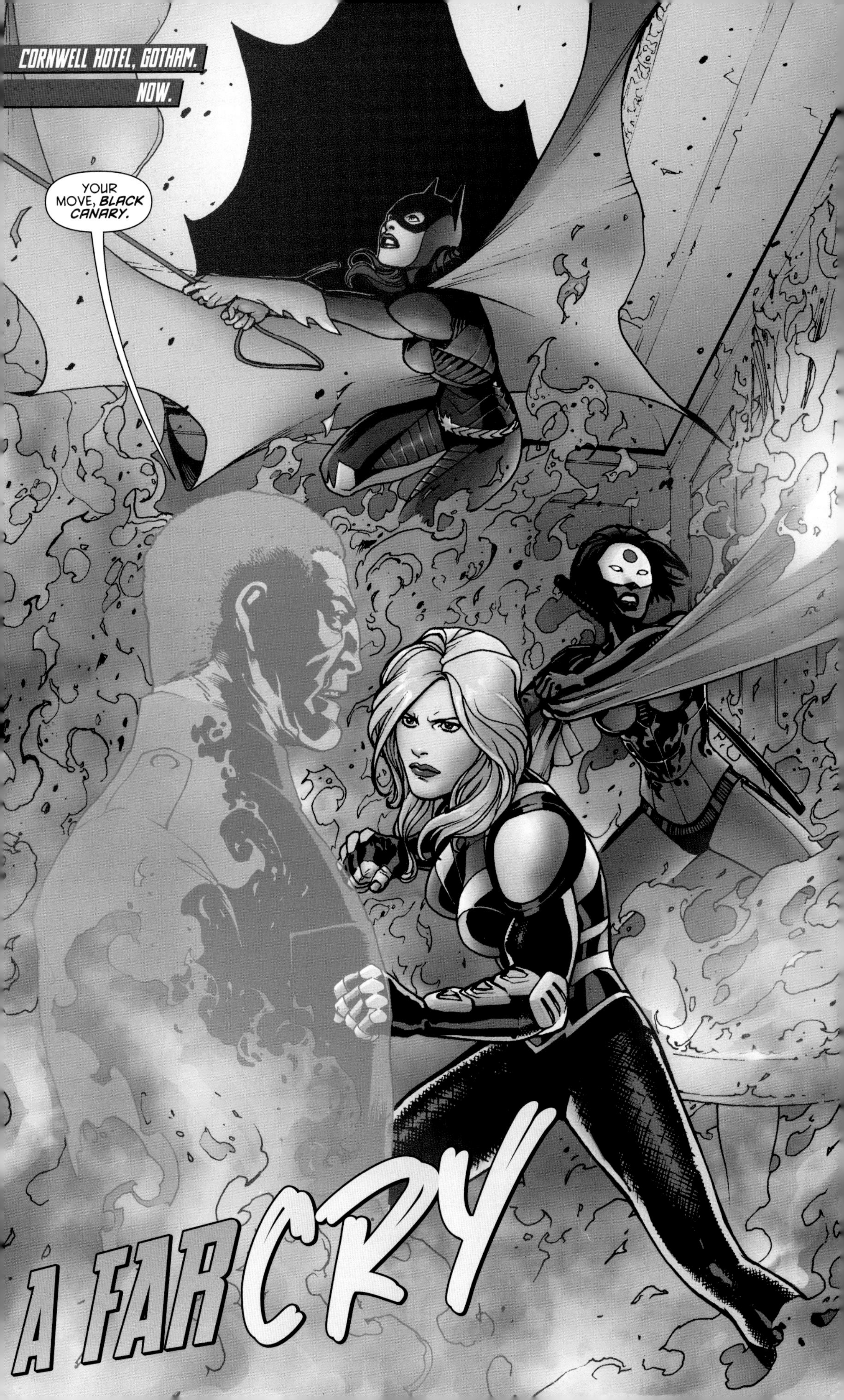
CORNWELL HOTEL, GOTHAM.
NOW.
YOUR MOVE, BLACK CANARY.
A FAR CRY

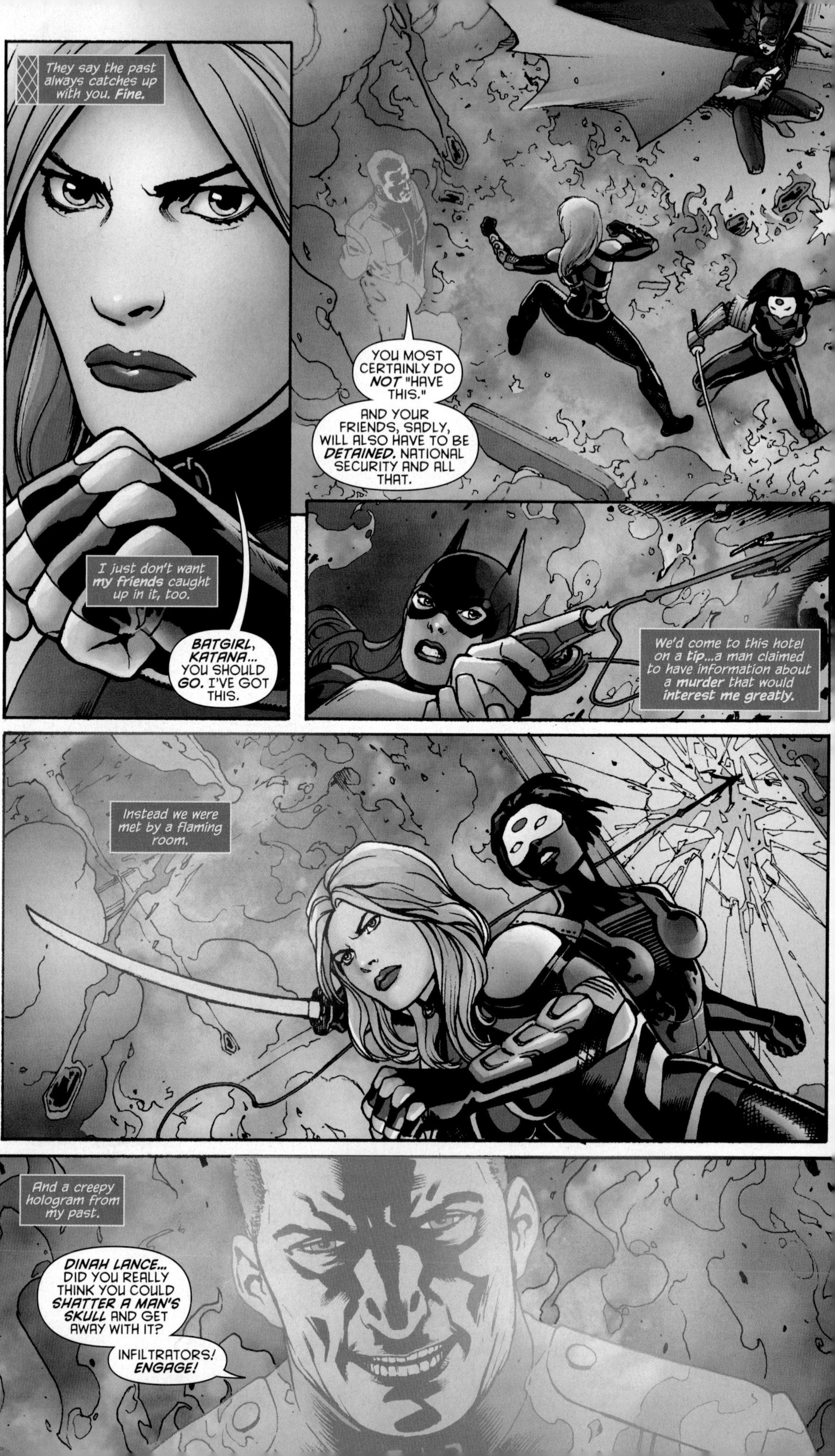

They say the past always catches up with you. Fine.
You most certainly do not "have this."
And your friends, sadly, will also have to be detained. National security and all that.
I just don't want my friends caught up in it, too.
Batgirl, Katana... you should go. I've got this.
We'd come to this hotel on a tip...a man claimed to have information about a murder that would interest me greatly.
Instead we were met by a flaming room.
And a creepy hologram from my past.
Dinah Lance... did you really think you could shatter a man's skull and get away with it?
Infiltrators! Engage!

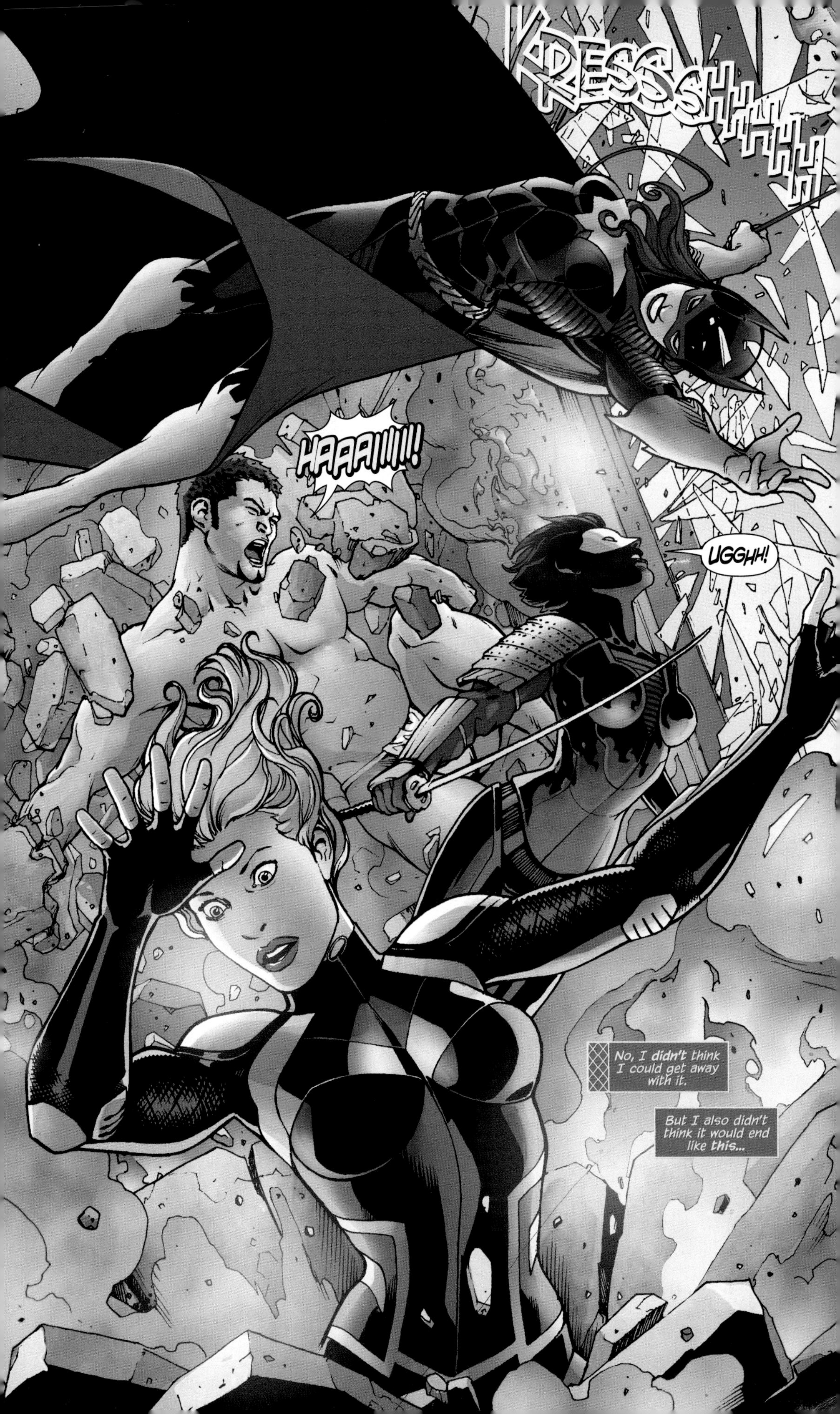
KRESSSHHHHH
HAAAIIIIIII!
UGGHH!
No, I didn't think I could get away with it.
But I also didn't think it would end like this...

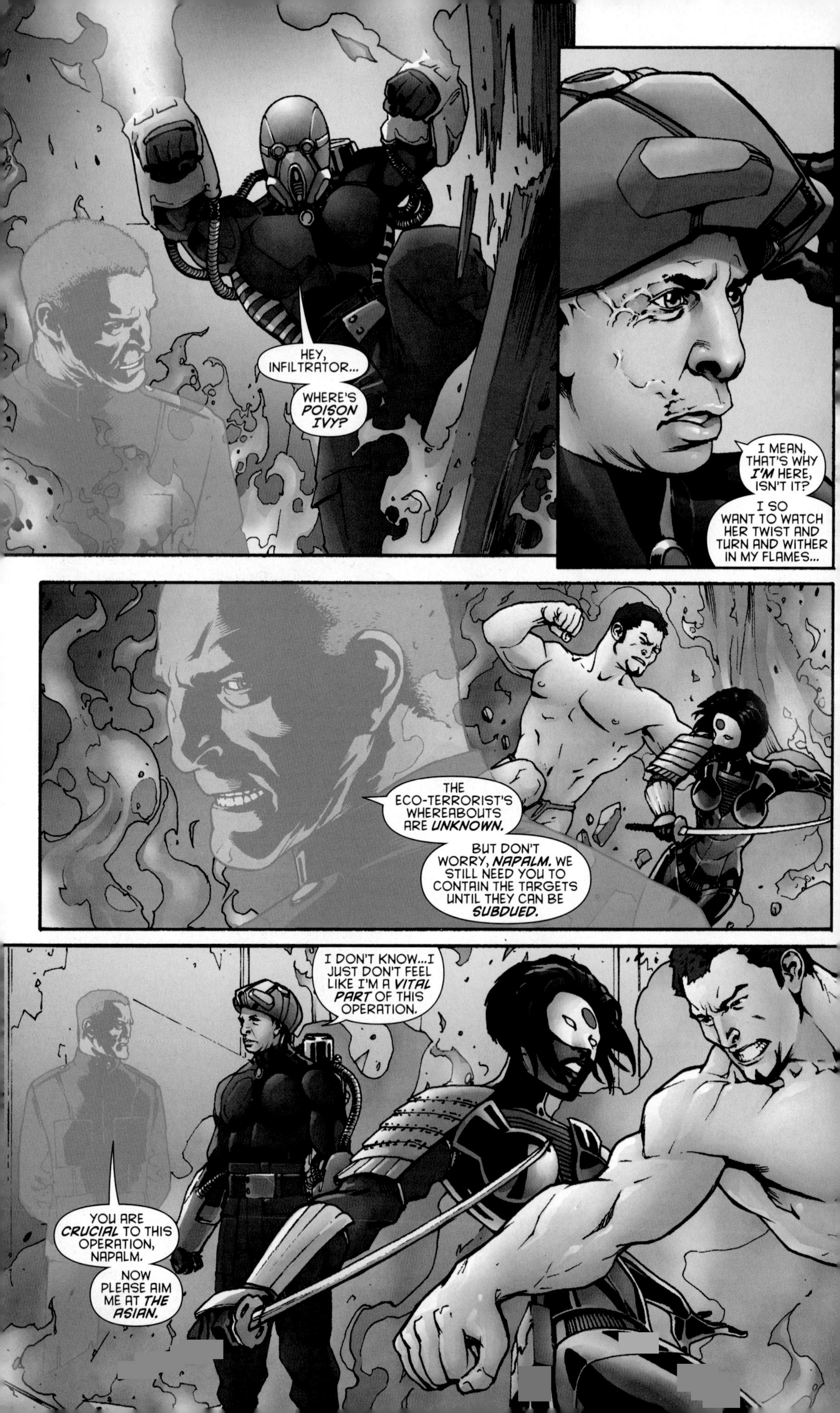
HEY, INFILTRATOR...
WHERE'S POISON IVY?
I MEAN, THAT'S WHY I'M HERE, ISN'T IT?
I SO WANT TO WATCH HER TWIST AND TURN AND WITHER IN MY FLAMES...
THE ECO-TERRORIST'S WHEREABOUTS ARE UNKNOWN.
BUT DON'T WORRY, NAPALM. WE STILL NEED YOU TO CONTAIN THE TARGETS UNTIL THEY CAN BE SUBDUED.
I DON'T KNOW...I JUST DON'T FEEL LIKE I'M A VITAL PART OF THIS OPERATION.
YOU ARE CRUCIAL TO THIS OPERATION, NAPALM.
NOW PLEASE AIM ME AT THE ASIAN.

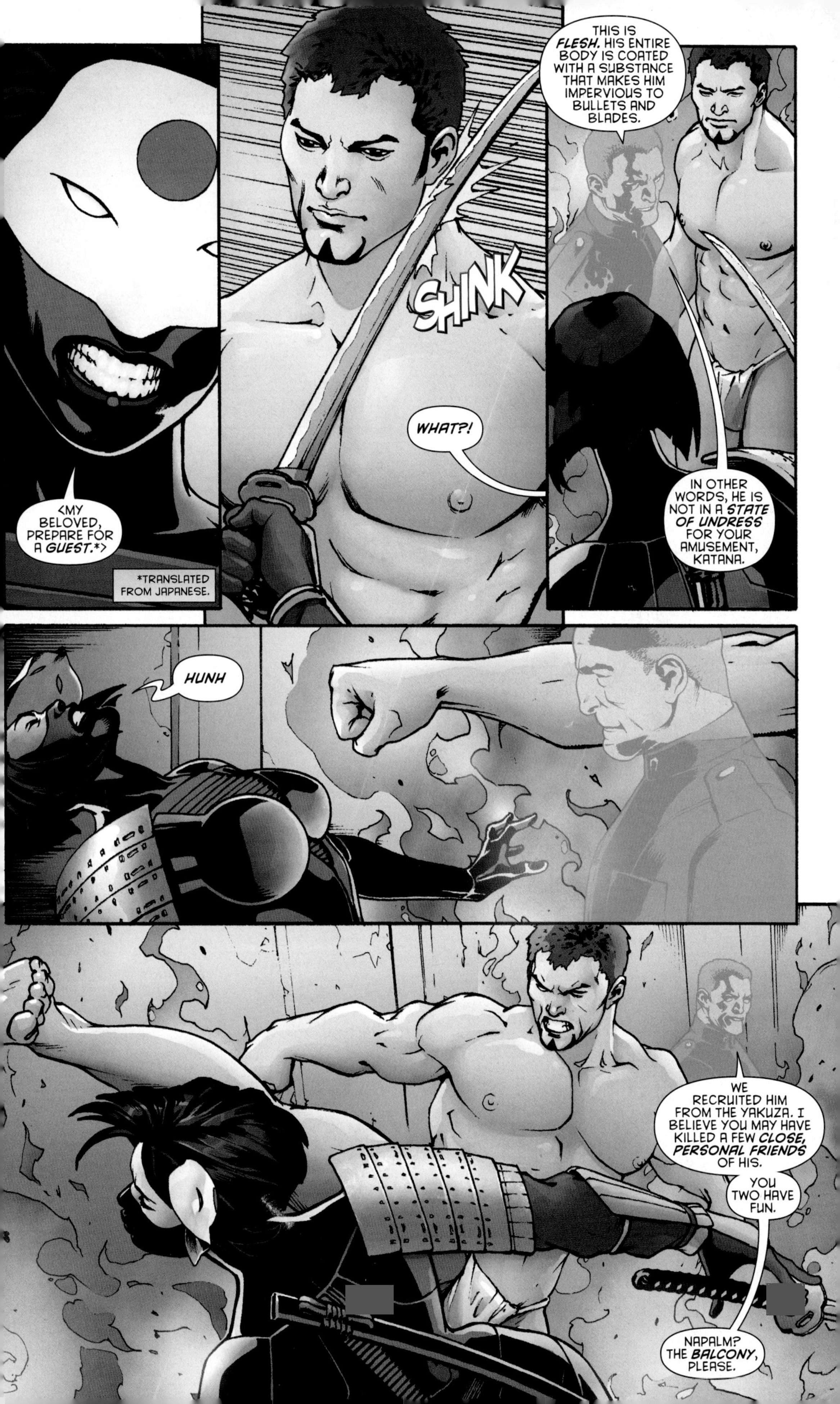

<MY BELOVED, PREPARE FOR A GUEST.*>
*TRANSLATED FROM JAPANESE.
SHINK
WHAT?!
THIS IS FLESH. HIS ENTIRE BODY IS COATED WITH A SUBSTANCE THAT MAKES HIM IMPERVIOUS TO BULLETS AND BLADES.
IN OTHER WORDS, HE IS NOT IN A STATE OF UNDRESS FOR YOUR AMUSEMENT, KATANA.
HUNH
WE RECRUITED HIM FROM THE YAKUZA. I BELIEVE YOU MAY HAVE KILLED A FEW CLOSE, PERSONAL FRIENDS OF HIS.
YOU TWO HAVE FUN.
NAPALM? THE BALCONY, PLEASE.

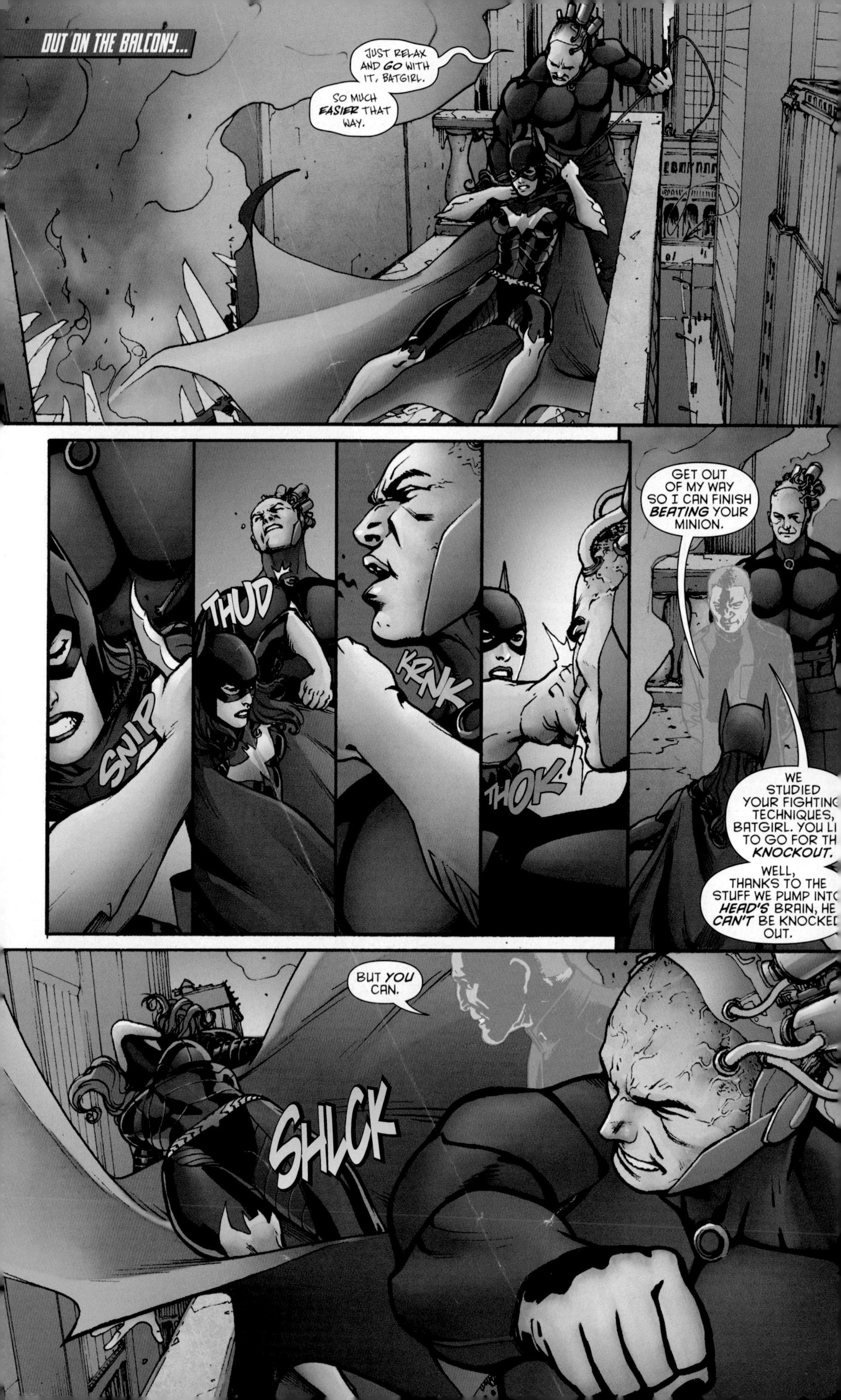

OUT ON THE BALCONY...
JUST RELAX AND GO WITH IT, BATGIRL.
SO MUCH EASIER THAT WAY.
SNIP
THUD
KRNK
THOK
GET OUT OF MY WAY SO I CAN FINISH BEATING YOUR MINION.
WE STUDIED YOUR FIGHTING TECHNIQUES, BATGIRL. YOU LI TO GO FOR TH KNOCKOUT.
WELL, THANKS TO THE STUFF WE PUMP INTO HEAD'S BRAIN, HE CAN'T BE KNOCKED OUT.
BUT YOU CAN.
SHLCK

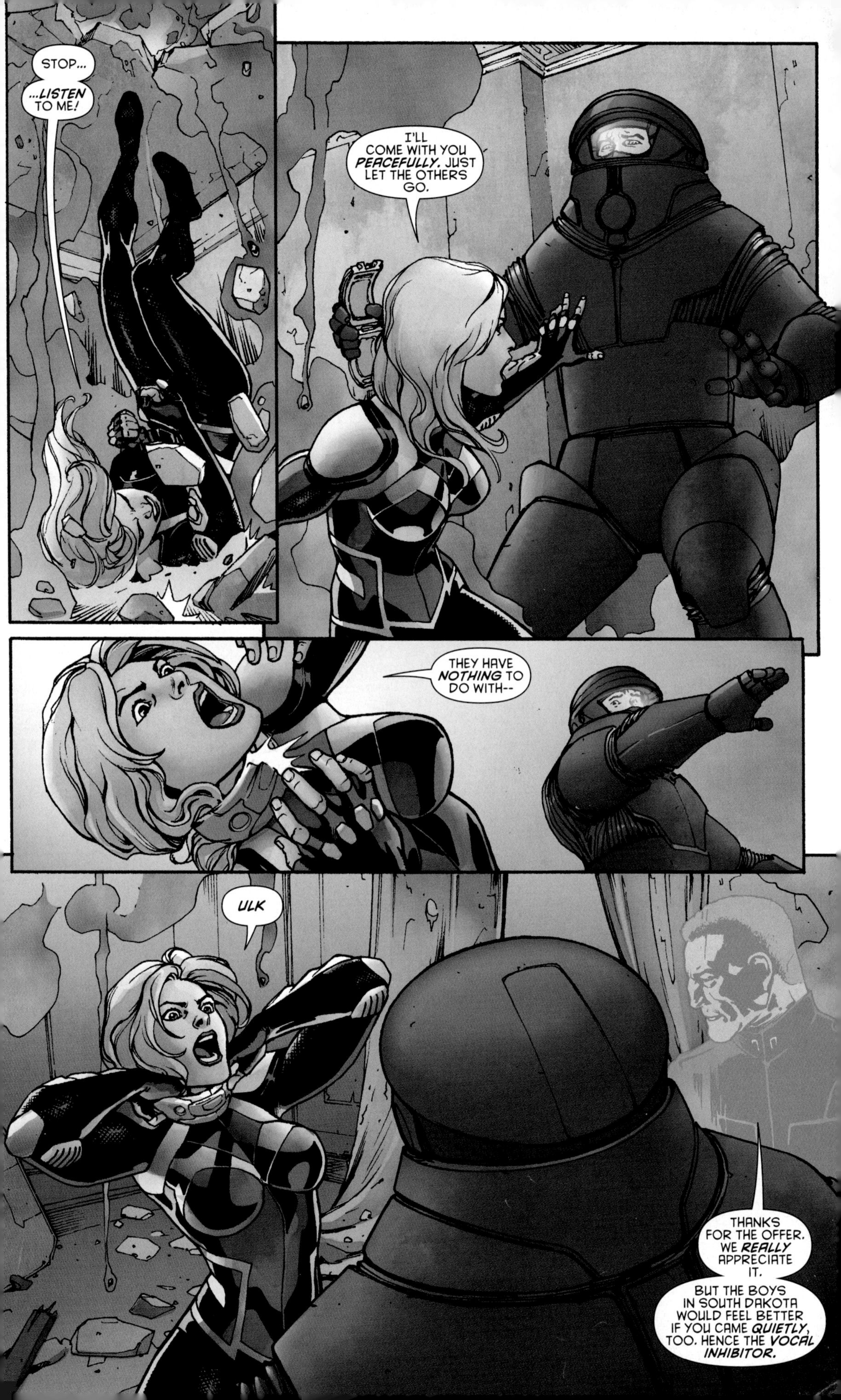

STOP... ...*LISTEN* TO ME!
I'LL COME WITH YOU *PEACEFULLY.* JUST LET THE OTHERS GO.
THEY HAVE *NOTHING* TO DO WITH--
ULK
THANKS FOR THE OFFER. WE *REALLY* APPRECIATE IT.
BUT THE BOYS IN SOUTH DAKOTA WOULD FEEL BETTER IF YOU CAME *QUIETLY,* TOO. HENCE THE *VOCAL INHIBITOR.*

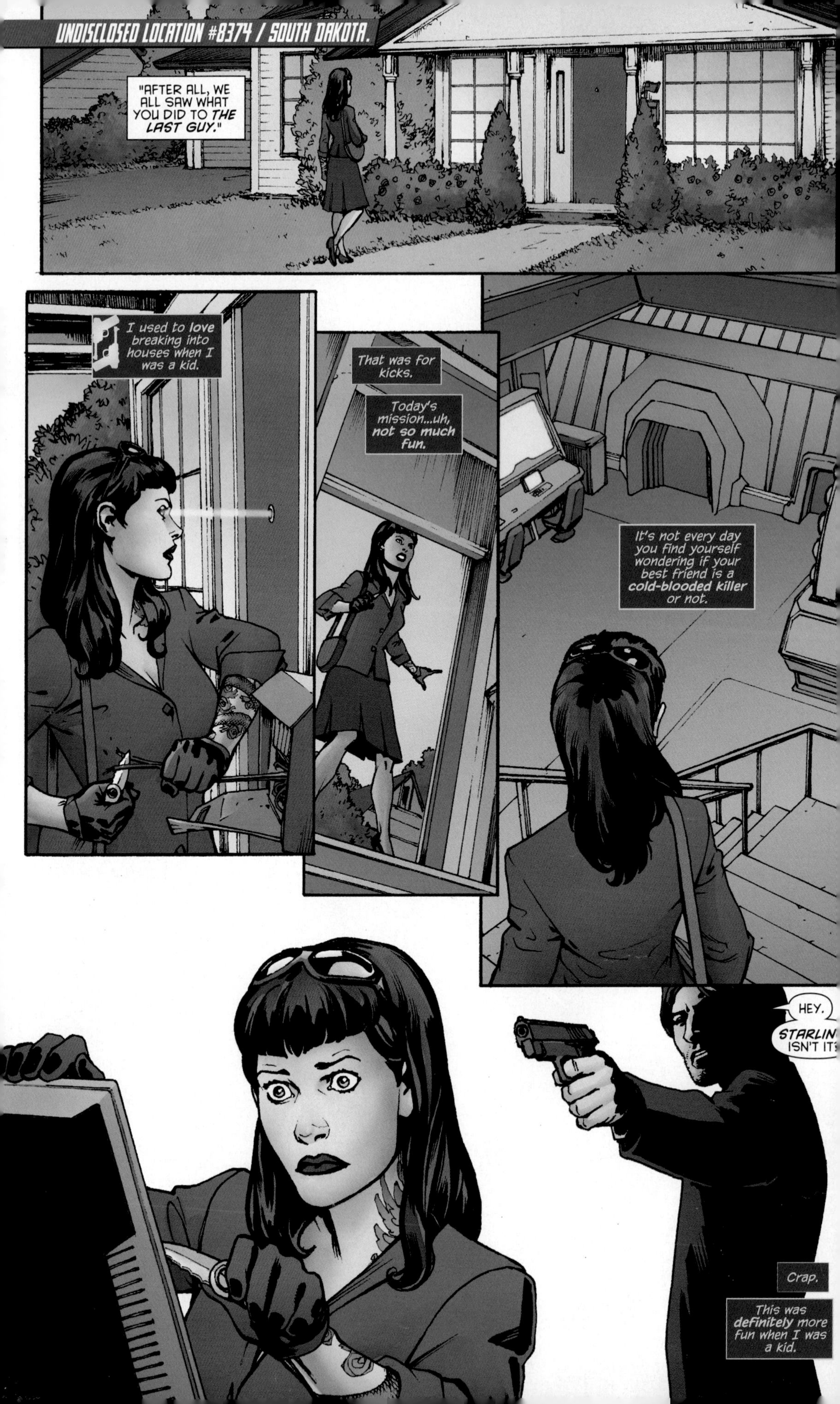

UNDISCLOSED LOCATION #8374 / SOUTH DAKOTA.
"AFTER ALL, WE ALL SAW WHAT YOU DID TO *THE LAST GUY.*"
I used to **love** breaking into houses when I was a kid.
That was for kicks.
Today's mission...uh, **not so much fun.**
It's not every day you find yourself wondering if your best friend is a **cold-blooded killer** or not.
HEY.
STARLIN ISN'T IT?
Crap.
This was **definitely** more fun when I was a kid.

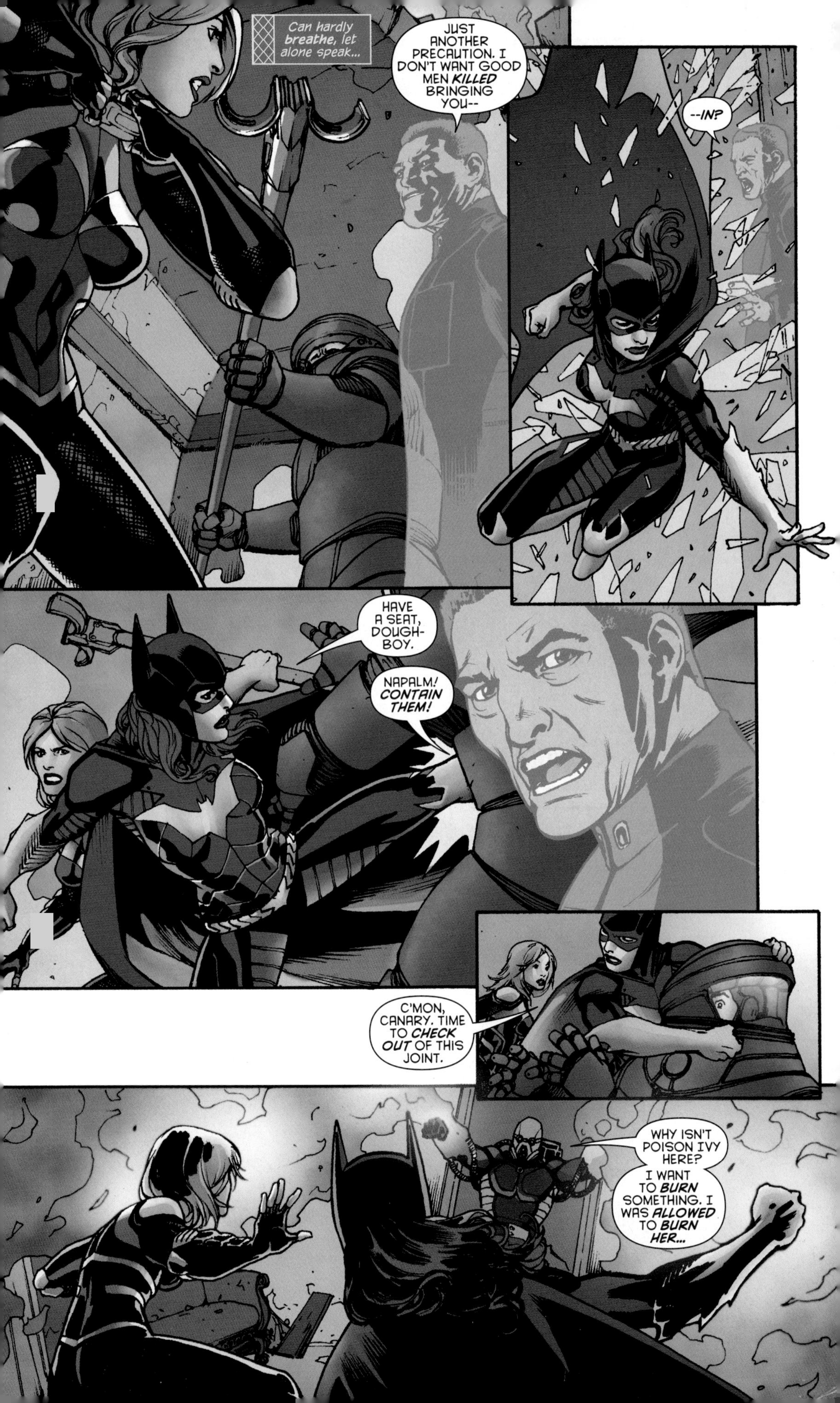

Can hardly breathe, let alone speak...
JUST ANOTHER PRECAUTION. I DON'T WANT GOOD MEN KILLED BRINGING YOU--
--IN?
HAVE A SEAT, DOUGH-BOY.
NAPALM! CONTAIN THEM!
C'MON, CANARY. TIME TO CHECK OUT OF THIS JOINT.
WHY ISN'T POISON IVY HERE?
I WANT TO BURN SOMETHING. I WAS ALLOWED TO BURN HER...

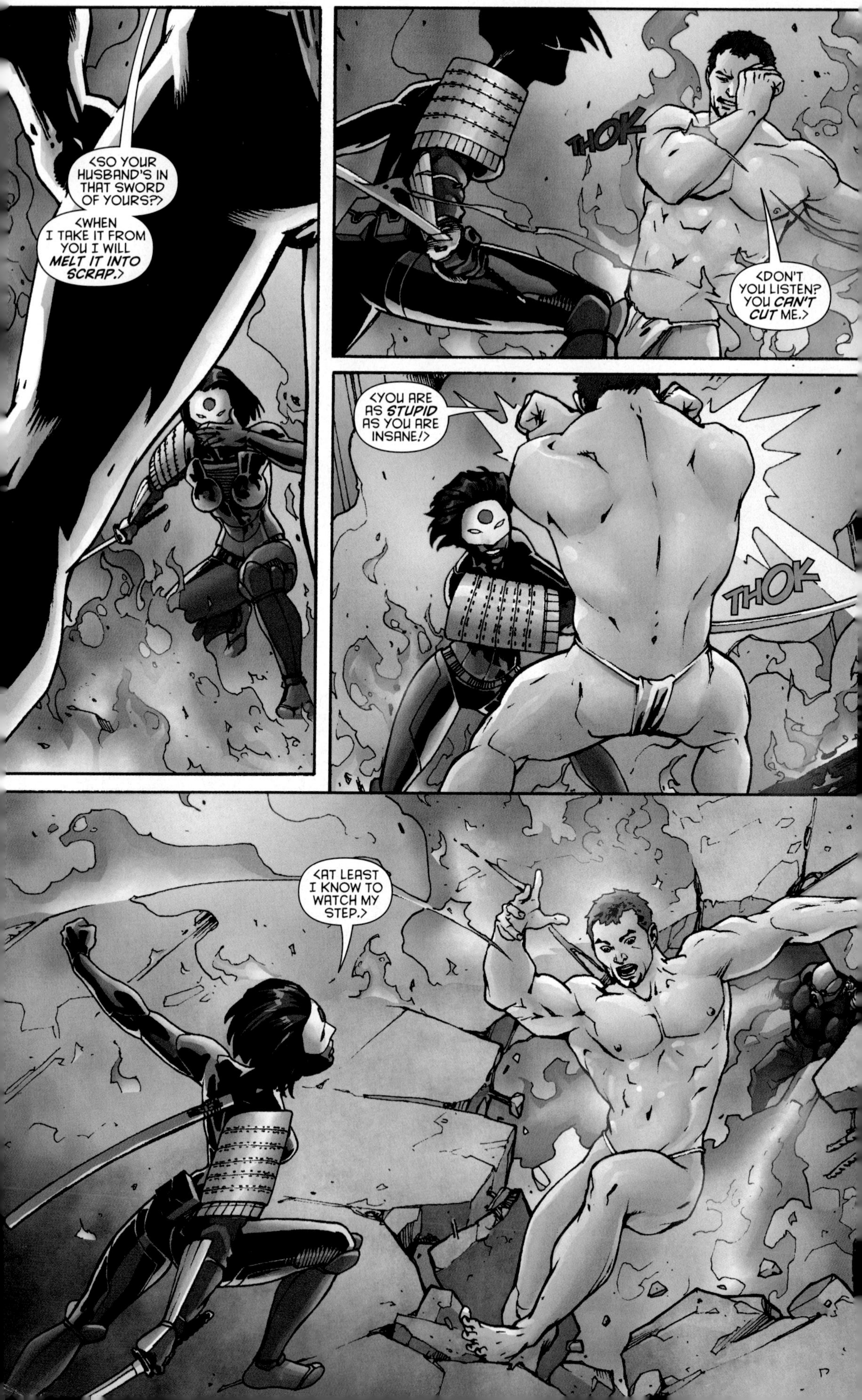

<SO YOUR HUSBAND'S IN THAT SWORD OF YOURS?>
<WHEN I TAKE IT FROM YOU I WILL *MELT IT INTO SCRAP.*>
THOK
<DON'T YOU LISTEN? YOU *CAN'T CUT* ME.>
<YOU ARE AS *STUPID* AS YOU ARE INSANE!>
THOK
<AT LEAST I KNOW TO WATCH MY STEP.>

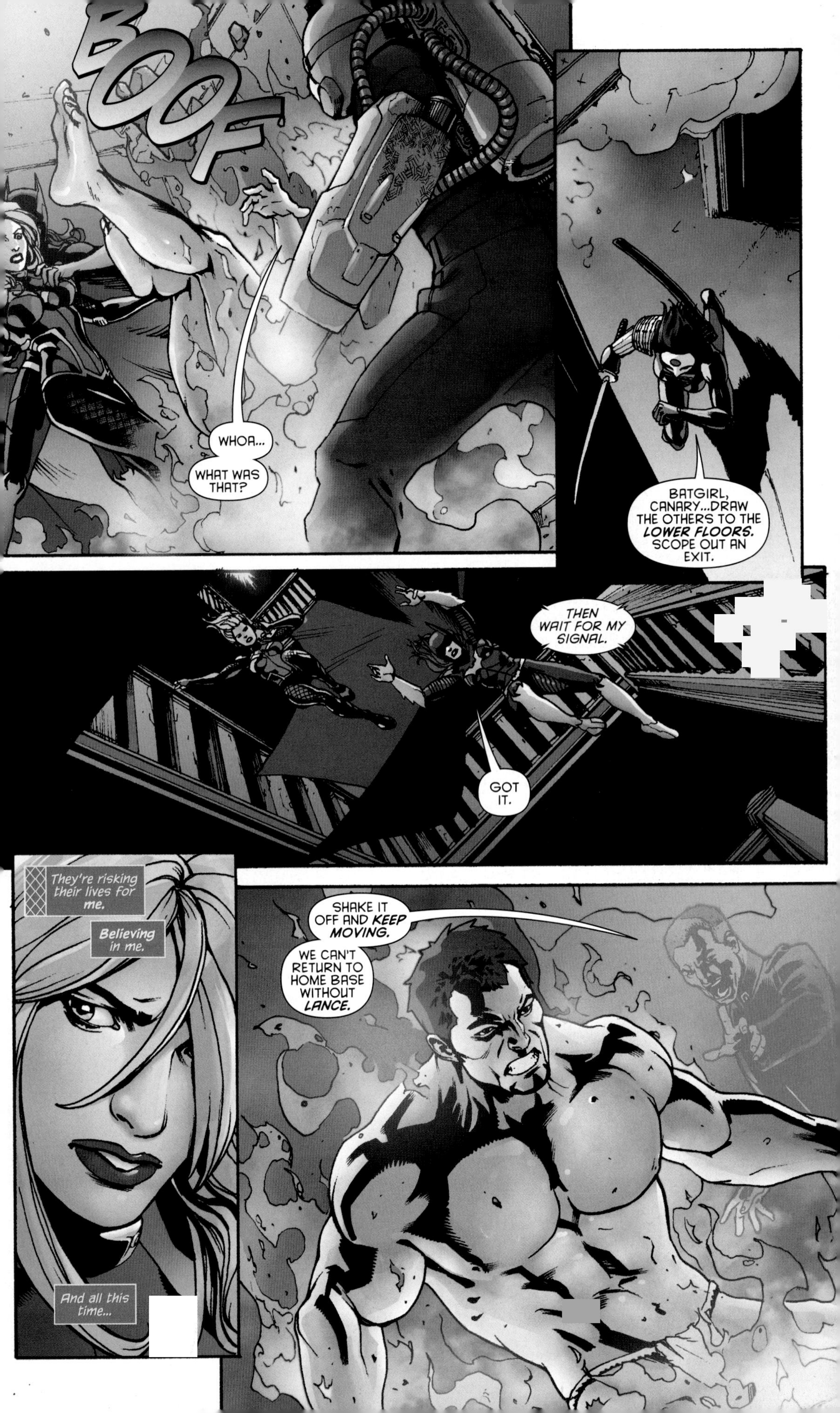
BOOF
WHOA...
WHAT WAS THAT?
BATGIRL, CANARY...DRAW THE OTHERS TO THE LOWER FLOORS. SCOPE OUT AN EXIT.
THEN WAIT FOR MY SIGNAL.
GOT IT.
They're risking their lives for me.
Believing in me.
SHAKE IT OFF AND KEEP MOVING.
WE CAN'T RETURN TO HOME BASE WITHOUT LANCE.
And all this time...

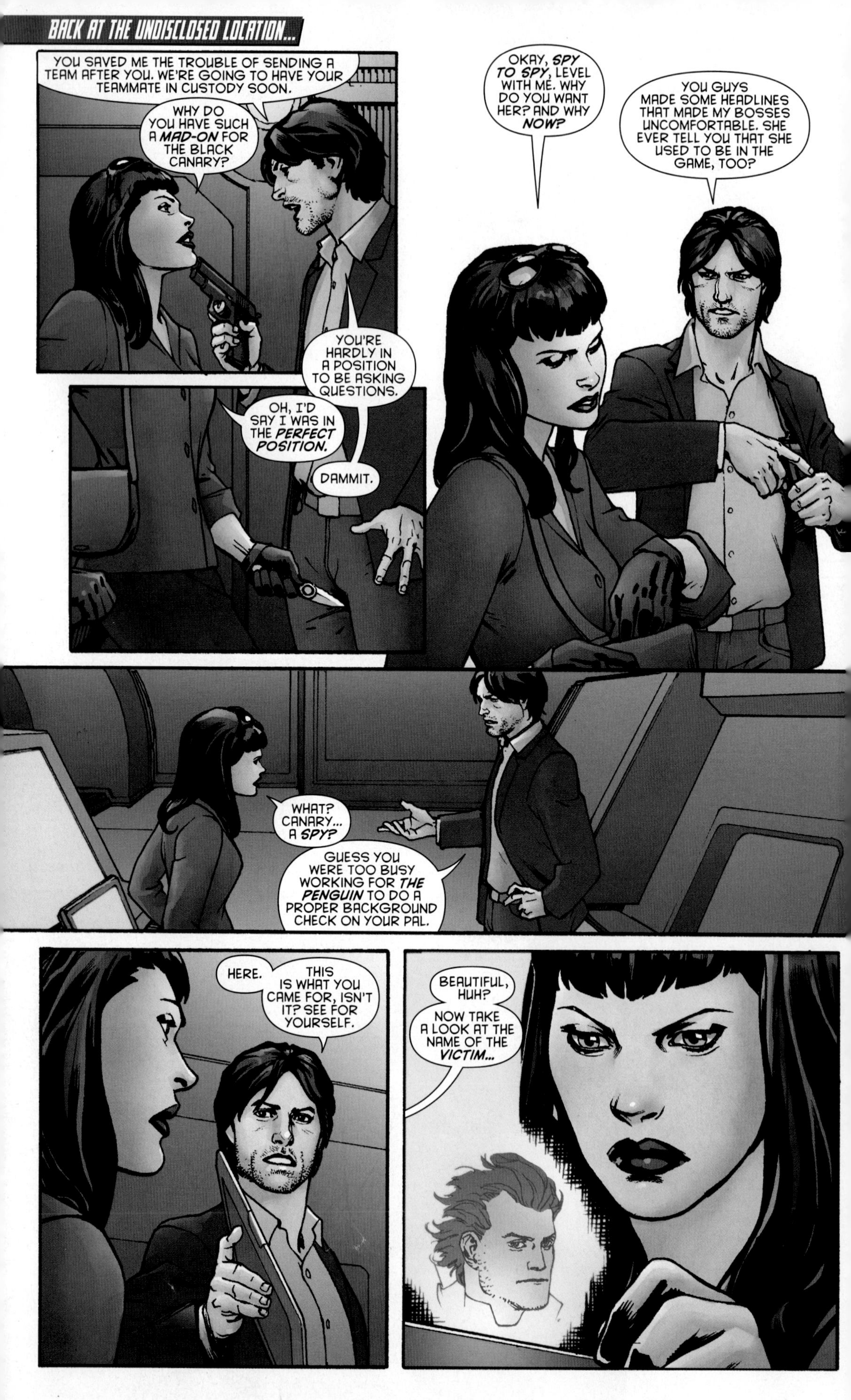
BACK AT THE UNDISCLOSED LOCATION...
YOU SAVED ME THE TROUBLE OF SENDING A TEAM AFTER YOU. WE'RE GOING TO HAVE YOUR TEAMMATE IN CUSTODY SOON.
WHY DO YOU HAVE SUCH A MAD-ON FOR THE BLACK CANARY?
YOU'RE HARDLY IN A POSITION TO BE ASKING QUESTIONS.
OH, I'D SAY I WAS IN THE PERFECT POSITION.
DAMMIT.
OKAY, SPY TO SPY, LEVEL WITH ME. WHY DO YOU WANT HER? AND WHY NOW?
YOU GUYS MADE SOME HEADLINES THAT MADE MY BOSSES UNCOMFORTABLE. SHE EVER TELL YOU THAT SHE USED TO BE IN THE GAME, TOO?
WHAT? CANARY... A SPY?
GUESS YOU WERE TOO BUSY WORKING FOR THE PENGUIN TO DO A PROPER BACKGROUND CHECK ON YOUR PAL.
HERE.
THIS IS WHAT YOU CAME FOR, ISN'T IT? SEE FOR YOURSELF.
BEAUTIFUL, HUH?
NOW TAKE A LOOK AT THE NAME OF THE VICTIM...

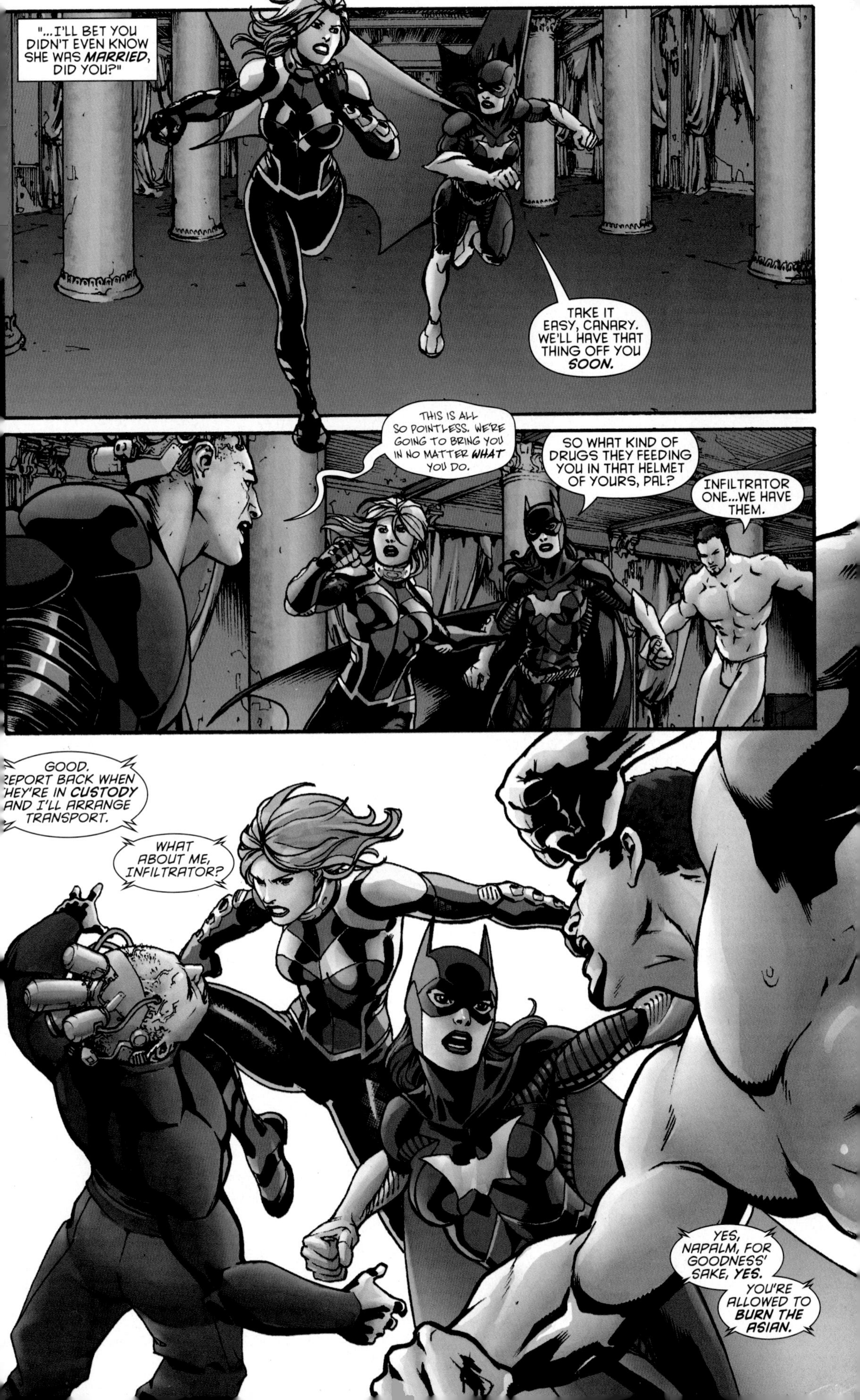
"...I'LL BET YOU DIDN'T EVEN KNOW SHE WAS MARRIED, DID YOU?"
TAKE IT EASY, CANARY. WE'LL HAVE THAT THING OFF YOU SOON.
THIS IS ALL SO POINTLESS. WE'RE GOING TO BRING YOU IN NO MATTER WHAT YOU DO.
SO WHAT KIND OF DRUGS THEY FEEDING YOU IN THAT HELMET OF YOURS, PAL?
INFILTRATOR ONE...WE HAVE THEM.
GOOD. REPORT BACK WHEN THEY'RE IN CUSTODY AND I'LL ARRANGE TRANSPORT.
WHAT ABOUT ME, INFILTRATOR?
YES, NAPALM, FOR GOODNESS' SAKE, YES.
YOU'RE ALLOWED TO BURN THE ASIAN.

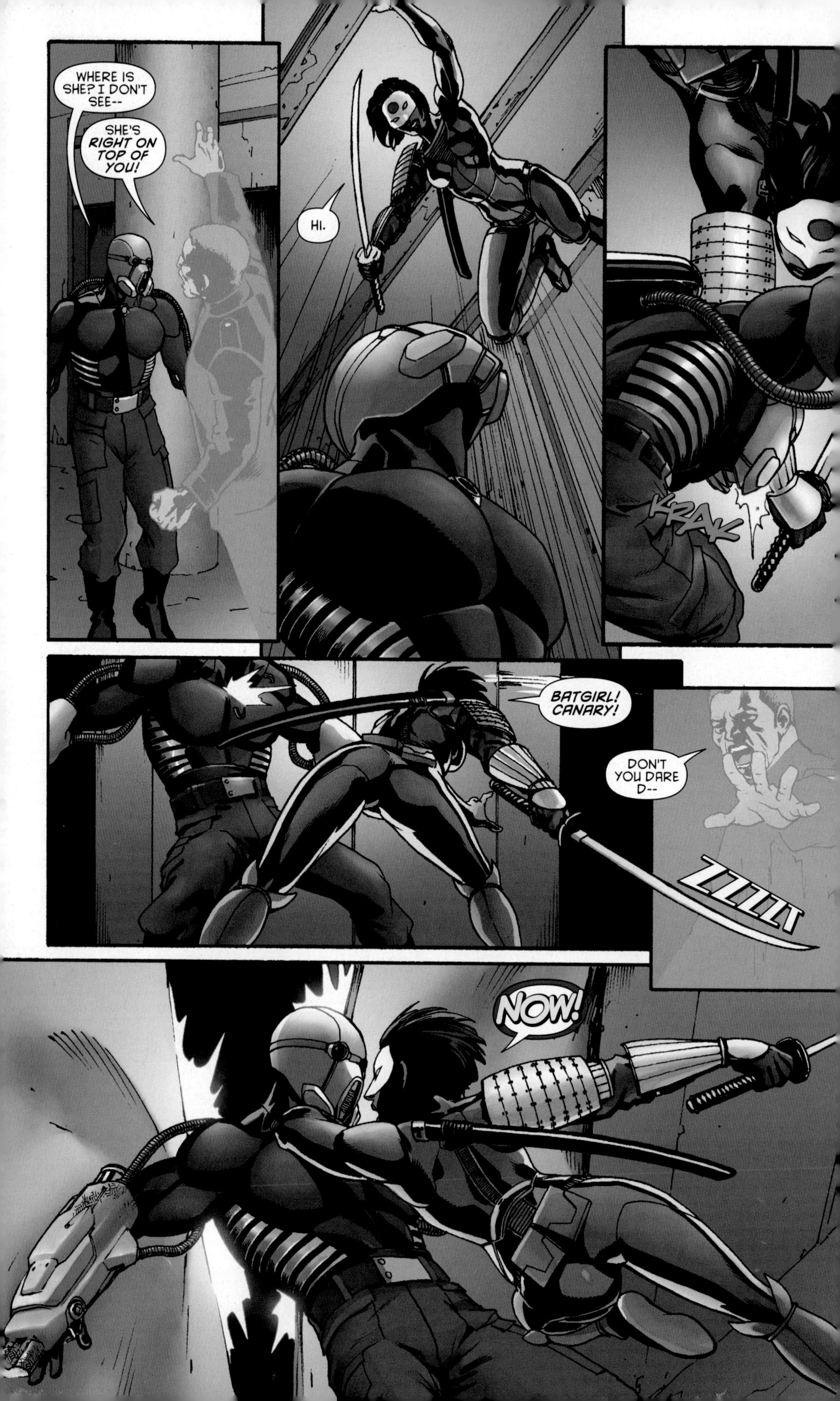
WHERE IS SHE? I DON'T SEE--
SHE'S RIGHT ON TOP OF YOU!
HI.
KRAK
BATGIRL! CANARY!
DON'T YOU DARE D--
ZZZZZT
NOW!

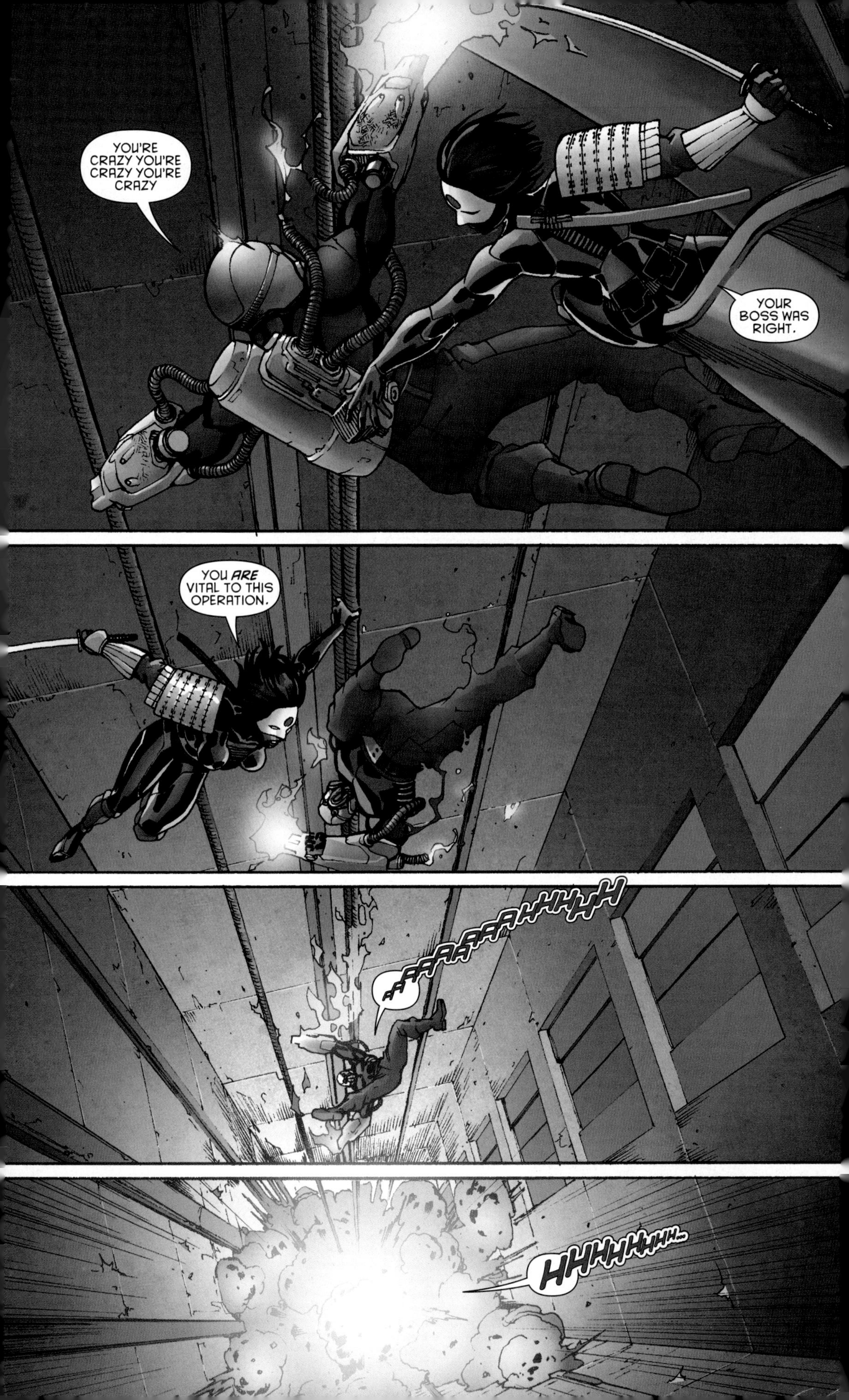

YOU'RE CRAZY YOU'RE CRAZY YOU'RE CRAZY
YOUR BOSS WAS RIGHT.
YOU *ARE* VITAL TO THIS OPERATION.
AAAAAAAAAHHHHHH
HHHHHHHHH...

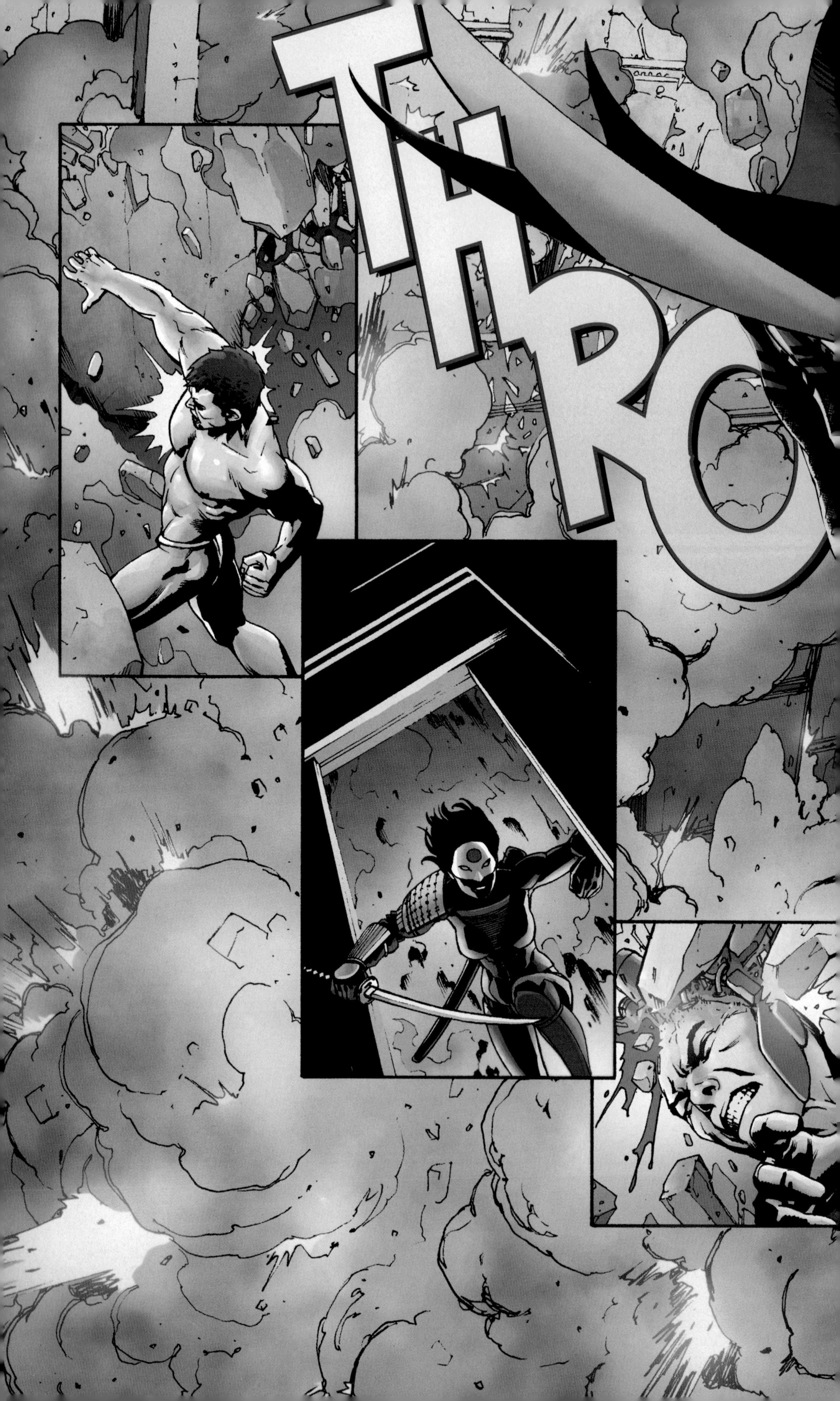
THRO

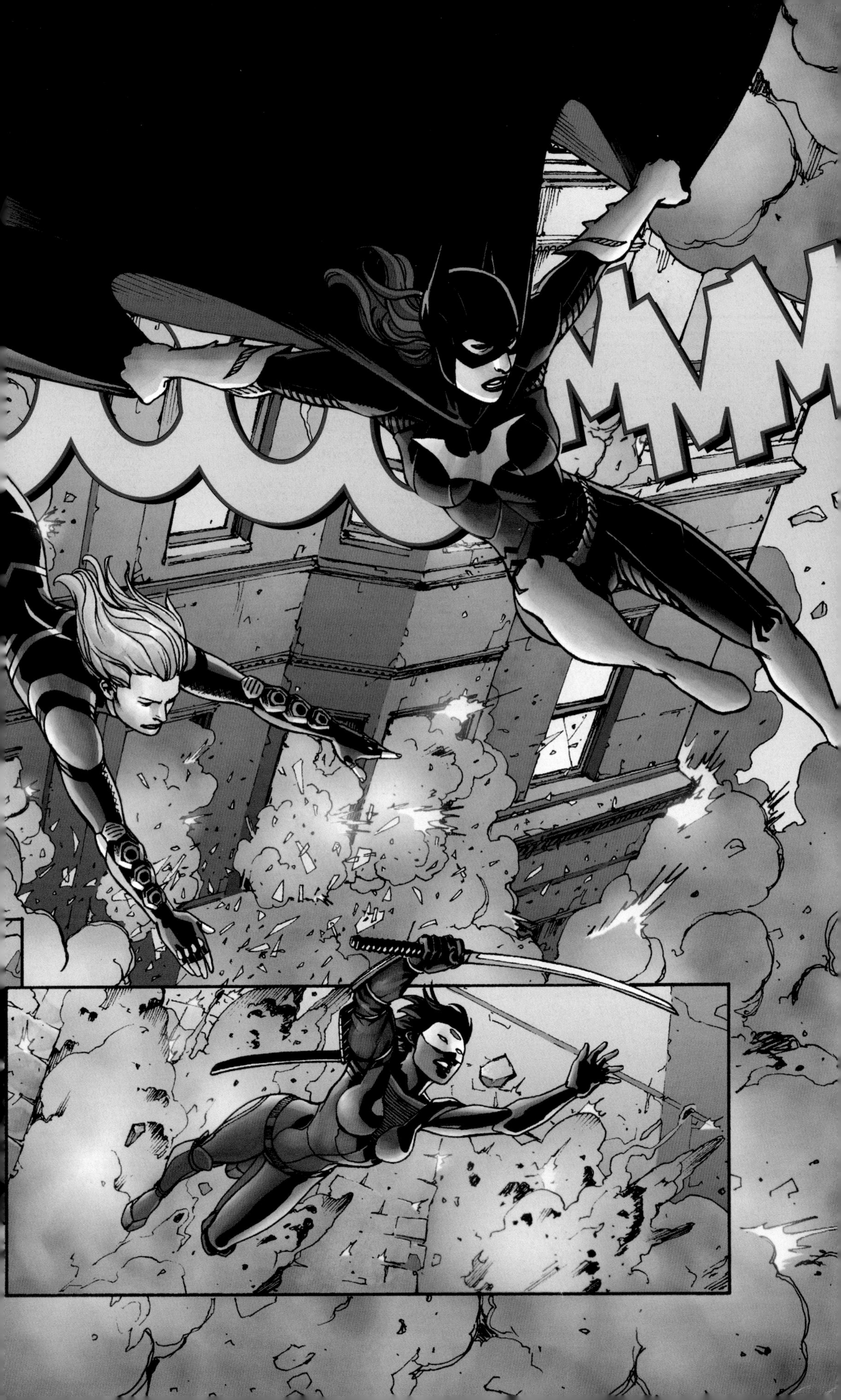

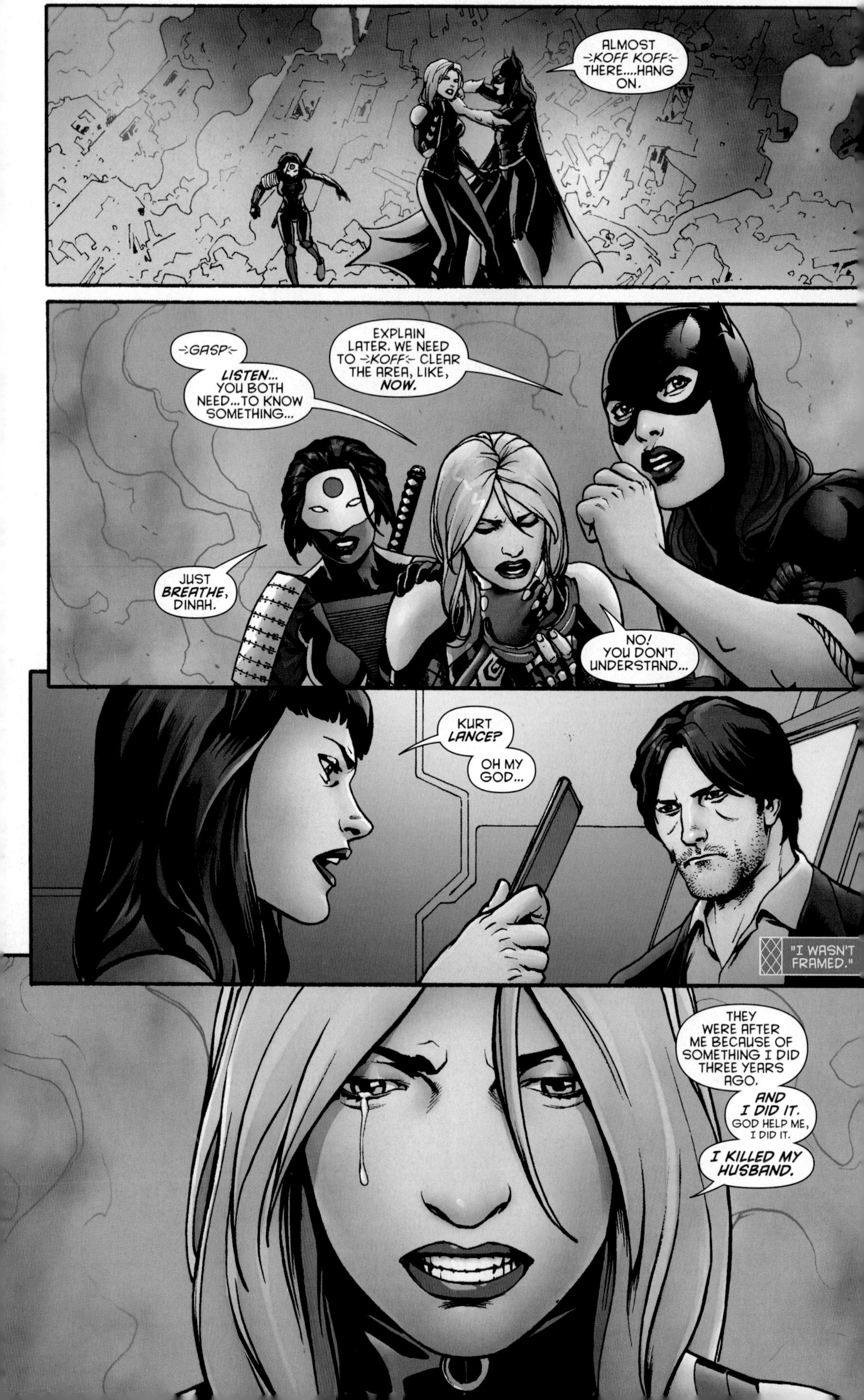
ALMOST -KOFF KOFF- THERE....HANG ON.
-GASP-
LISTEN... YOU BOTH NEED...TO KNOW SOMETHING...
EXPLAIN LATER. WE NEED TO -KOFF- CLEAR THE AREA, LIKE, NOW.
JUST BREATHE, DINAH.
NO! YOU DON'T UNDERSTAND...
KURT LANCE?
OH MY GOD...
"I WASN'T FRAMED."
THEY WERE AFTER ME BECAUSE OF SOMETHING I DID THREE YEARS AGO.
AND I DID IT. GOD HELP ME, I DID IT.
I KILLED MY HUSBAND.

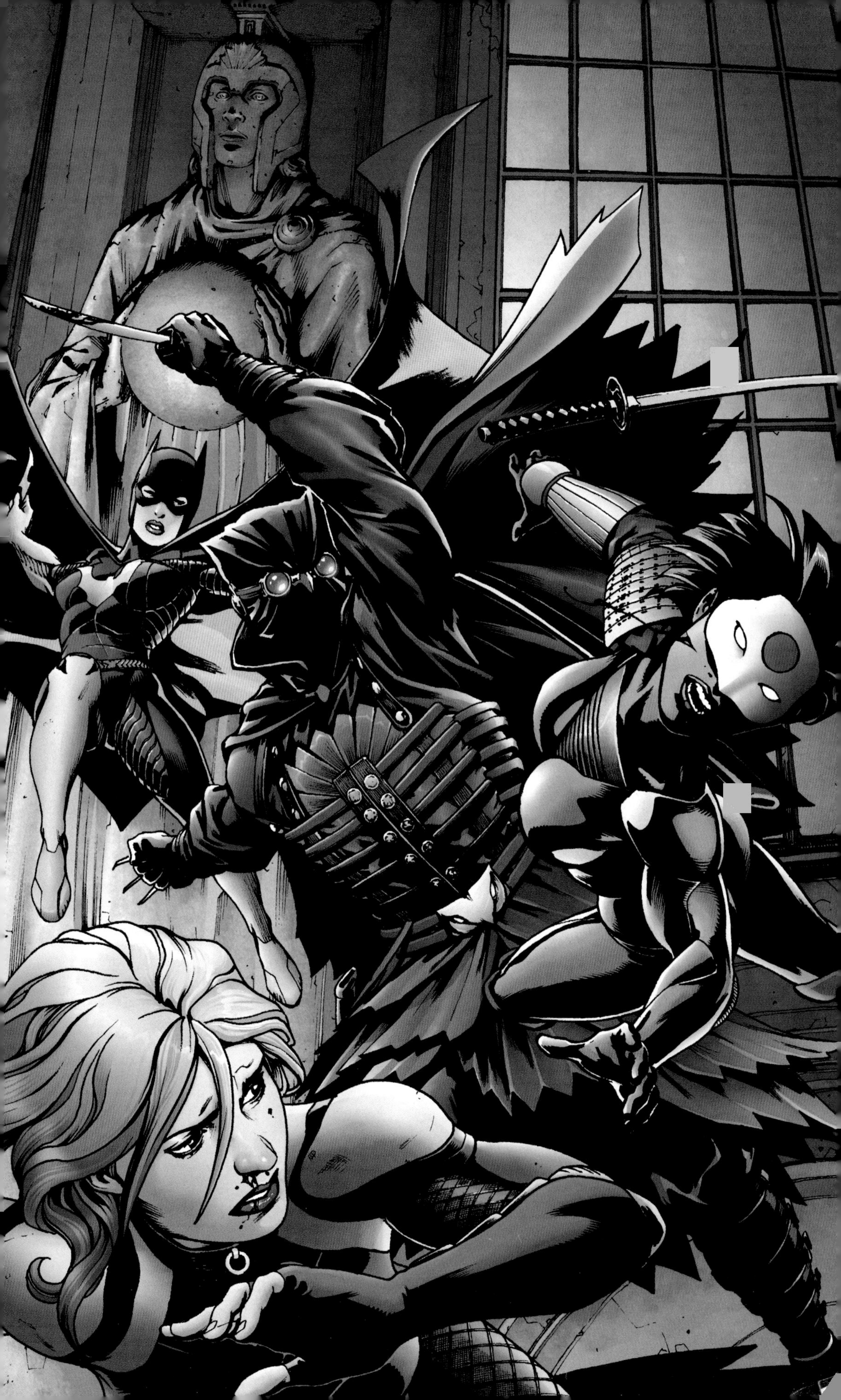

GANGLAND STYLE

DUANE SWIERCZYNSKI writer **TRAVEL FOREMAN** penciller **JEFF HUET** inker cover art by **JESUS SAIZ & JUNE CHUNG**

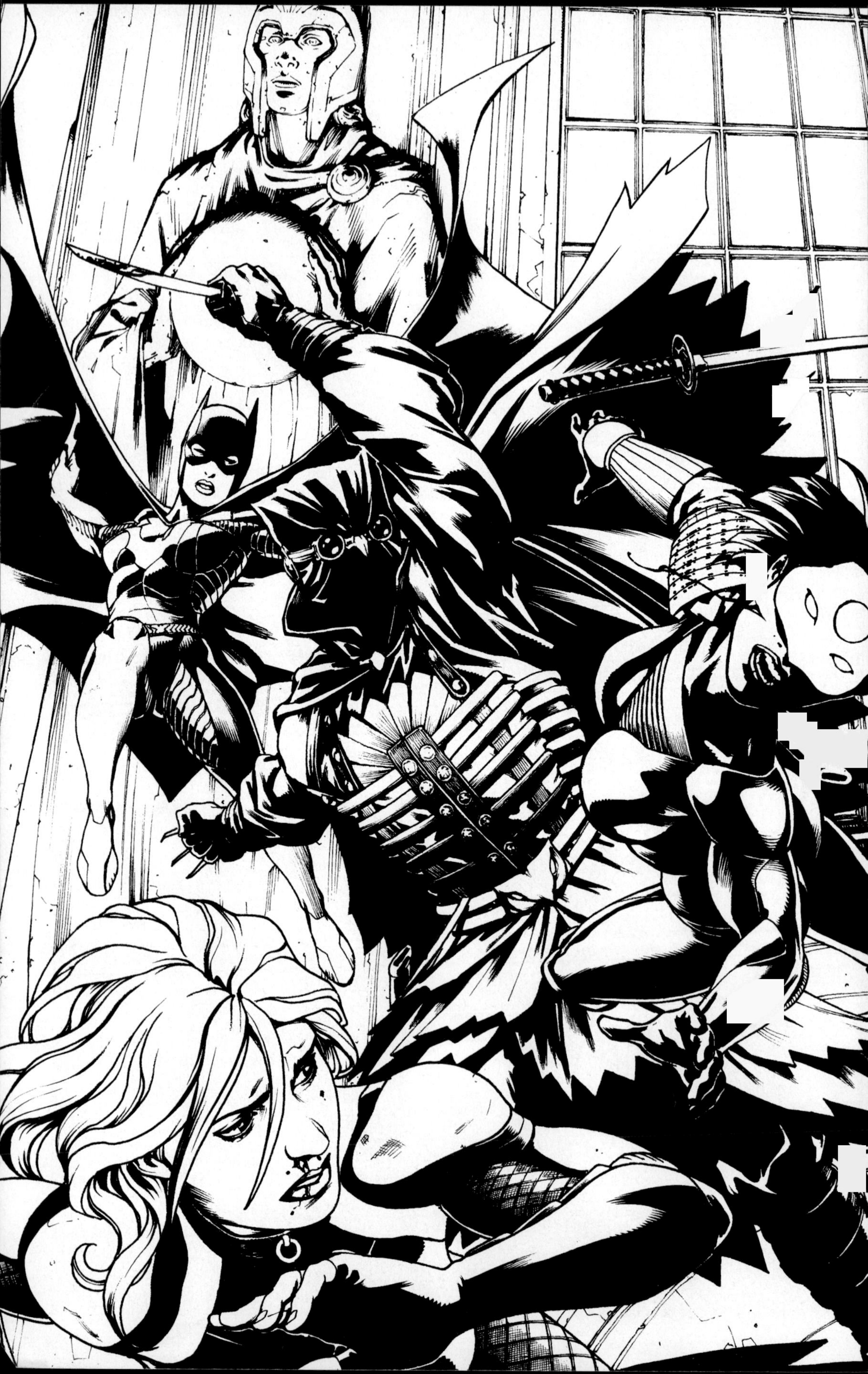

THE CITY OF GOTHAM IN THE YEAR OF OUR LORD 1842.

THE STREETS ARE RULED BY CRUEL MEN WITH LITTLE MORE THAN SHARP KNIVES AND A LACK OF REMORSE.

THEY BAND TOGETHER IN GANGS TO ROB AND RAPE AND FILL THE GUTTERS WITH BLOOD.

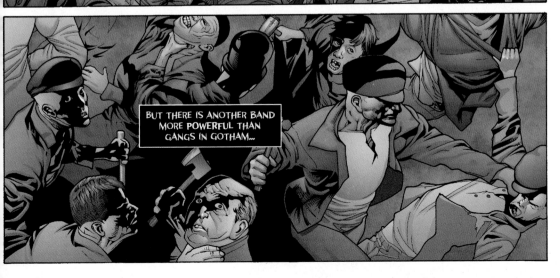

BUT THERE IS ANOTHER BAND MORE POWERFUL THAN GANGS IN GOTHAM...

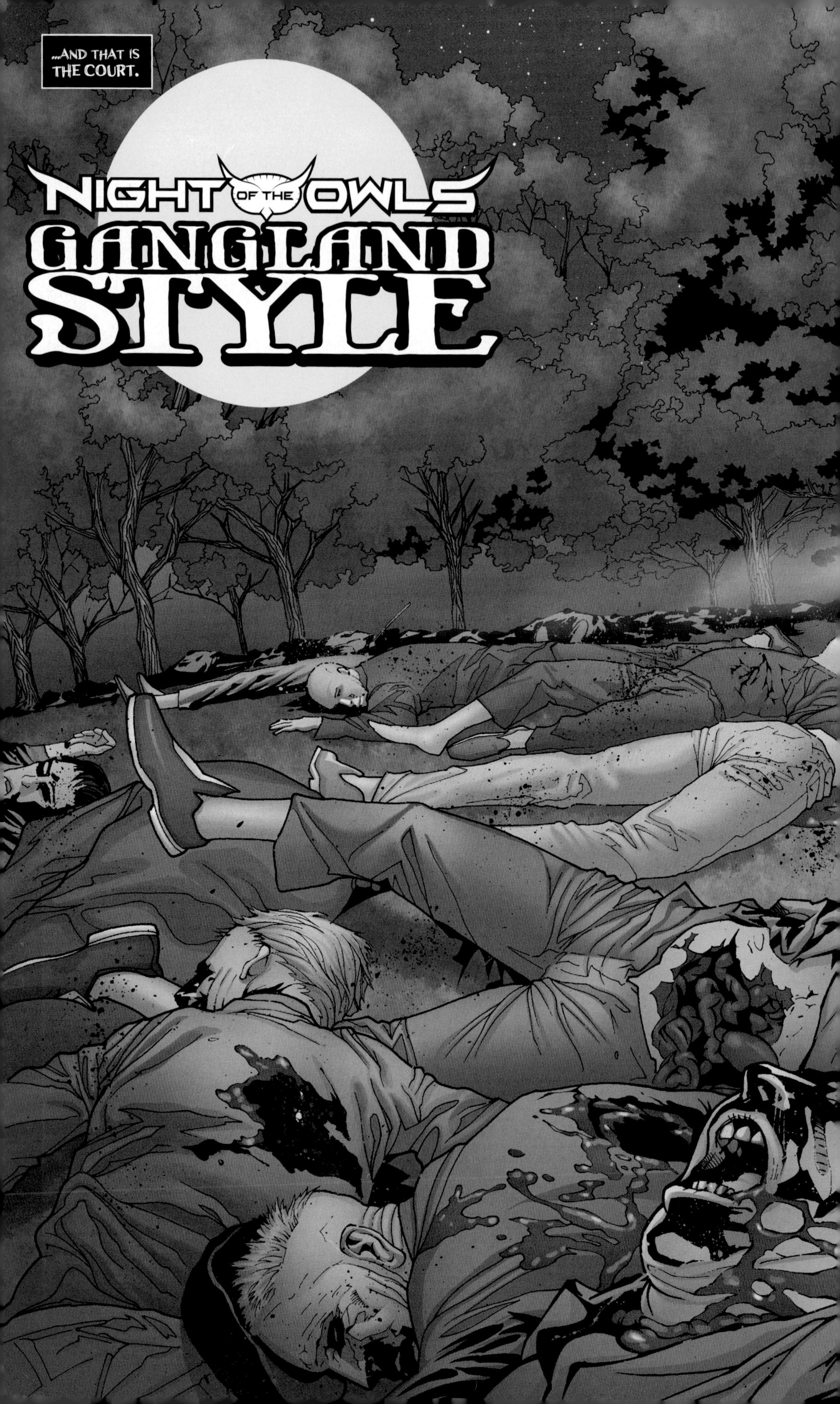
...AND THAT IS THE COURT.
NIGHT OF THE OWLS
GANGLAND STYLE

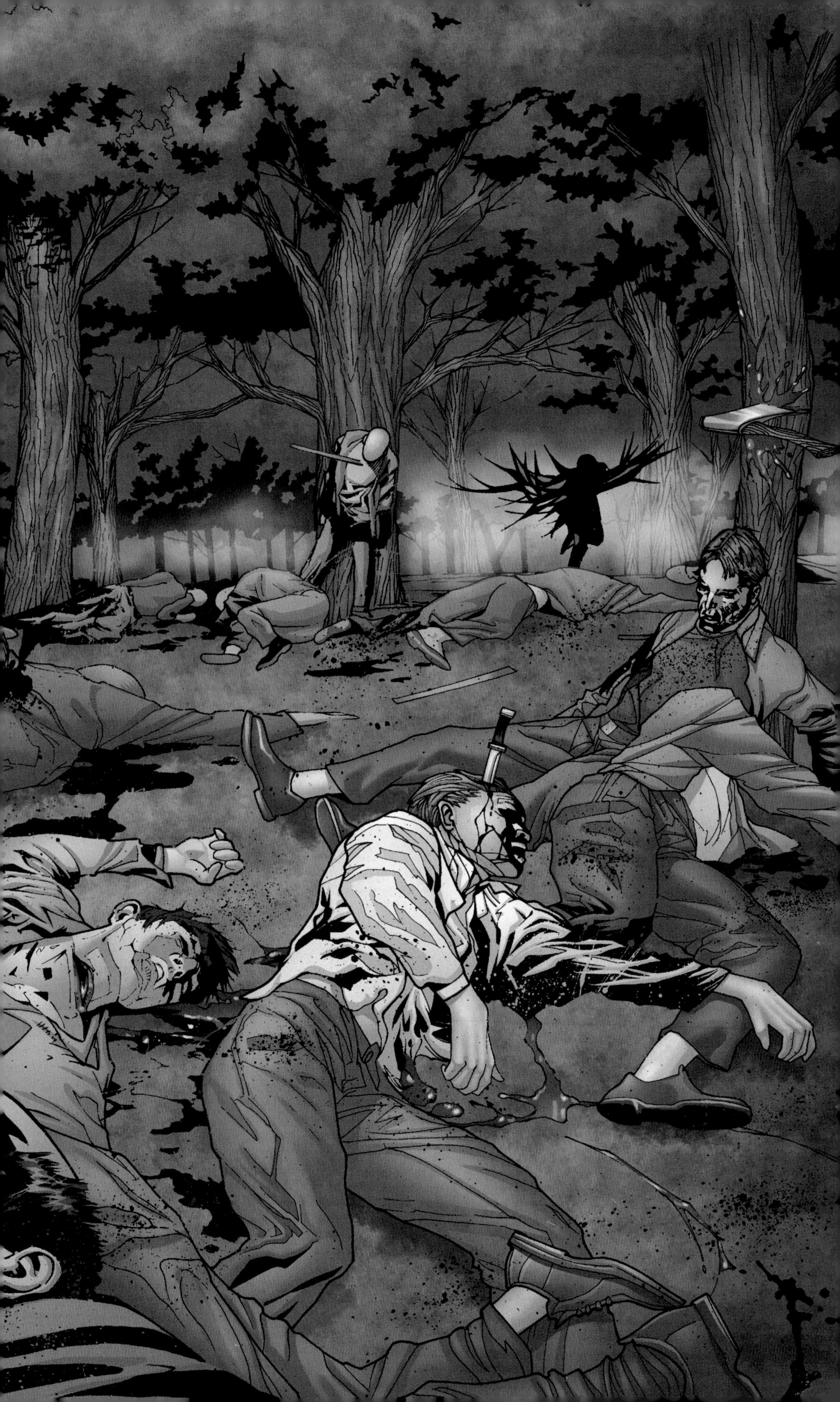

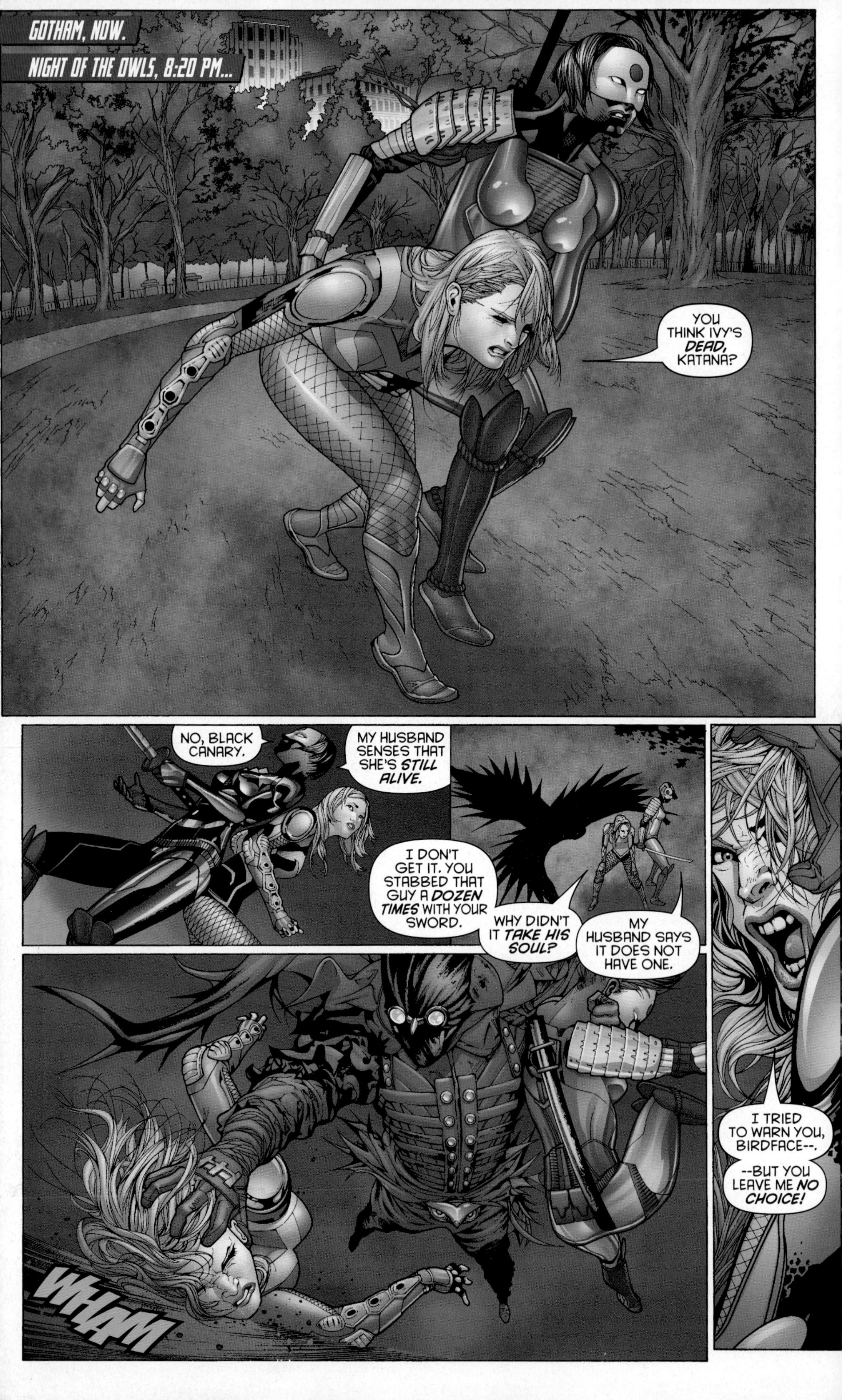
GOTHAM, NOW.
NIGHT OF THE OWLS, 8:20 PM...
YOU THINK IVY'S DEAD, KATANA?
NO, BLACK CANARY.
MY HUSBAND SENSES THAT SHE'S STILL ALIVE.
I DON'T GET IT. YOU STABBED THAT GUY A DOZEN TIMES WITH YOUR SWORD.
WHY DIDN'T IT TAKE HIS SOUL?
MY HUSBAND SAYS IT DOES NOT HAVE ONE.
WHAM
I TRIED TO WARN YOU, BIRDFACE--.
--BUT YOU LEAVE ME NO CHOICE!

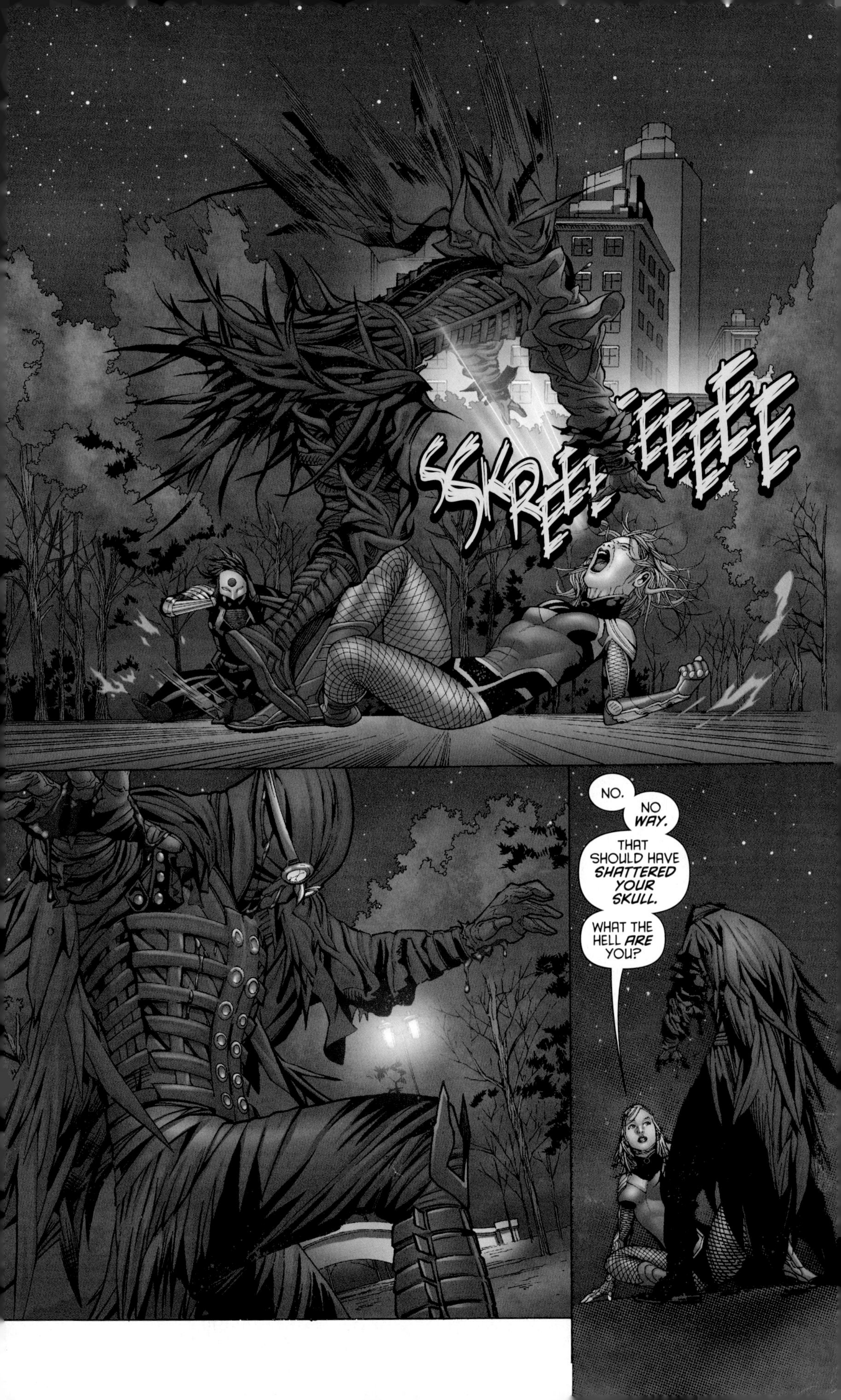
SKREEEEEEEEE
NO.
NO WAY.
THAT SHOULD HAVE SHATTERED YOUR SKULL.
WHAT THE HELL ARE YOU?

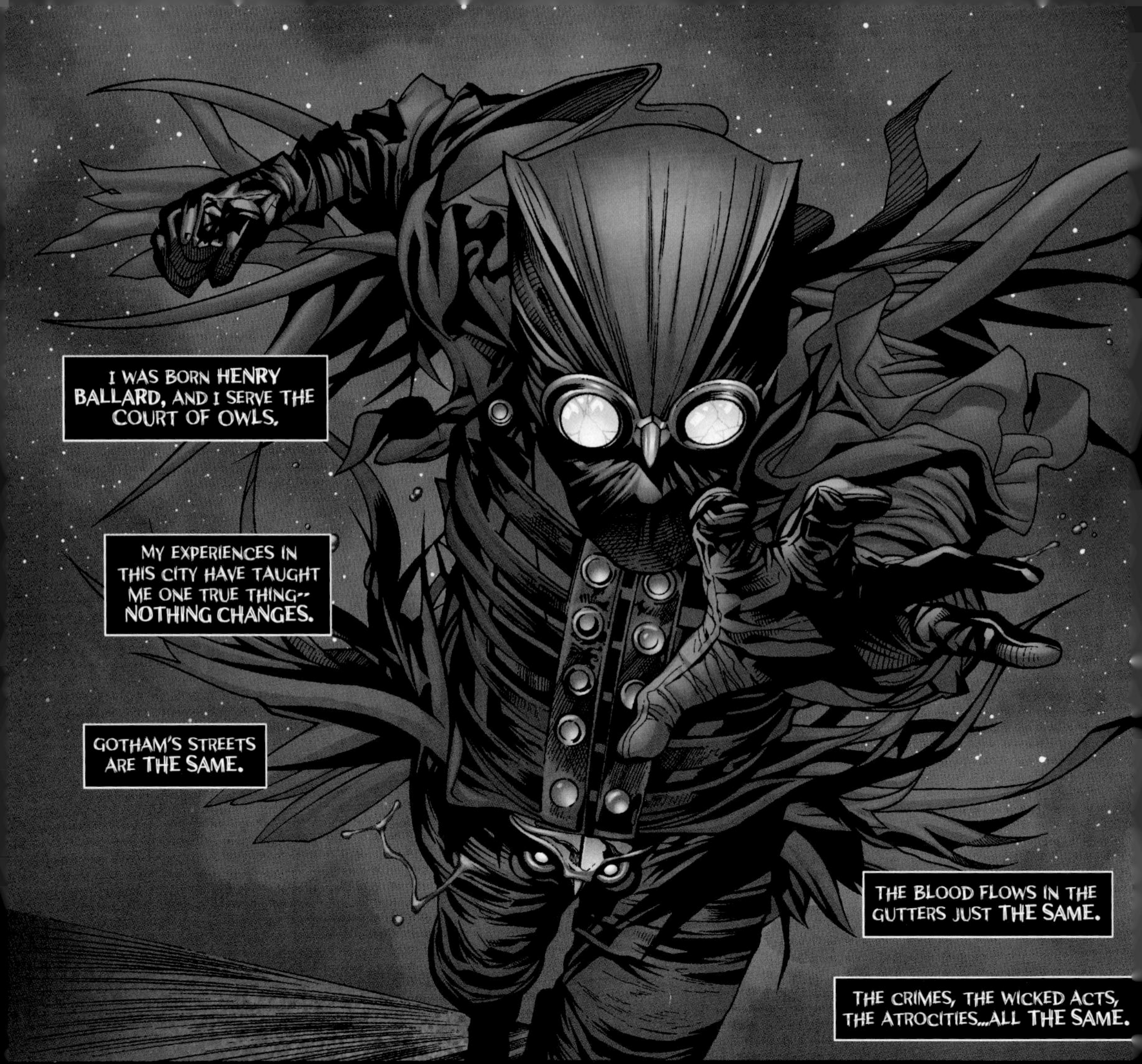
I WAS BORN HENRY BALLARD, AND I SERVE THE COURT OF OWLS.
MY EXPERIENCES IN THIS CITY HAVE TAUGHT ME ONE TRUE THING--NOTHING CHANGES.
GOTHAM'S STREETS ARE THE SAME.
THE BLOOD FLOWS IN THE GUTTERS JUST THE SAME.
THE CRIMES, THE WICKED ACTS, THE ATROCITIES...ALL THE SAME.
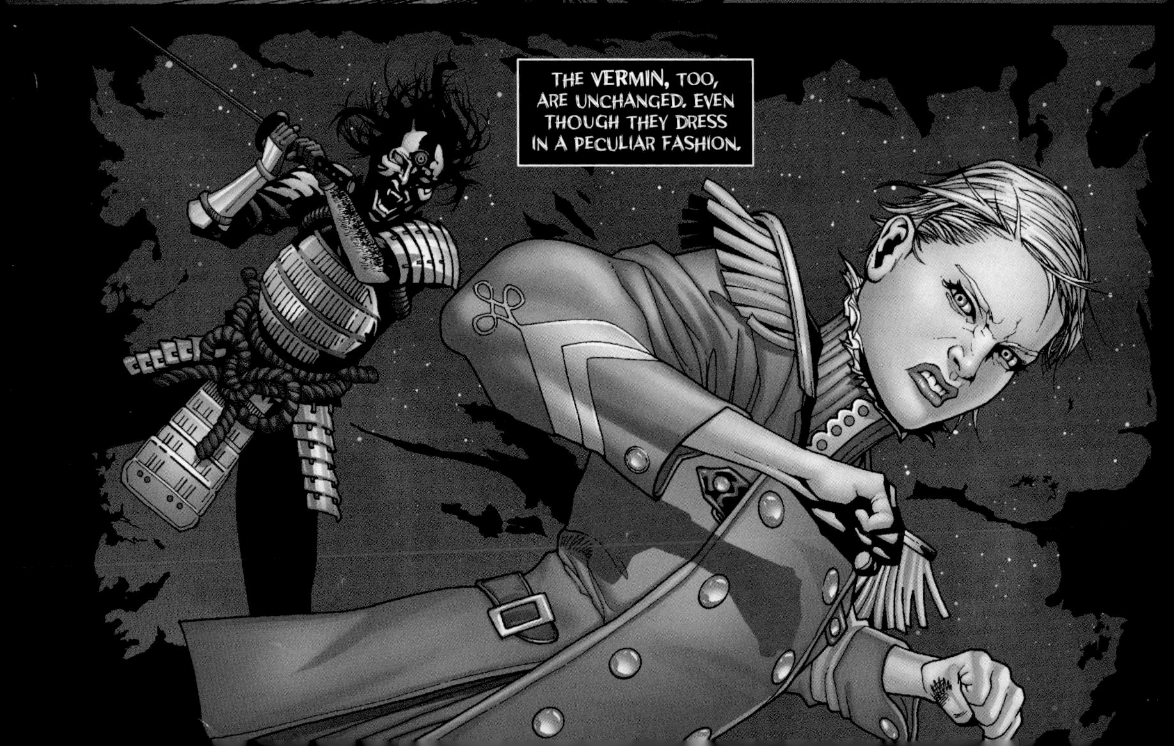
THE VERMIN, TOO, ARE UNCHANGED. EVEN THOUGH THEY DRESS IN A PECULIAR FASHION.

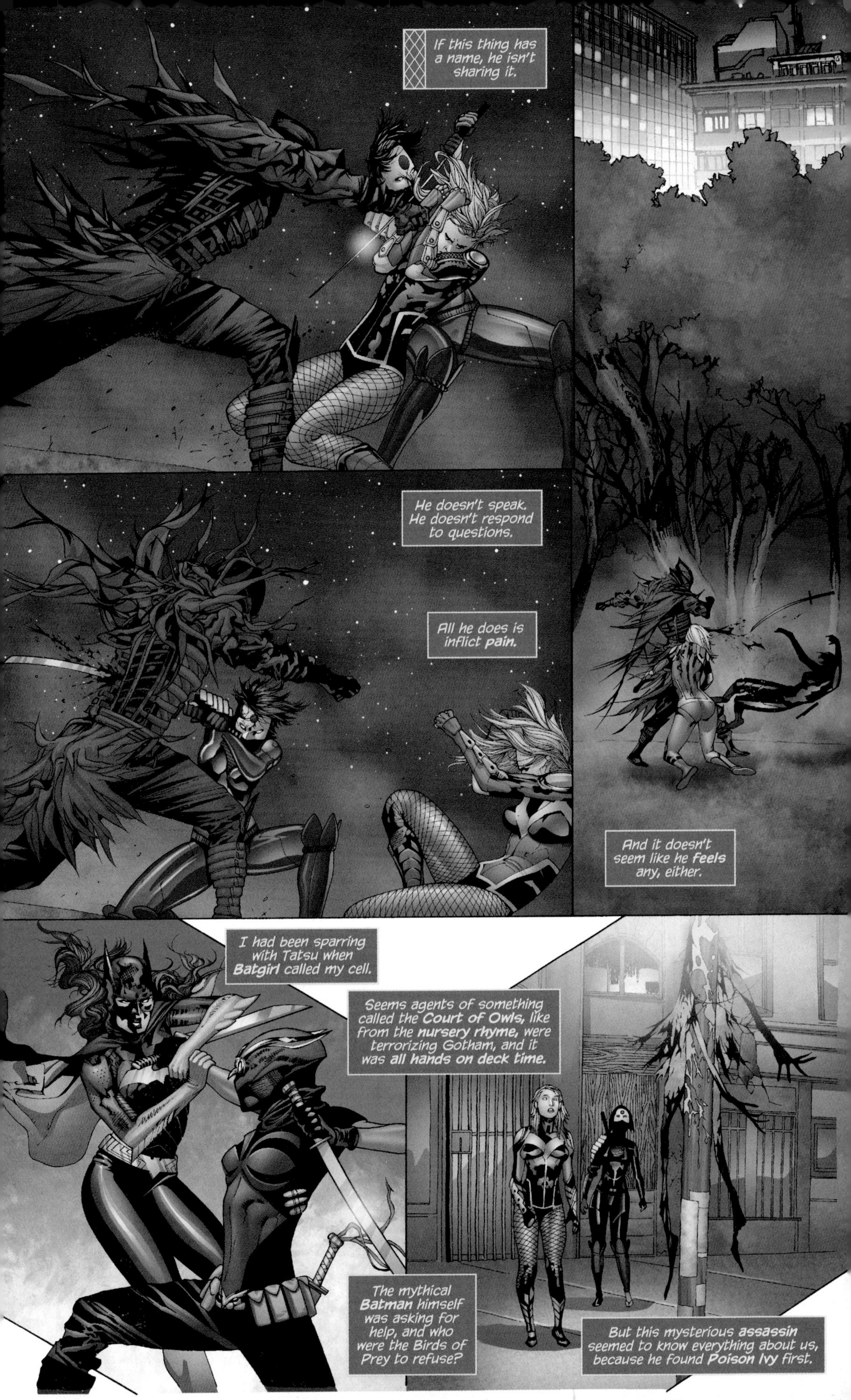

If this thing has a name, he isn't sharing it.
He doesn't speak. He doesn't respond to questions.
All he does is inflict **pain.**
And it doesn't seem like he **feels** any, either.
I had been sparring with Tatsu when **Batgirl** called my cell.
Seems agents of something called the **Court of Owls,** like from the **nursery rhyme,** were terrorizing Gotham, and it was **all hands on deck time.**
The mythical **Batman** himself was asking for help, and who were the Birds of Prey to refuse?
But this mysterious **assassin** seemed to know everything about us, because he found **Poison Ivy** first.

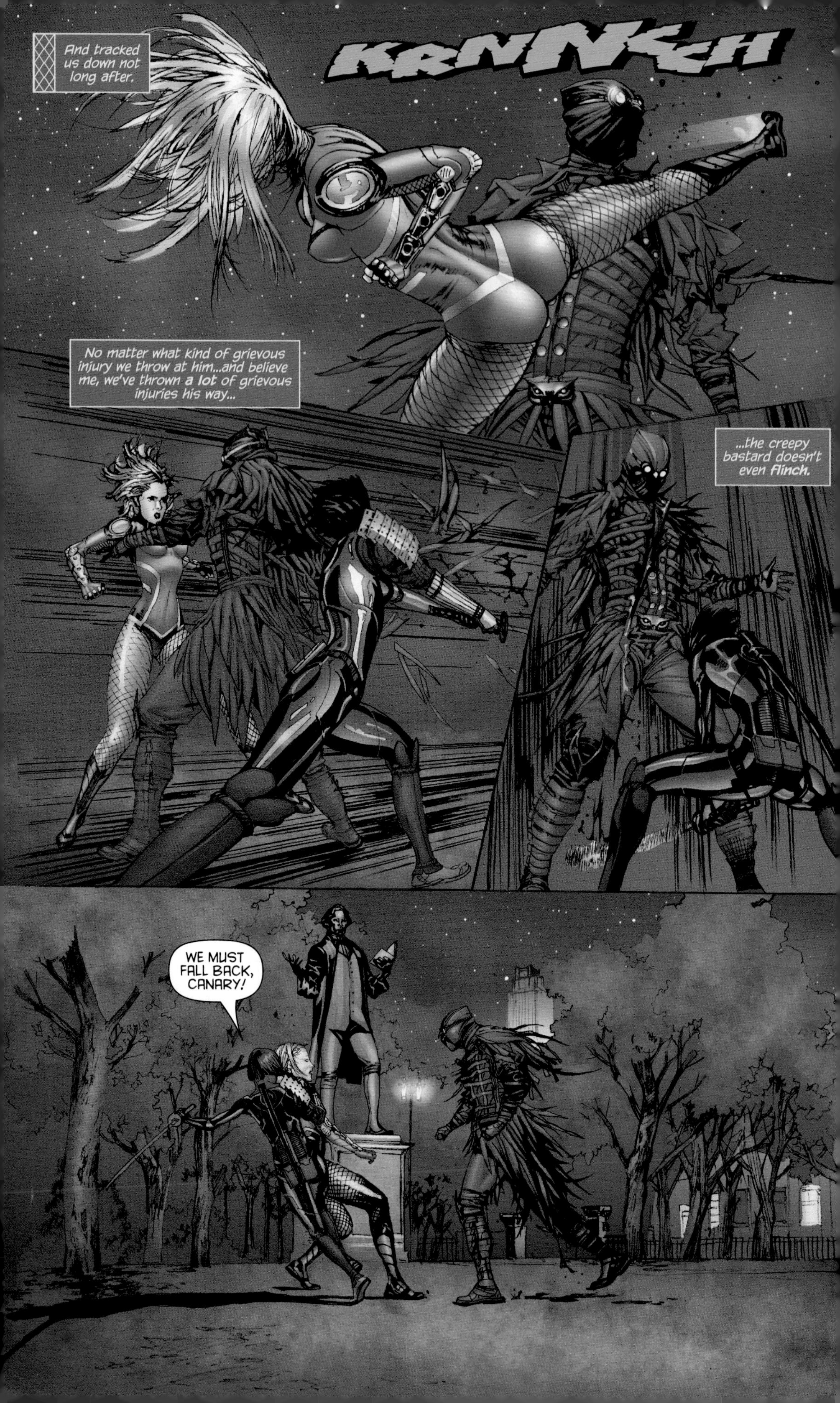
And tracked us down not long after.
KRNNKCH
No matter what kind of grievous injury we throw at him...and believe me, we've thrown a **lot** of grievous injuries his way...
...the creepy bastard doesn't even **flinch.**
WE MUST FALL BACK, CANARY!

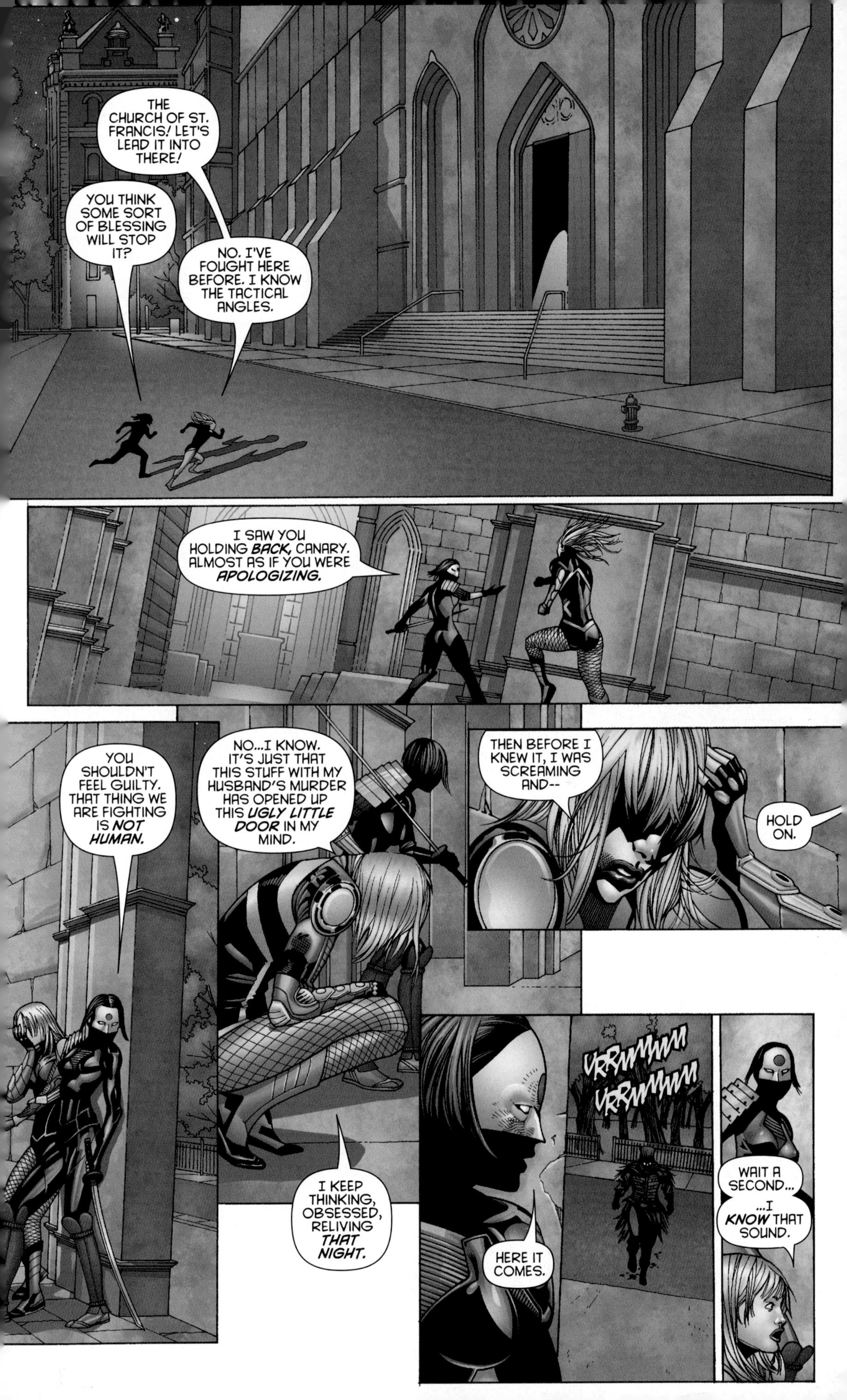
THE CHURCH OF ST. FRANCIS! LET'S LEAD IT INTO THERE!
YOU THINK SOME SORT OF BLESSING WILL STOP IT?
NO. I'VE FOUGHT HERE BEFORE. I KNOW THE TACTICAL ANGLES.
I SAW YOU HOLDING BACK, CANARY. ALMOST AS IF YOU WERE APOLOGIZING.
YOU SHOULDN'T FEEL GUILTY. THAT THING WE ARE FIGHTING IS NOT HUMAN.
NO...I KNOW. IT'S JUST THAT THIS STUFF WITH MY HUSBAND'S MURDER HAS OPENED UP THIS UGLY LITTLE DOOR IN MY MIND.
I KEEP THINKING, OBSESSED, RELIVING THAT NIGHT.
THEN BEFORE I KNEW IT, I WAS SCREAMING AND--
HOLD ON.
HERE IT COMES.
VRRMMMM
VRRMMMM
WAIT A SECOND...
...I KNOW THAT SOUND.

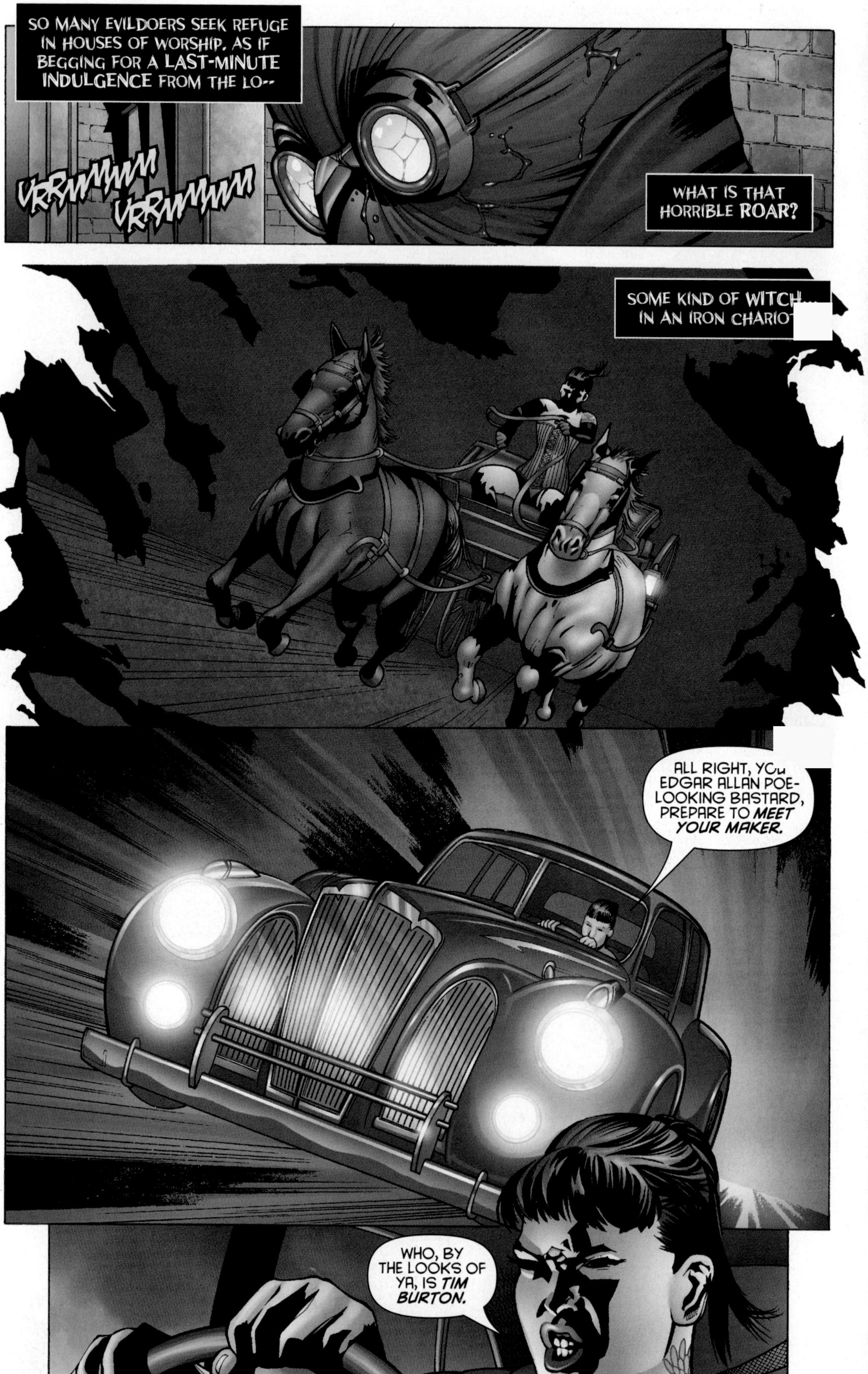

SO MANY EVILDOERS SEEK REFUGE IN HOUSES OF WORSHIP, AS IF BEGGING FOR A LAST-MINUTE INDULGENCE FROM THE LO--
VRRMMMM
VRRMMMM
WHAT IS THAT HORRIBLE ROAR?
SOME KIND OF WITCH
IN AN IRON CHARIO
ALL RIGHT, YO
EDGAR ALLAN POE-LOOKING BASTARD, PREPARE TO MEET YOUR MAKER.
WHO, BY THE LOOKS OF YA, IS TIM BURTON.

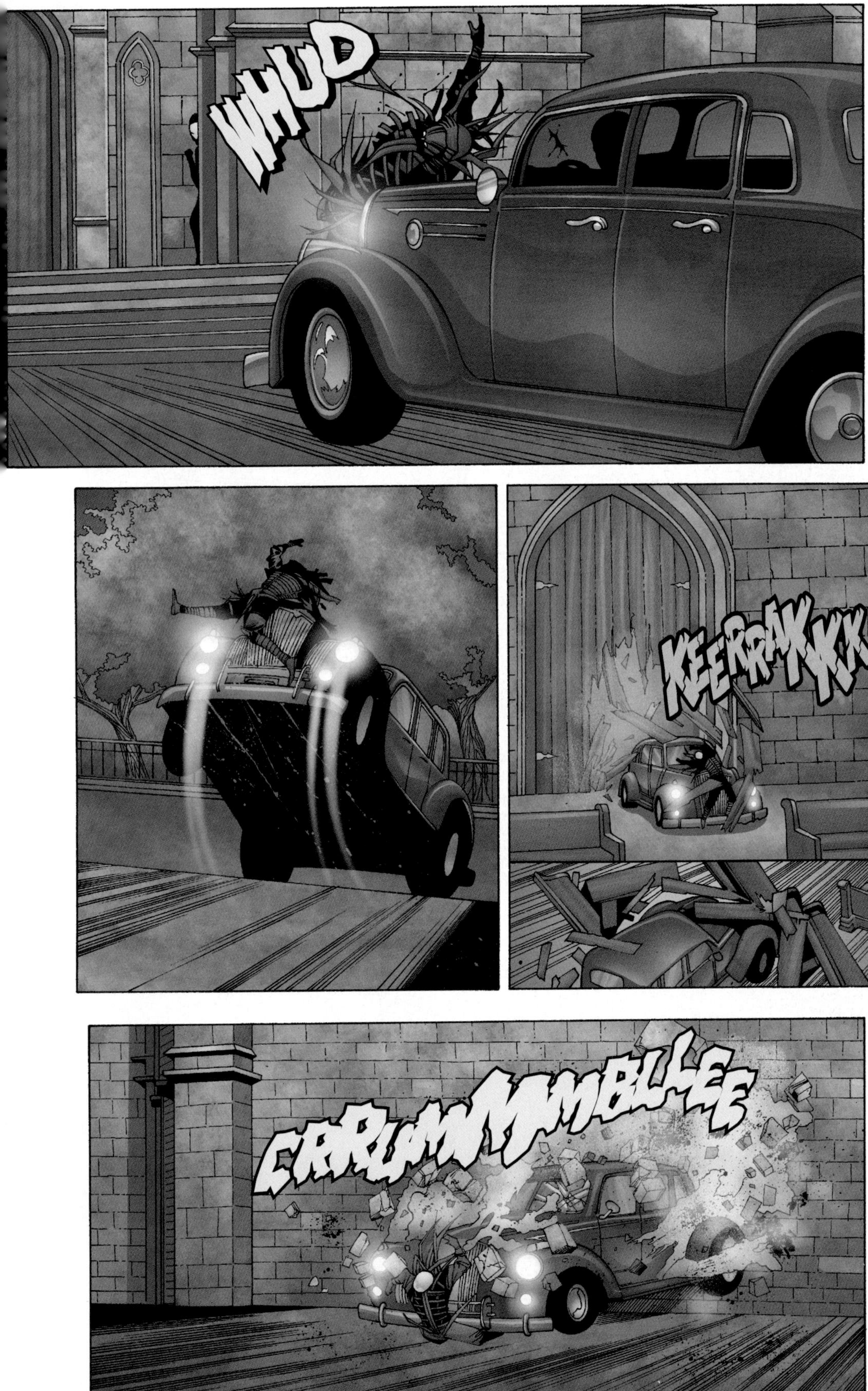
WHUD
KEERRAKKKK
CRRUMMMMBLLEE

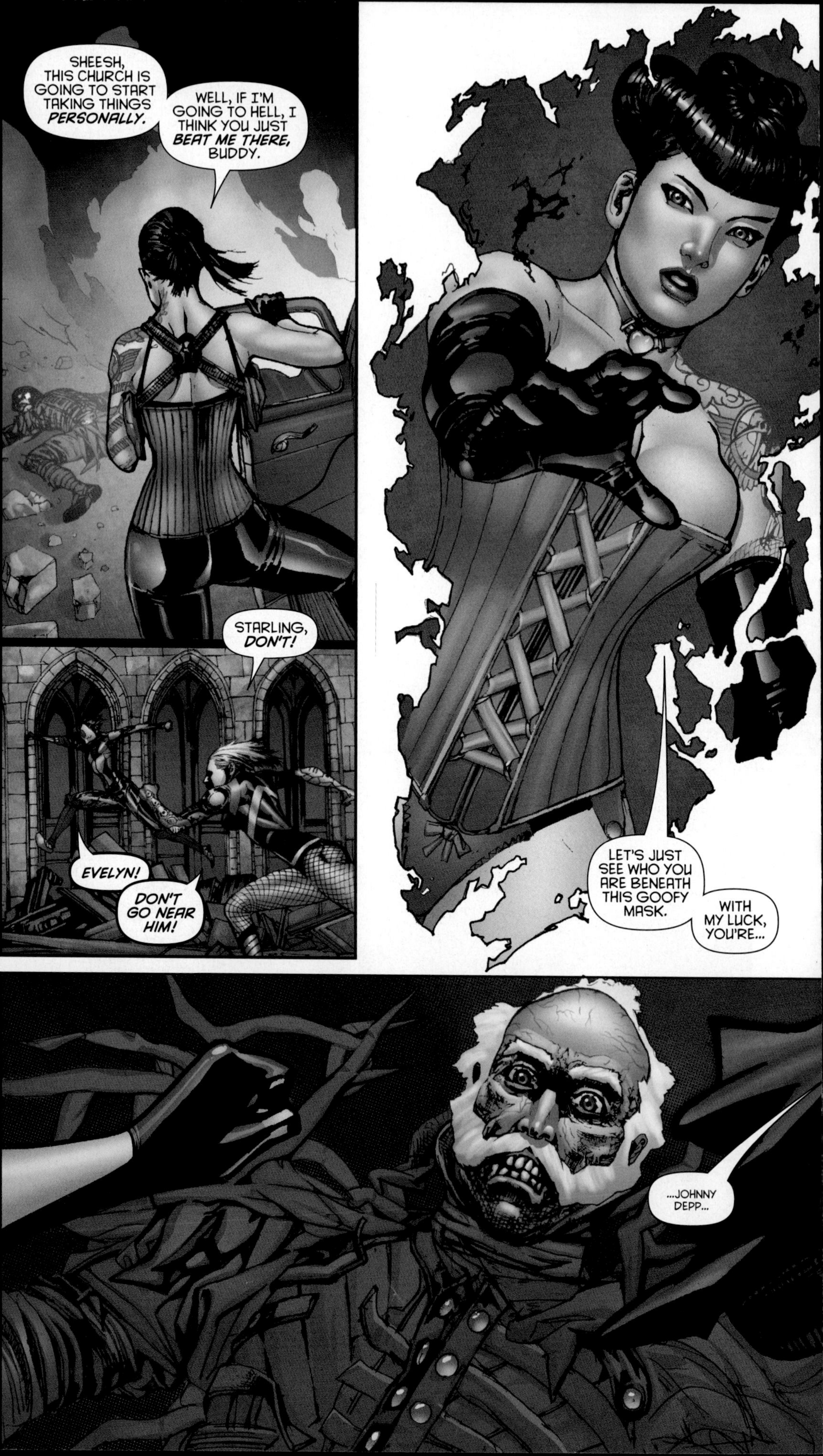
SHEESH, THIS CHURCH IS GOING TO START TAKING THINGS PERSONALLY.
WELL, IF I'M GOING TO HELL, I THINK YOU JUST BEAT ME THERE, BUDDY.
STARLING, DON'T!
EVELYN!
DON'T GO NEAR HIM!
LET'S JUST SEE WHO YOU ARE BENEATH THIS GOOFY MASK.
WITH MY LUCK, YOU'RE...
...JOHNNY DEPP...

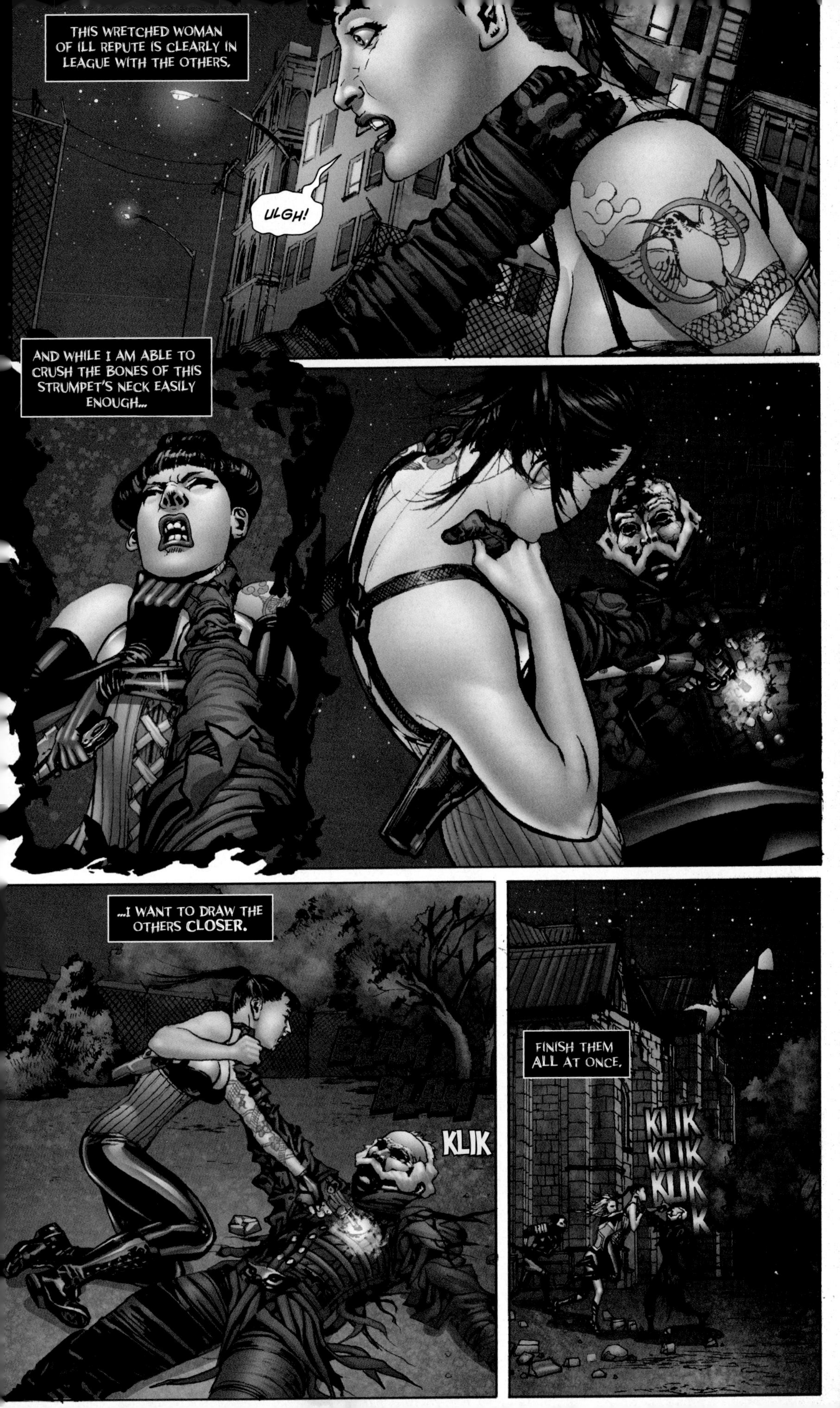

THIS WRETCHED WOMAN OF ILL REPUTE IS CLEARLY IN LEAGUE WITH THE OTHERS.
ULGH!
AND WHILE I AM ABLE TO CRUSH THE BONES OF THIS STRUMPET'S NECK EASILY ENOUGH...
...I WANT TO DRAW THE OTHERS CLOSER.
KLIK
FINISH THEM ALL AT ONCE.
KLIK
KLIK
KLIK
K

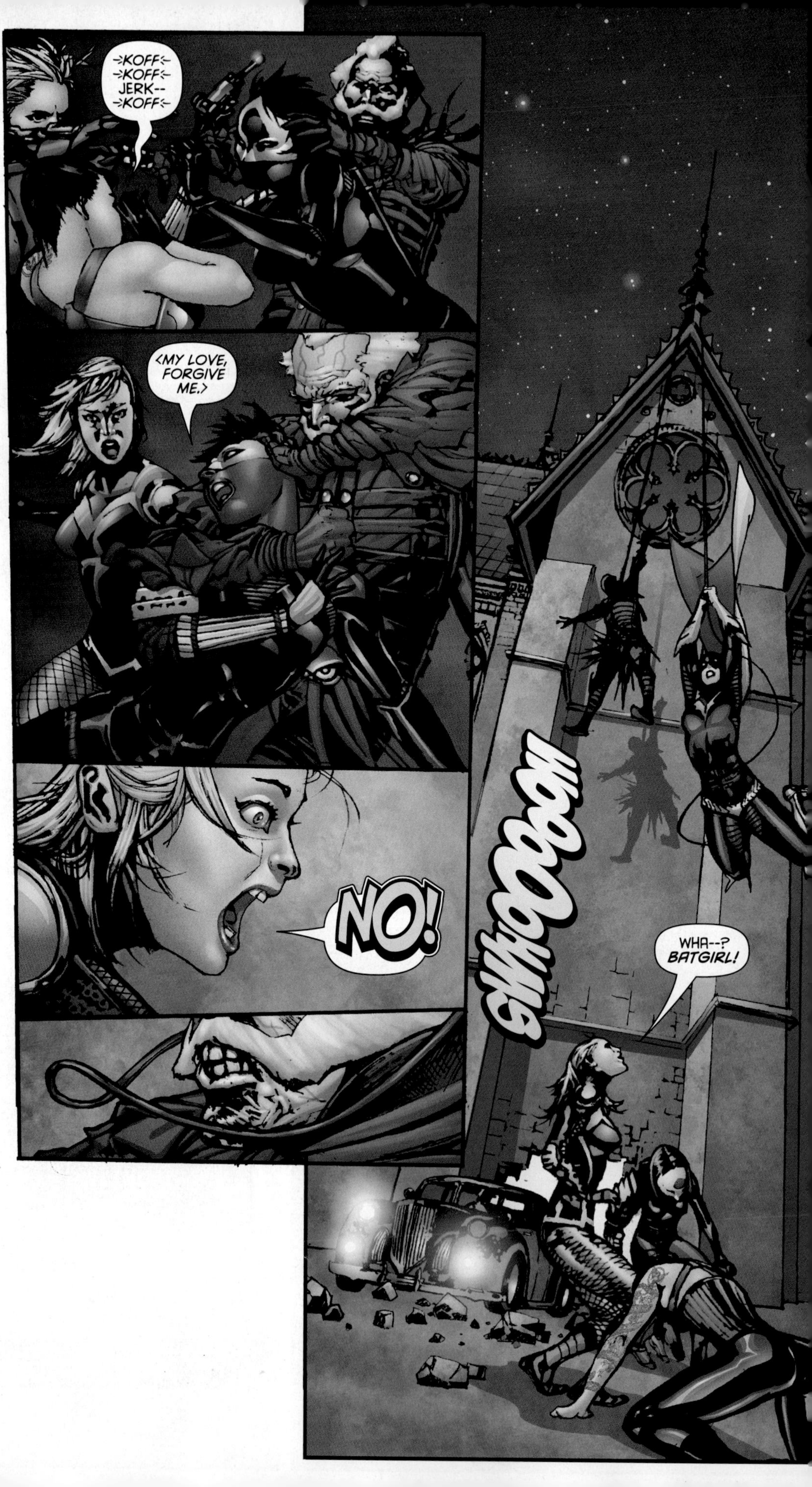

-KOFF- -KOFF- JERK-- -KOFF-
<MY LOVE, FORGIVE ME.>
NO!
SHWOOOOM
WHA--? BATGIRL!

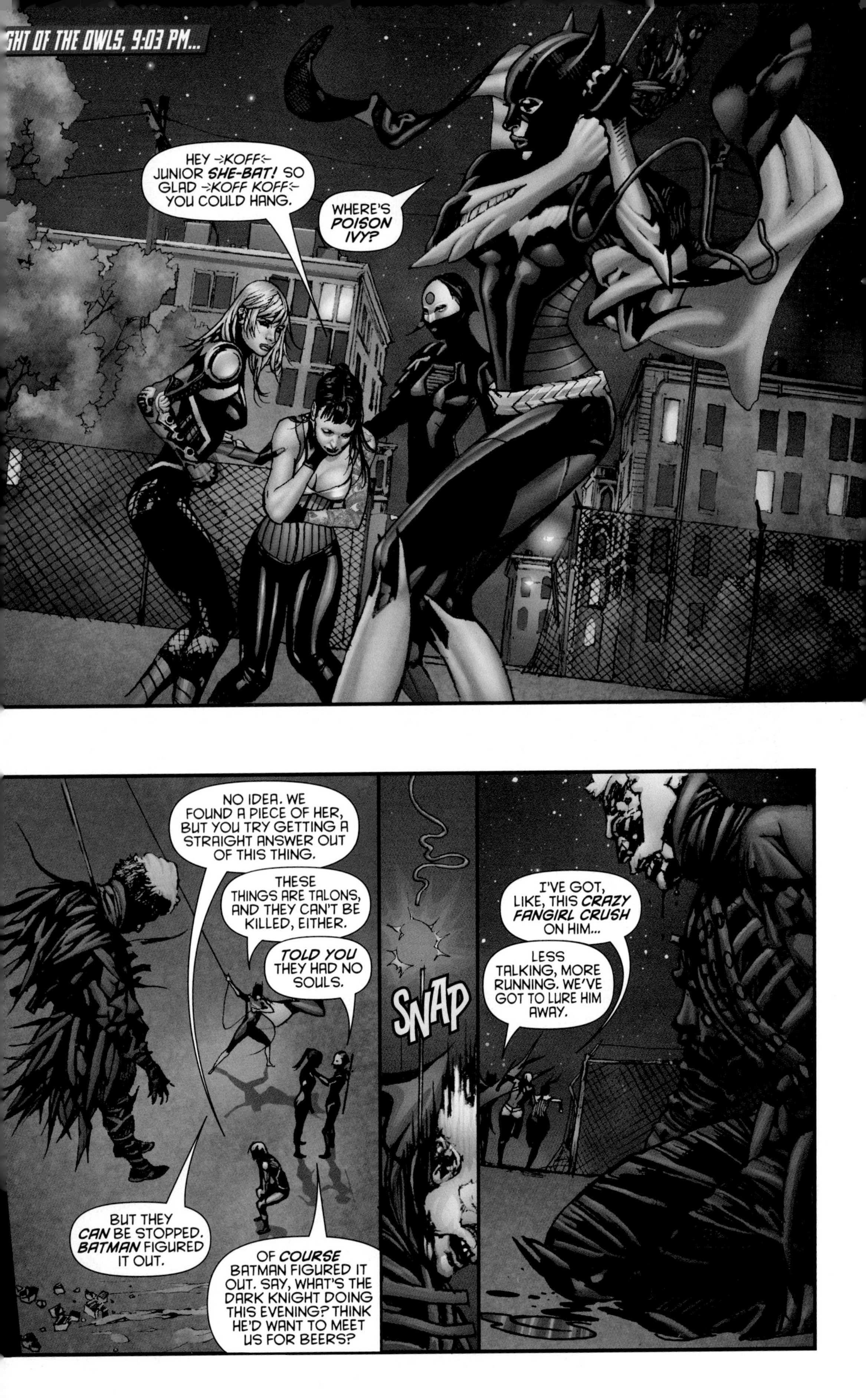
GHT OF THE OWLS, 9:03 PM...
HEY ⇢KOFF⇠ JUNIOR SHE-BAT! SO GLAD ⇢KOFF KOFF⇠ YOU COULD HANG.
WHERE'S POISON IVY?
NO IDEA. WE FOUND A PIECE OF HER, BUT YOU TRY GETTING A STRAIGHT ANSWER OUT OF THIS THING.
THESE THINGS ARE TALONS, AND THEY CAN'T BE KILLED, EITHER.
TOLD YOU THEY HAD NO SOULS.
BUT THEY CAN BE STOPPED. BATMAN FIGURED IT OUT.
OF COURSE BATMAN FIGURED IT OUT. SAY, WHAT'S THE DARK KNIGHT DOING THIS EVENING? THINK HE'D WANT TO MEET US FOR BEERS?
SNAP
I'VE GOT, LIKE, THIS CRAZY FANGIRL CRUSH ON HIM...
LESS TALKING, MORE RUNNING. WE'VE GOT TO LURE HIM AWAY.

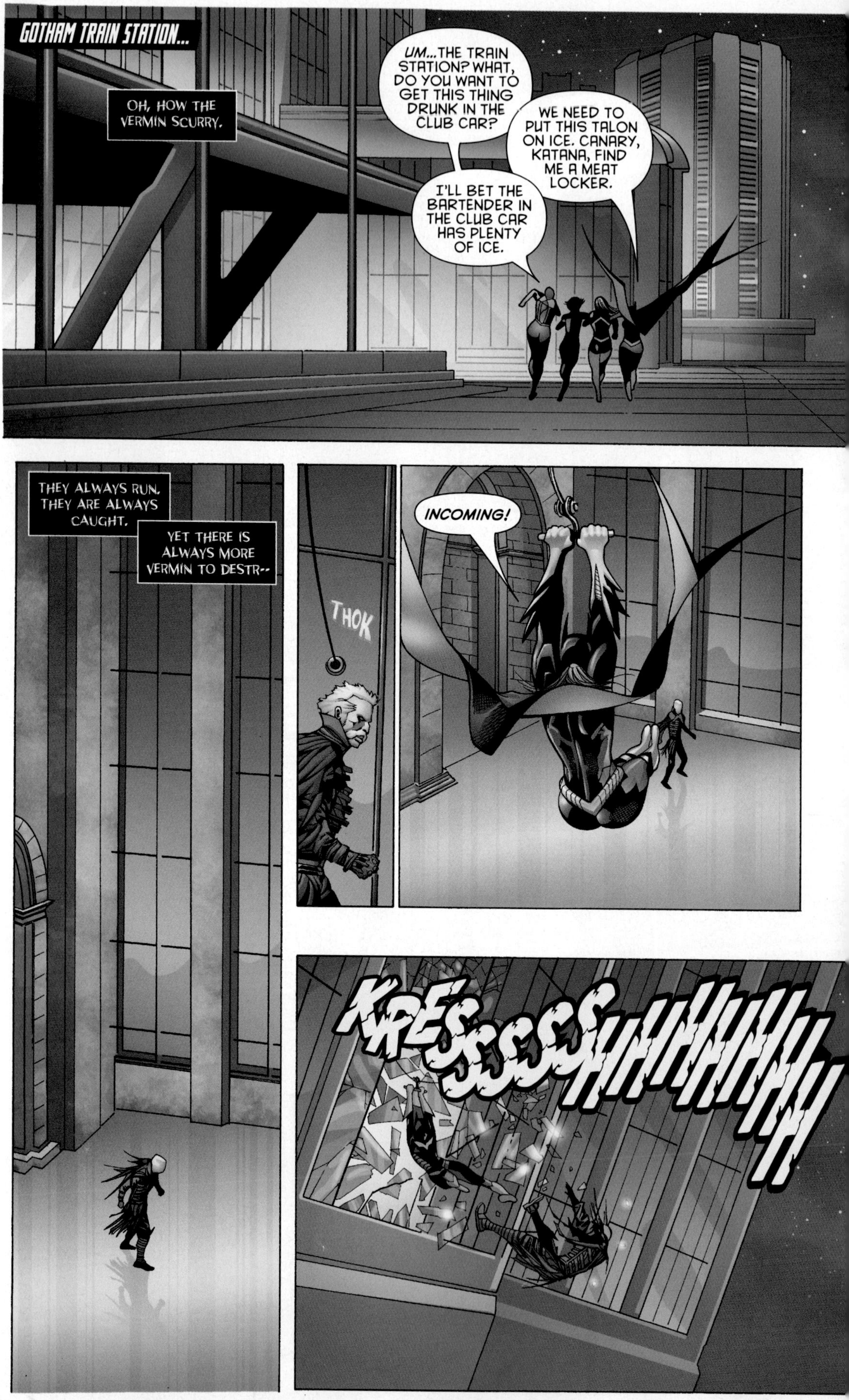
GOTHAM TRAIN STATION...
OH, HOW THE VERMIN SCURRY.
UM...THE TRAIN STATION? WHAT, DO YOU WANT TO GET THIS THING DRUNK IN THE CLUB CAR?
WE NEED TO PUT THIS TALON ON ICE. CANARY, KATANA, FIND ME A MEAT LOCKER.
I'LL BET THE BARTENDER IN THE CLUB CAR HAS PLENTY OF ICE.
THEY ALWAYS RUN. THEY ARE ALWAYS CAUGHT.
YET THERE IS ALWAYS MORE VERMIN TO DESTR--
THOK
INCOMING!
KRESSSSSSHHHHHHHH

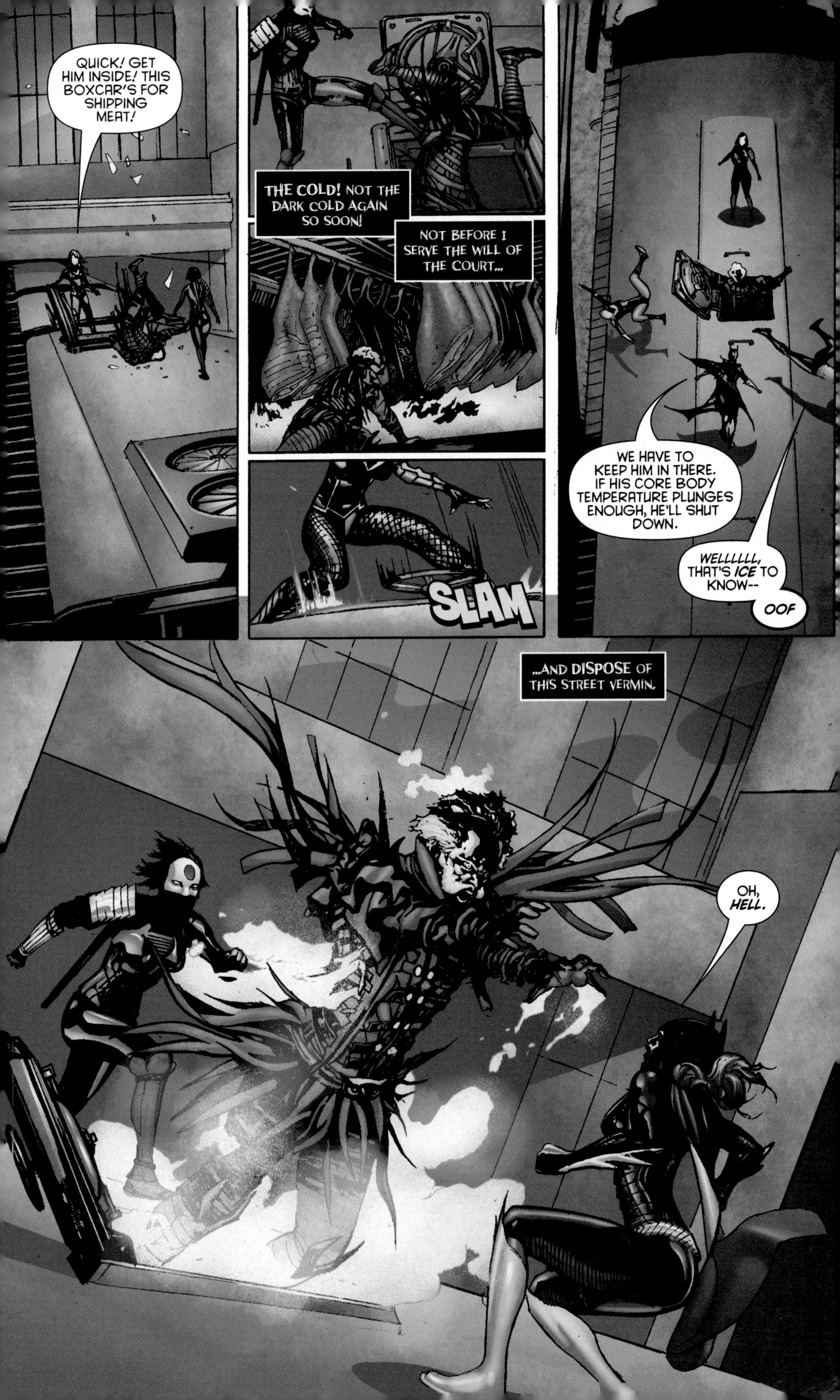
QUICK! GET HIM INSIDE! THIS BOXCAR'S FOR SHIPPING MEAT!
THE COLD! NOT THE DARK COLD AGAIN SO SOON!
NOT BEFORE I SERVE THE WILL OF THE COURT...
SLAM
WE HAVE TO KEEP HIM IN THERE. IF HIS CORE BODY TEMPERATURE PLUNGES ENOUGH, HE'LL SHUT DOWN.
WELLLLLLL, THAT'S ICE TO KNOW--
OOF
...AND DISPOSE OF THIS STREET VERMIN.
OH, HELL.

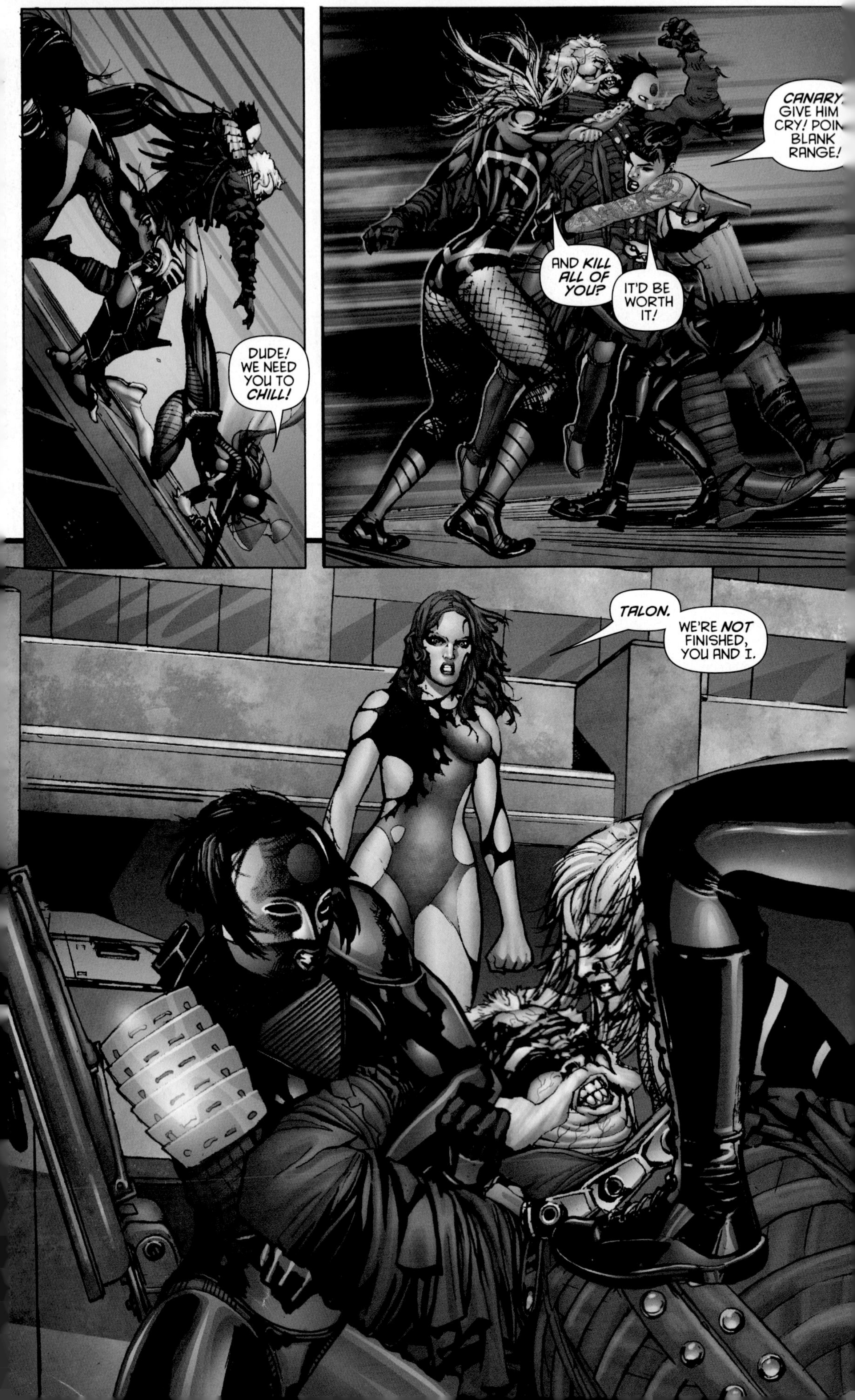
DUDE! WE NEED YOU TO CHILL!
CANARY! GIVE HIM CRY! POIN BLANK RANGE!
AND KILL ALL OF YOU?
IT'D BE WORTH IT!
TALON.
WE'RE NOT FINISHED, YOU AND I.

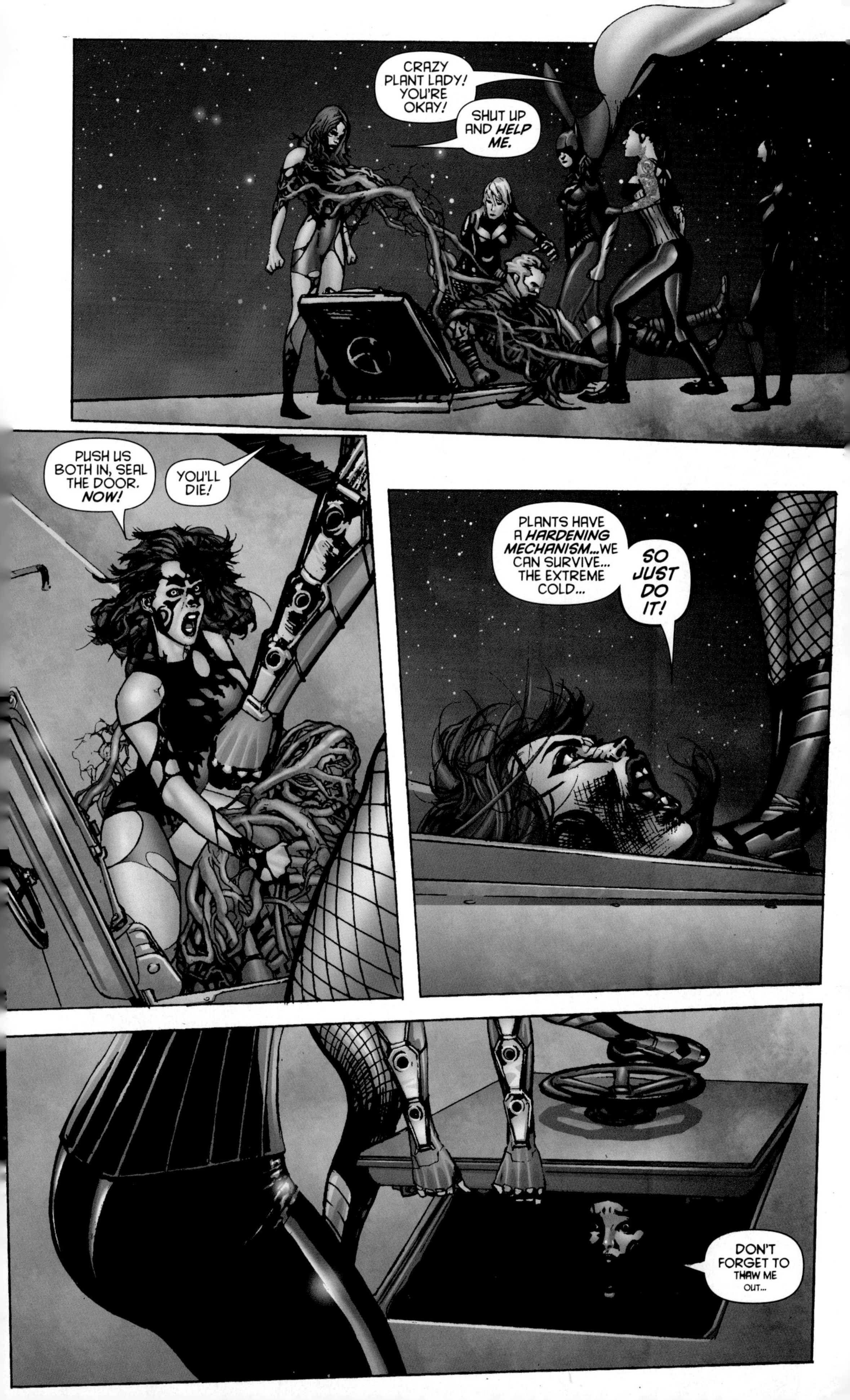
CRAZY PLANT LADY! YOU'RE OKAY!
SHUT UP AND *HELP ME.*
PUSH US BOTH IN, SEAL THE DOOR. *NOW!*
YOU'LL DIE!
PLANTS HAVE A *HARDENING MECHANISM*...WE CAN SURVIVE... THE EXTREME COLD...
SO JUST DO IT!
DON'T FORGET TO THAW ME OUT...

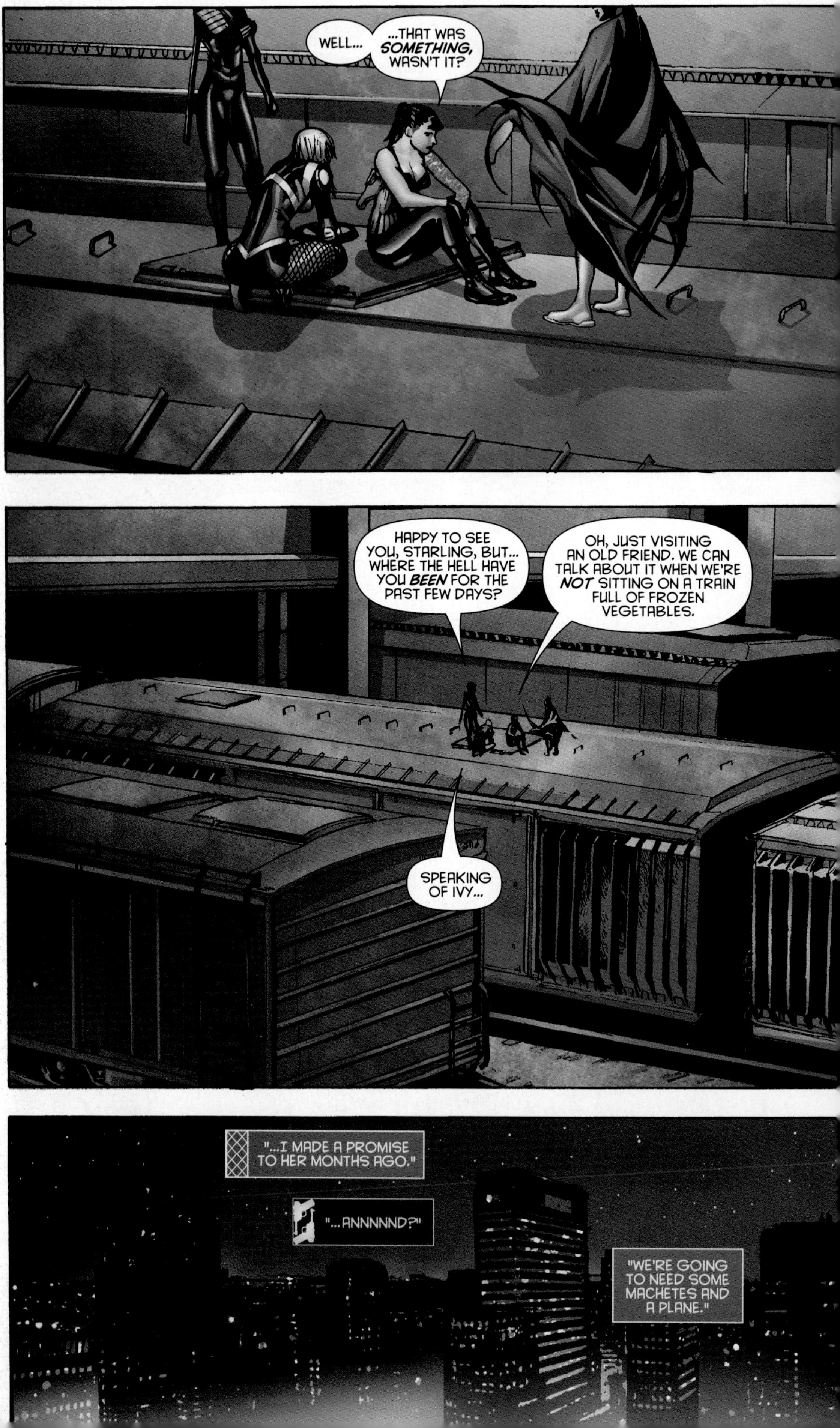
WELL...
...THAT WAS SOMETHING, WASN'T IT?
HAPPY TO SEE YOU, STARLING, BUT... WHERE THE HELL HAVE YOU BEEN FOR THE PAST FEW DAYS?
OH, JUST VISITING AN OLD FRIEND. WE CAN TALK ABOUT IT WHEN WE'RE NOT SITTING ON A TRAIN FULL OF FROZEN VEGETABLES.
SPEAKING OF IVY...
"...I MADE A PROMISE TO HER MONTHS AGO."
"...ANNNNND?"
"WE'RE GOING TO NEED SOME MACHETES AND A PLANE."

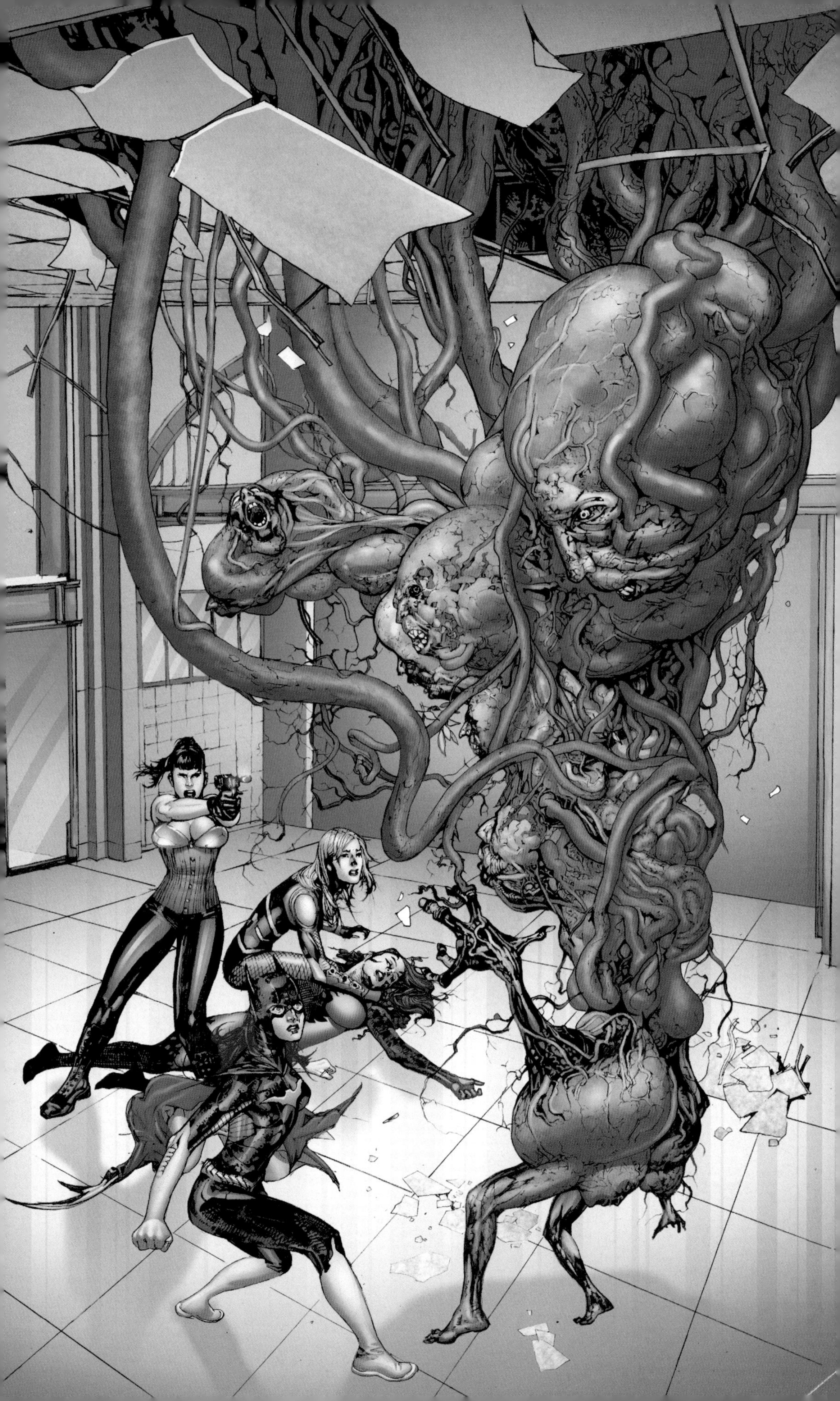

DUANE SWIERCZYNSKI writer TRAVEL FOREMAN artist cover art by TRAVEL FOREMAN & GABE ELTAEB

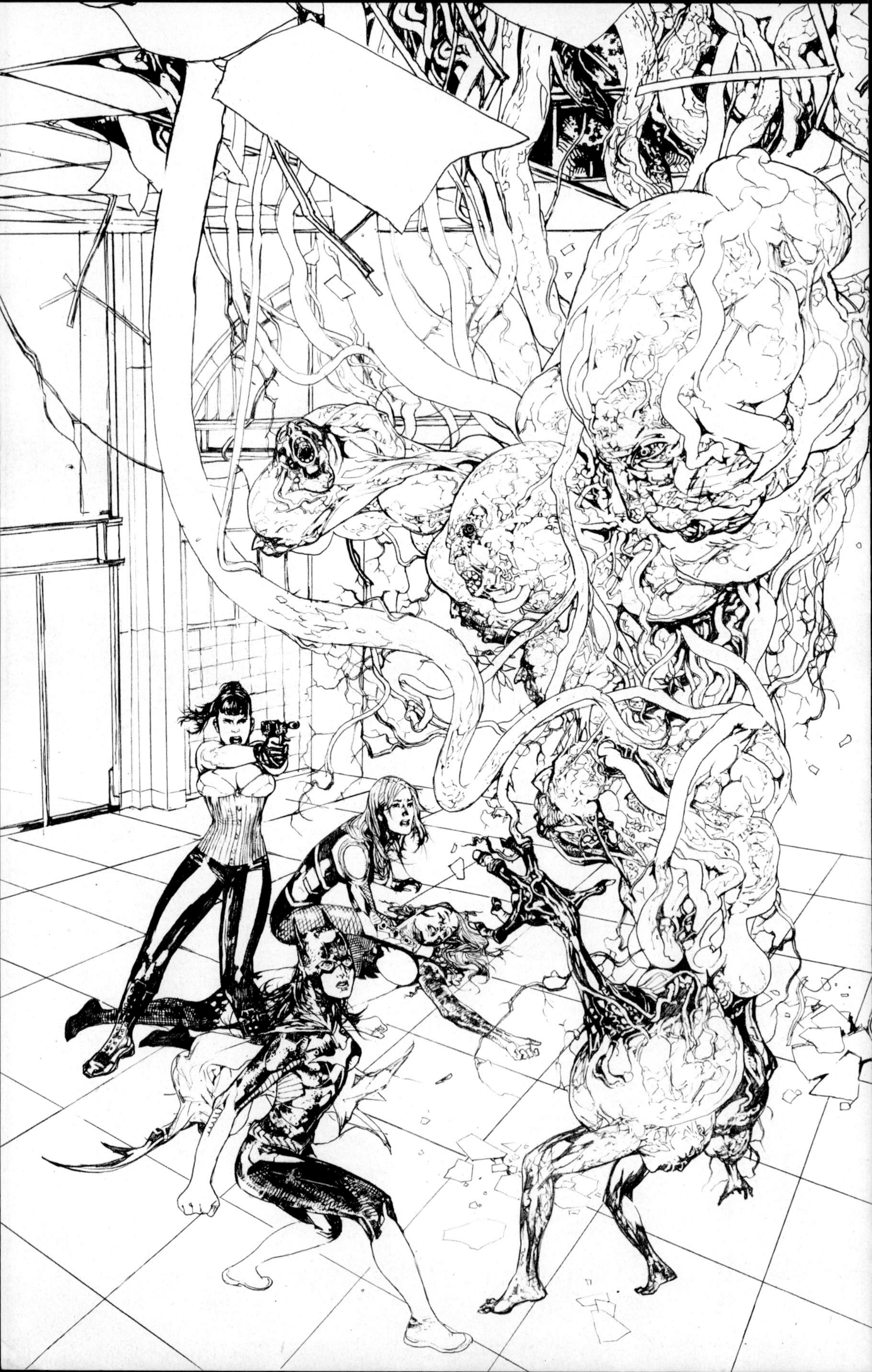

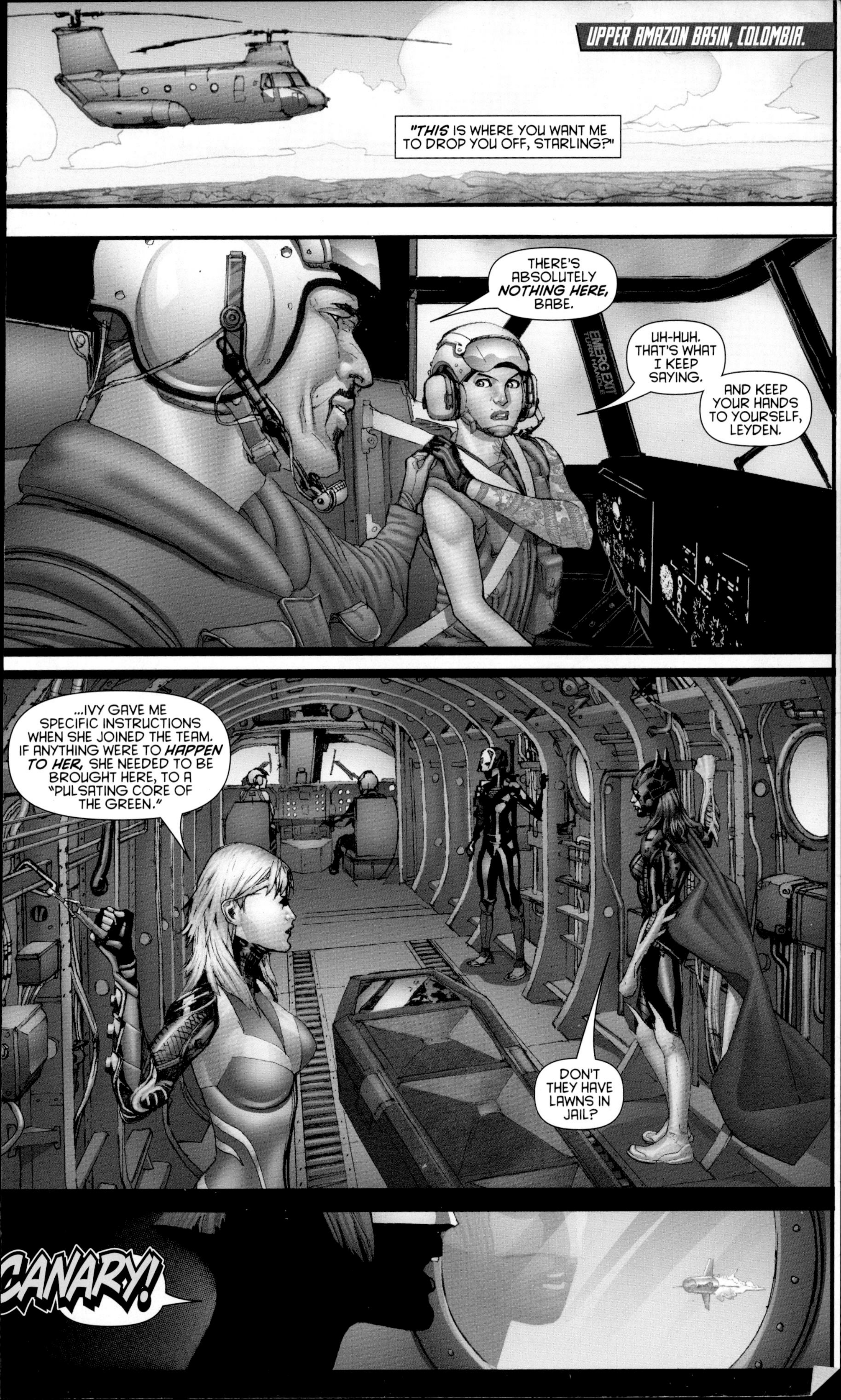
UPPER AMAZON BASIN, COLOMBIA.
"THIS IS WHERE YOU WANT ME TO DROP YOU OFF, STARLING?"
THERE'S ABSOLUTELY NOTHING HERE, BABE.
UH-HUH. THAT'S WHAT I KEEP SAYING.
AND KEEP YOUR HANDS TO YOURSELF, LEYDEN.
EMERG EXIT TURN HANDLE
...IVY GAVE ME SPECIFIC INSTRUCTIONS WHEN SHE JOINED THE TEAM. IF ANYTHING WERE TO HAPPEN TO HER, SHE NEEDED TO BE BROUGHT HERE, TO A "PULSATING CORE OF THE GREEN."
DON'T THEY HAVE LAWNS IN JAIL?
CANARY!

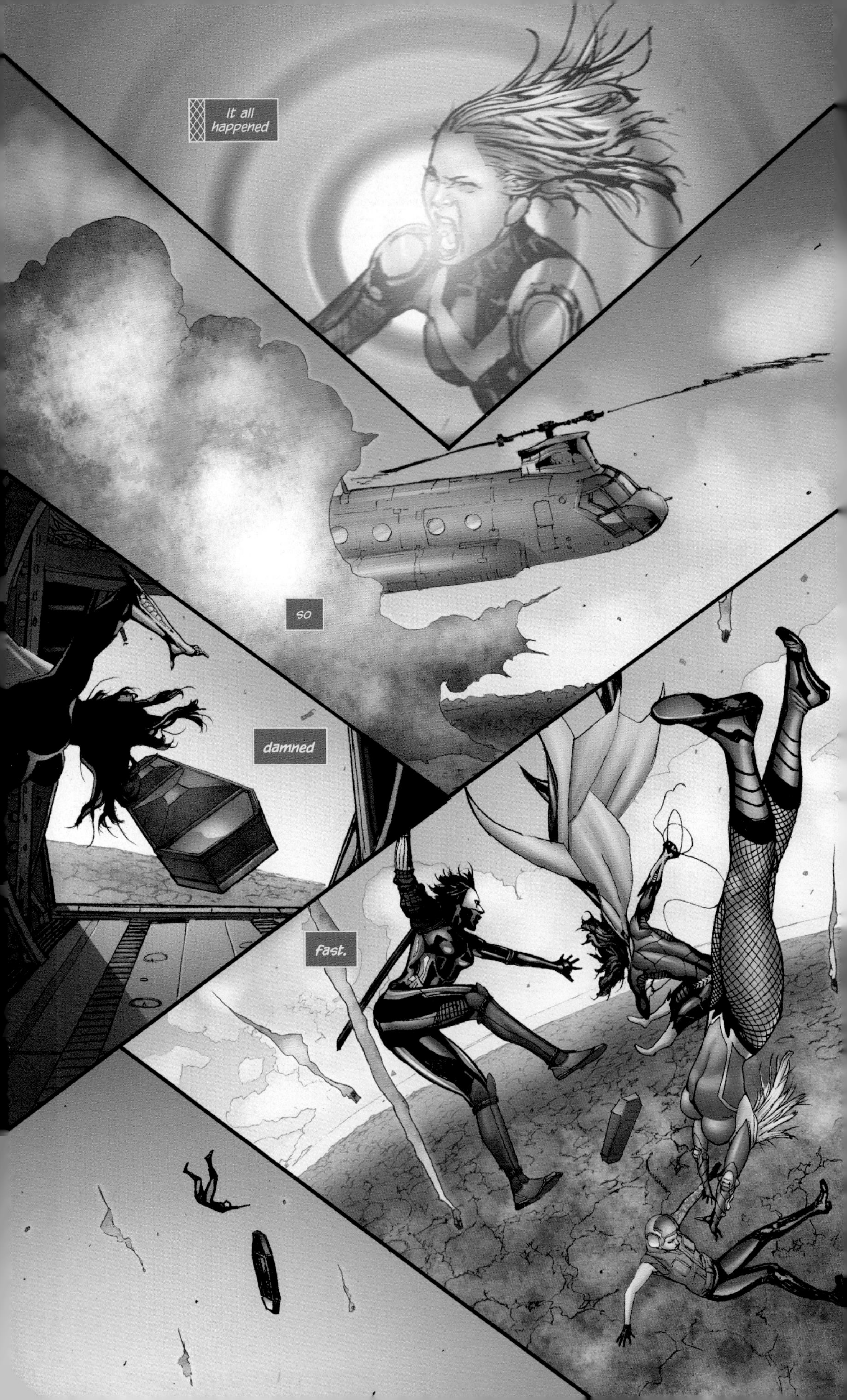
It all happened
so
damned
fast.

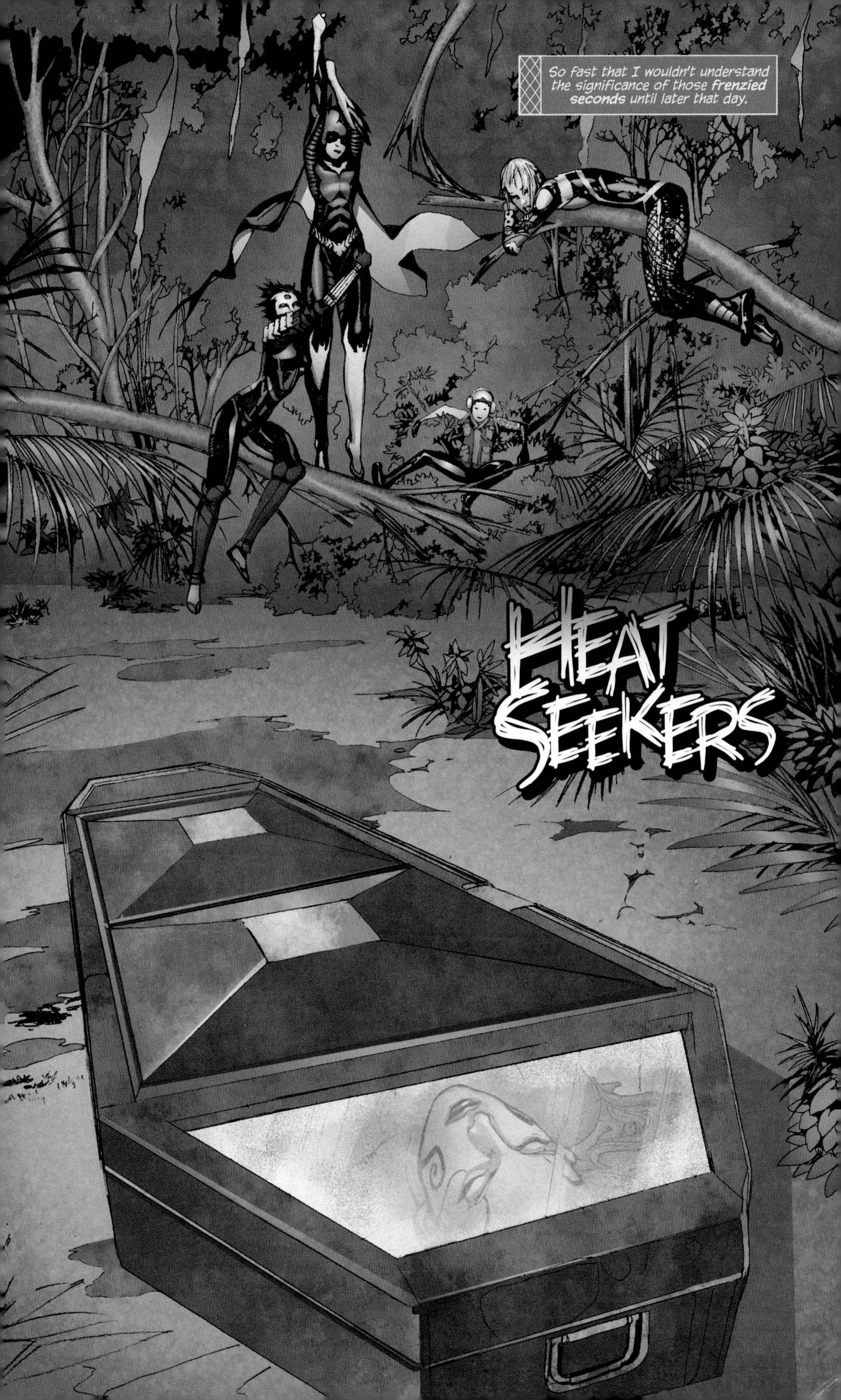
So fast that I wouldn't understand the significance of those frenzied seconds until later that day.
HEAT SEEKERS

AGH, MY EARS...ANYONE ELSE HAVE THIS AWFUL *RINGING THING* GOING ON?

SORRY? DID YOU SAY SOMETHING, BATGIRL?

OH, HELL... ANYBODY SEE *LEYDEN?* DID HE MAKE IT OUT OF THE CHOPPER?

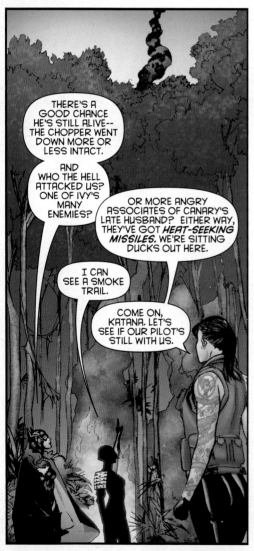

THERE'S A GOOD CHANCE HE'S STILL ALIVE-- THE CHOPPER WENT DOWN MORE OR LESS INTACT.

AND WHO THE HELL ATTACKED US? ONE OF IVY'S MANY ENEMIES?

OR MORE ANGRY ASSOCIATES OF CANARY'S LATE HUSBAND? EITHER WAY, THEY'VE GOT *HEAT-SEEKING MISSILES.* WE'RE SITTING DUCKS OUT HERE.

I CAN SEE A SMOKE TRAIL.

COME ON, KATANA. LET'S SEE IF OUR PILOT'S STILL WITH US.

CANARY... YOU OKAY? I MEAN, ASIDE FROM BEING KNOCKED OUT OF A HELICOPTER AND ALMOST *DYING.*

YEAH. I'M... FINE.

WE NEED TO GET IVY OUT OF THAT *BOX.*

THE HINGES... MUST HAVE BENT... IN THE FALL...

*Poison Ivy was supposed to be our navigator. I thought we'd have a **full day** to thaw her out and rejuvenate her...*

...not a matter of seconds.

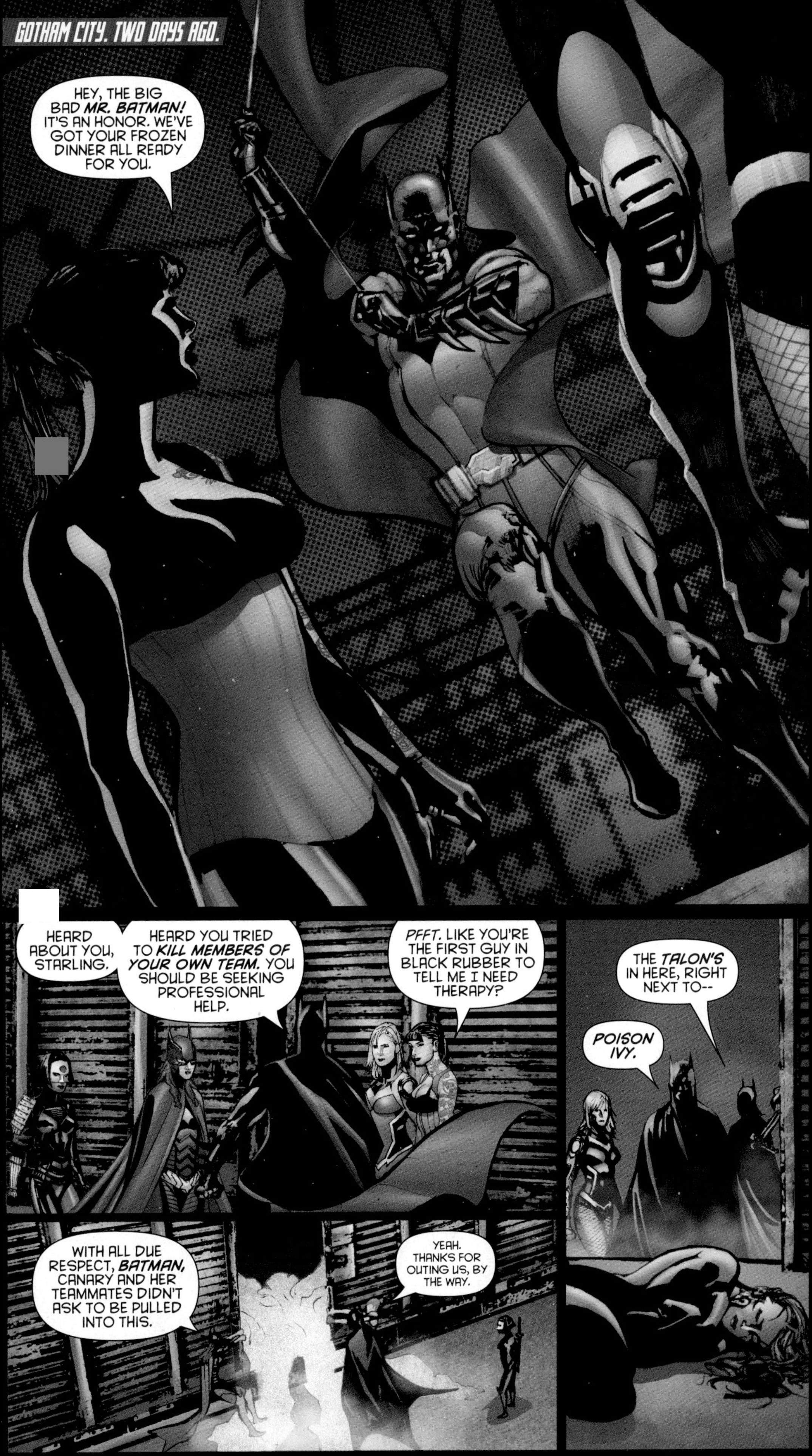
GOTHAM CITY. TWO DAYS AGO.
HEY, THE BIG BAD MR. BATMAN! IT'S AN HONOR. WE'VE GOT YOUR FROZEN DINNER ALL READY FOR YOU.
HEARD ABOUT YOU, STARLING.
HEARD YOU TRIED TO KILL MEMBERS OF YOUR OWN TEAM. YOU SHOULD BE SEEKING PROFESSIONAL HELP.
PFFT. LIKE YOU'RE THE FIRST GUY IN BLACK RUBBER TO TELL ME I NEED THERAPY?
THE TALON'S IN HERE, RIGHT NEXT TO--
POISON IVY.
WITH ALL DUE RESPECT, BATMAN, CANARY AND HER TEAMMATES DIDN'T ASK TO BE PULLED INTO THIS.
YEAH. THANKS FOR OUTING US, BY THE WAY.

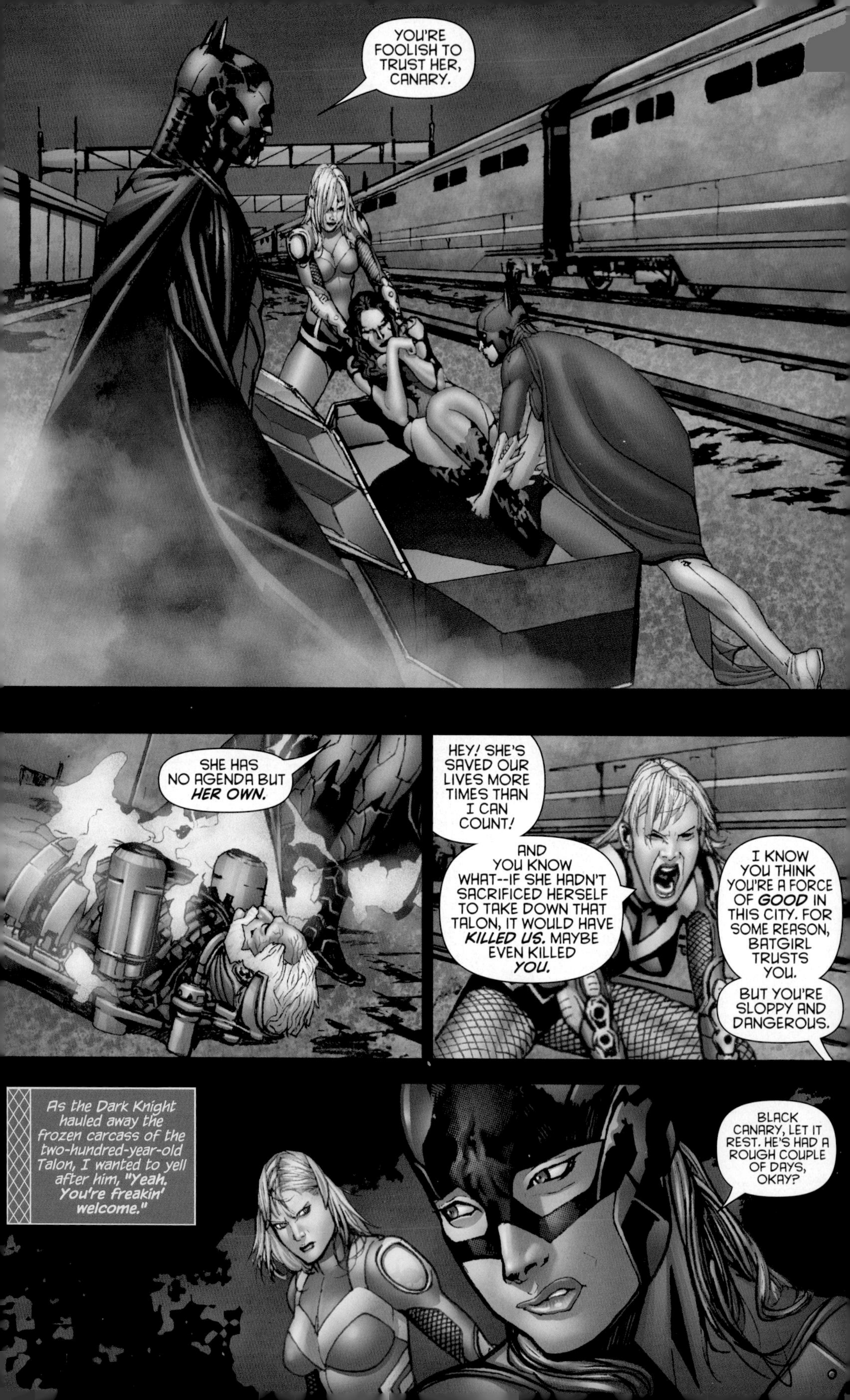

YOU'RE FOOLISH TO TRUST HER, CANARY.
SHE HAS NO AGENDA BUT *HER OWN.*
HEY! SHE'S SAVED OUR LIVES MORE TIMES THAN I CAN COUNT!
AND YOU KNOW WHAT--IF SHE HADN'T SACRIFICED HERSELF TO TAKE DOWN THAT TALON, IT WOULD HAVE *KILLED US.* MAYBE EVEN KILLED *YOU.*
I KNOW YOU THINK YOU'RE A FORCE OF *GOOD* IN THIS CITY. FOR SOME REASON, BATGIRL TRUSTS YOU.
BUT YOU'RE SLOPPY AND DANGEROUS.
*As the Dark Knight hauled away the frozen carcass of the two-hundred-year-old Talon, I wanted to yell after him, **"Yeah. You're freakin' welcome."***
BLACK CANARY, LET IT REST. HE'S HAD A ROUGH COUPLE OF DAYS, OKAY?

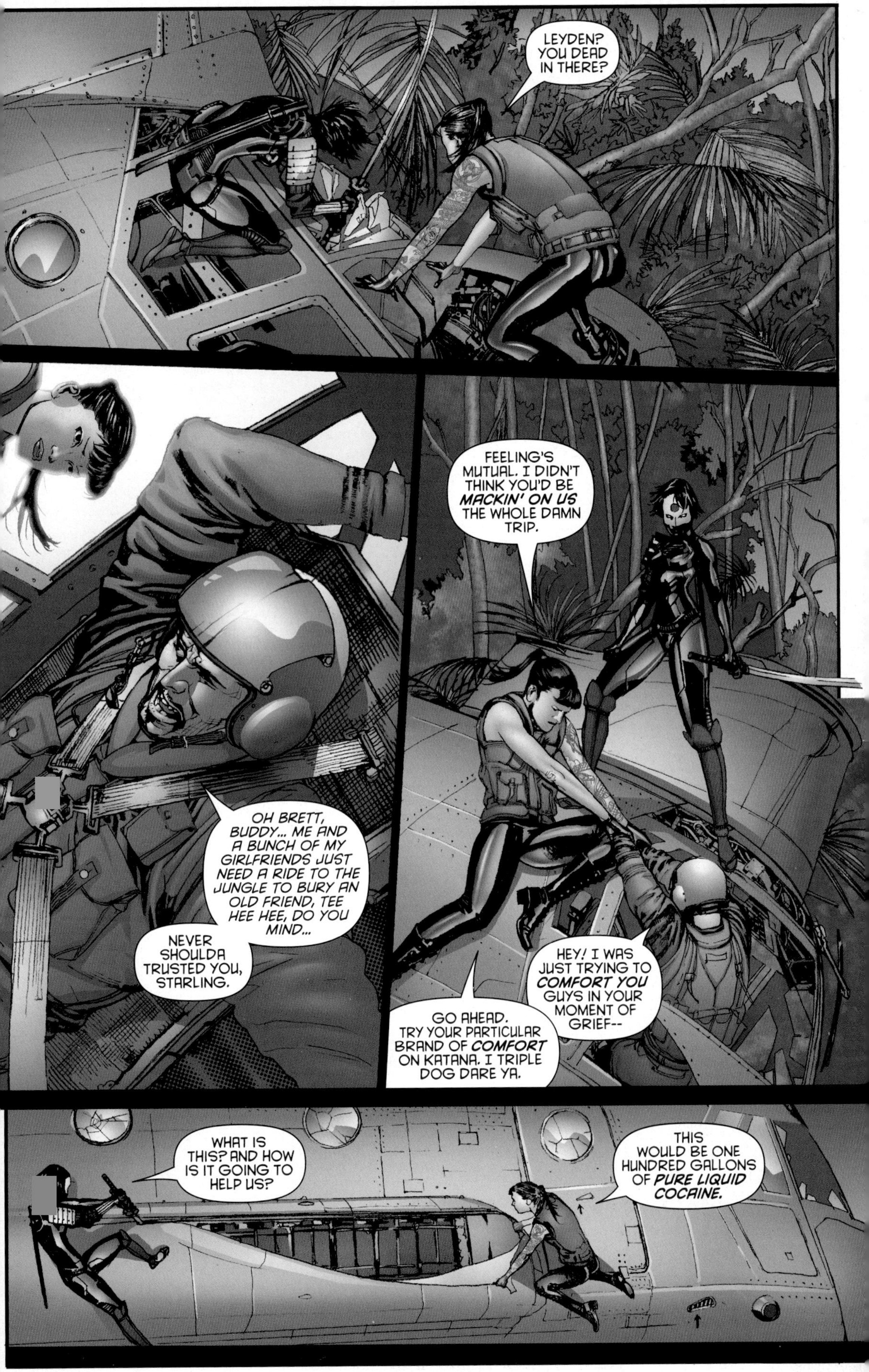

LEYDEN? YOU DEAD IN THERE?
OH BRETT, BUDDY... ME AND A BUNCH OF MY GIRLFRIENDS JUST NEED A RIDE TO THE JUNGLE TO BURY AN OLD FRIEND, TEE HEE HEE, DO YOU MIND...
NEVER SHOULDA TRUSTED YOU, STARLING.
FEELING'S MUTUAL. I DIDN'T THINK YOU'D BE *MACKIN' ON US* THE WHOLE DAMN TRIP.
HEY! I WAS JUST TRYING TO *COMFORT YOU* GUYS IN YOUR MOMENT OF GRIEF--
GO AHEAD. TRY YOUR PARTICULAR BRAND OF *COMFORT* ON KATANA. I TRIPLE DOG DARE YA.
WHAT IS THIS? AND HOW IS IT GOING TO HELP US?
THIS WOULD BE ONE HUNDRED GALLONS OF *PURE LIQUID COCAINE.*

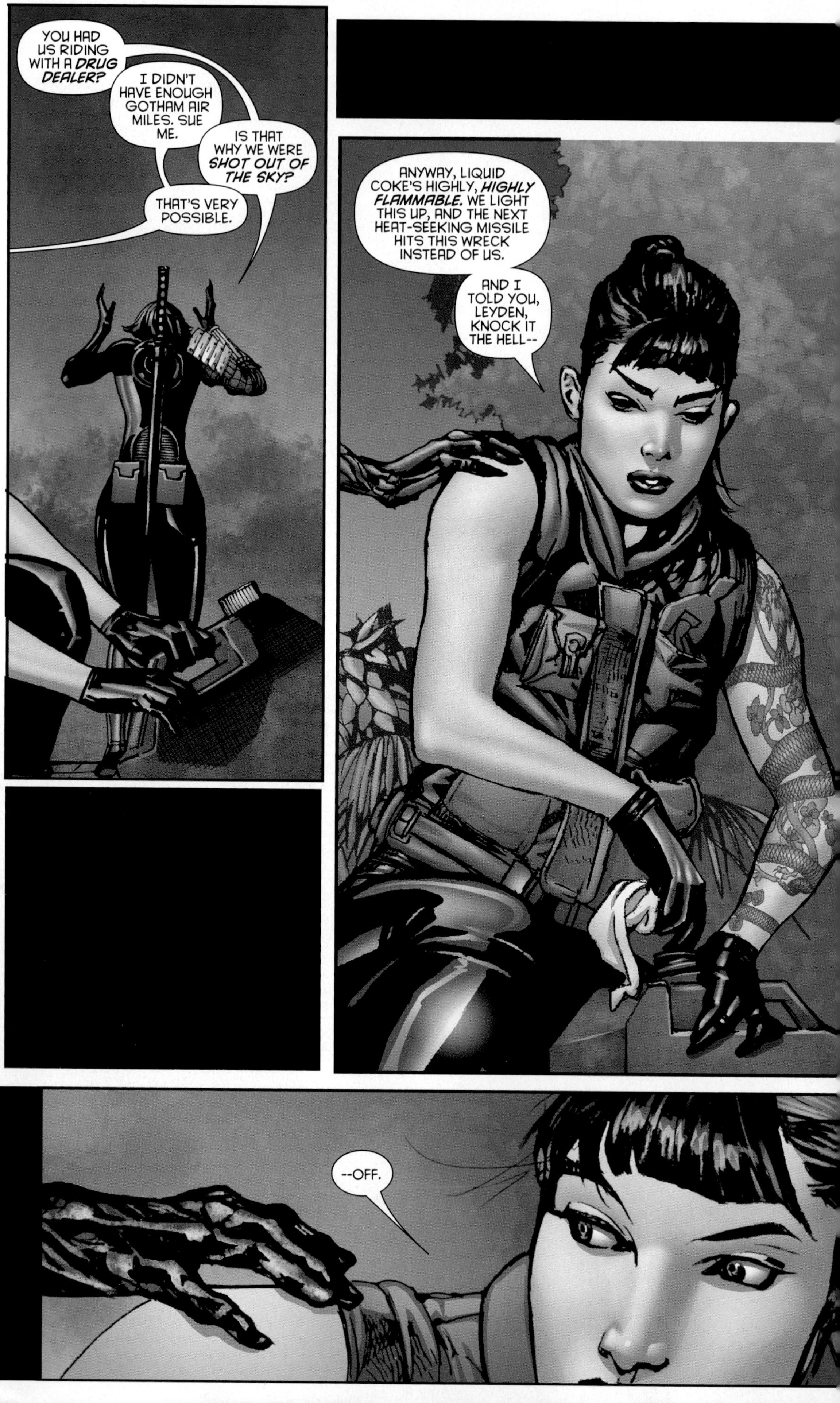
YOU HAD US RIDING WITH A DRUG DEALER?
I DIDN'T HAVE ENOUGH GOTHAM AIR MILES. SUE ME.
IS THAT WHY WE WERE SHOT OUT OF THE SKY?
THAT'S VERY POSSIBLE.
ANYWAY, LIQUID COKE'S HIGHLY, HIGHLY FLAMMABLE. WE LIGHT THIS UP, AND THE NEXT HEAT-SEEKING MISSILE HITS THIS WRECK INSTEAD OF US.
AND I TOLD YOU, LEYDEN, KNOCK IT THE HELL--
--OFF.

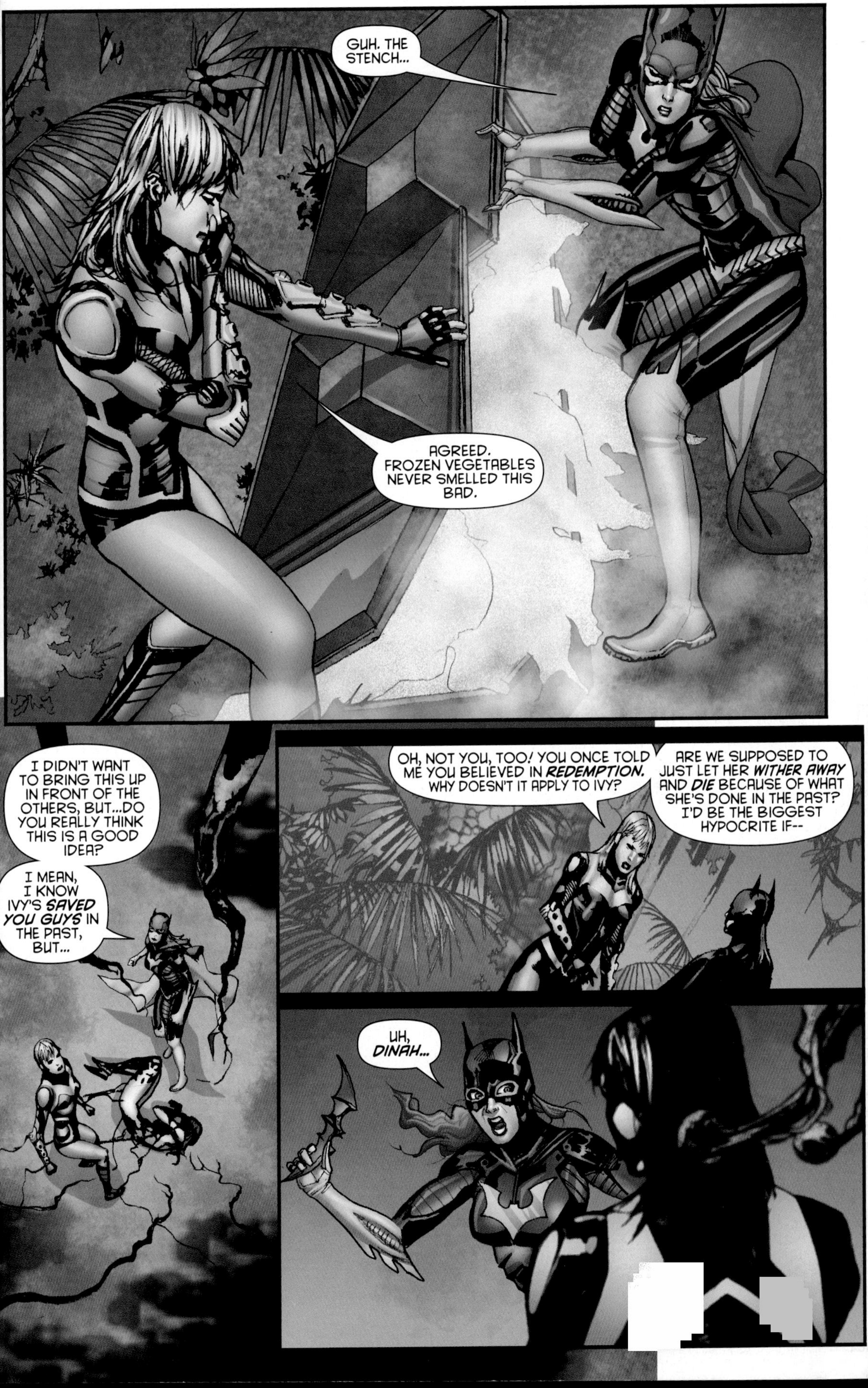
GUH. THE STENCH...
AGREED. FROZEN VEGETABLES NEVER SMELLED THIS BAD.
I DIDN'T WANT TO BRING THIS UP IN FRONT OF THE OTHERS, BUT...DO YOU REALLY THINK THIS IS A GOOD IDEA?
I MEAN, I KNOW IVY'S SAVED YOU GUYS IN THE PAST, BUT...
OH, NOT YOU, TOO! YOU ONCE TOLD ME YOU BELIEVED IN REDEMPTION. WHY DOESN'T IT APPLY TO IVY?
ARE WE SUPPOSED TO JUST LET HER WITHER AWAY AND DIE BECAUSE OF WHAT SHE'S DONE IN THE PAST? I'D BE THE BIGGEST HYPOCRITE IF--
UH, DINAH...

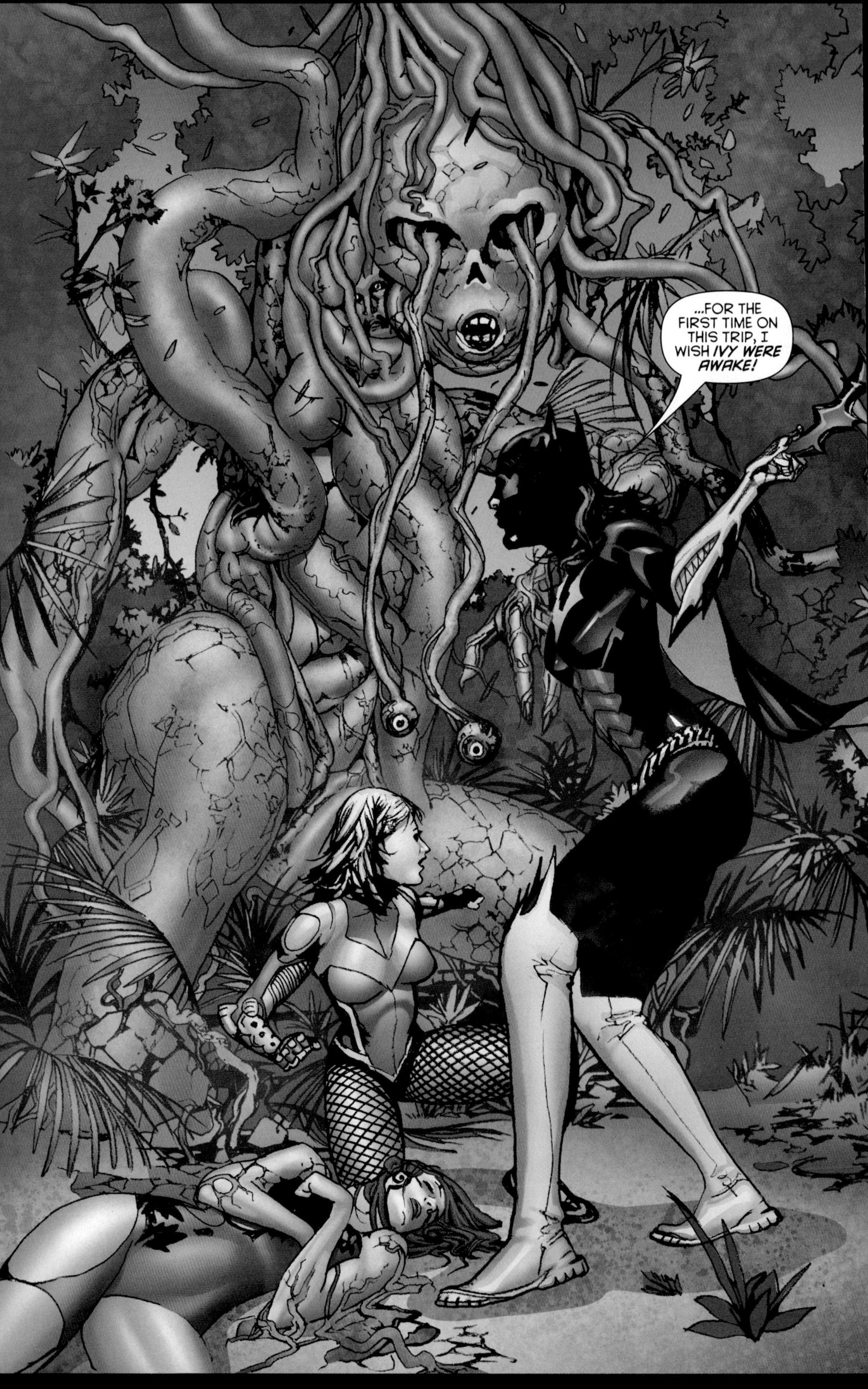
...FOR THE FIRST TIME ON THIS TRIP, I WISH IVY WERE AWAKE!

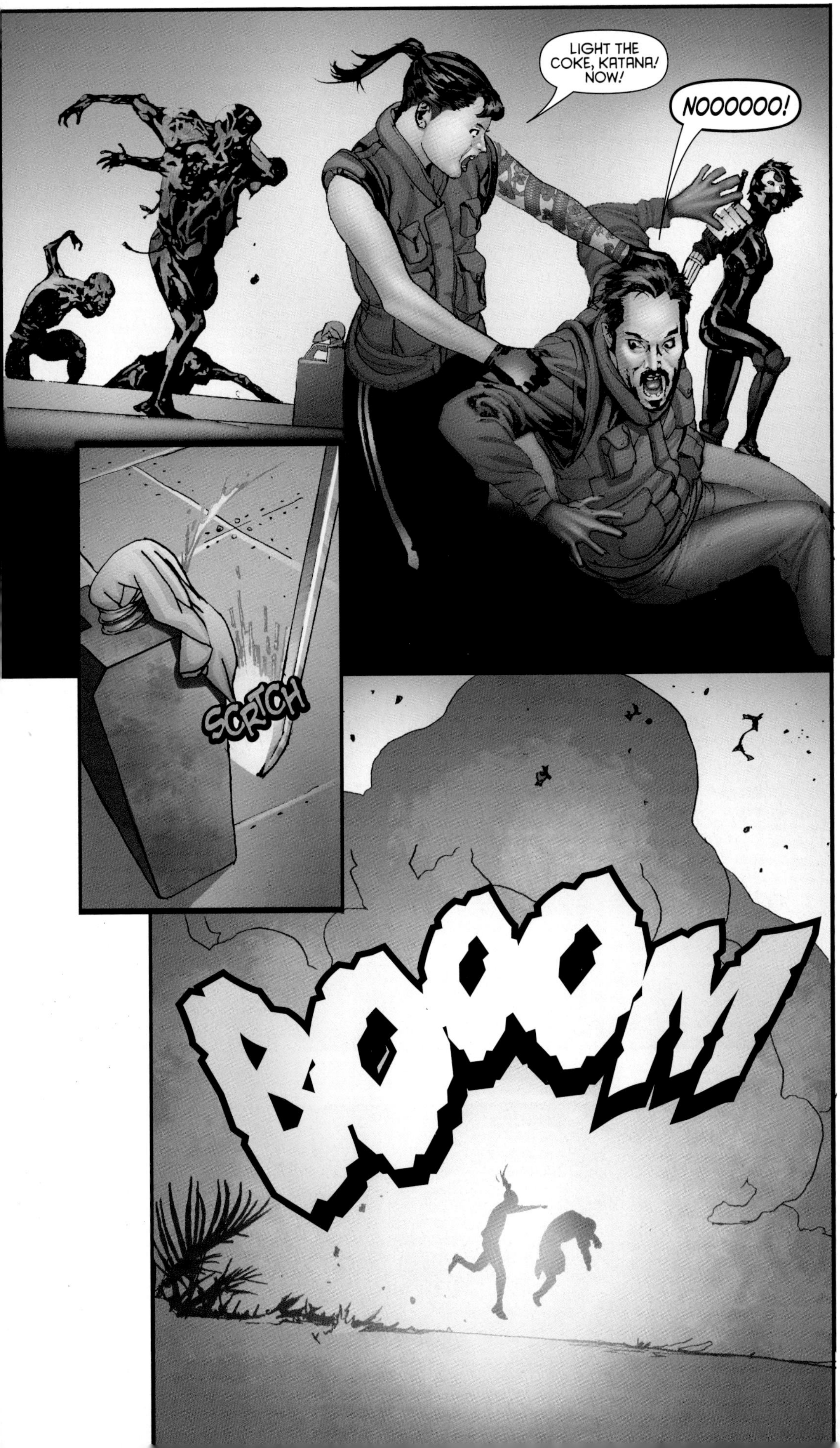
LIGHT THE COKE, KATANA! NOW!
NOOOOOO!
SCRTCH
BOOM

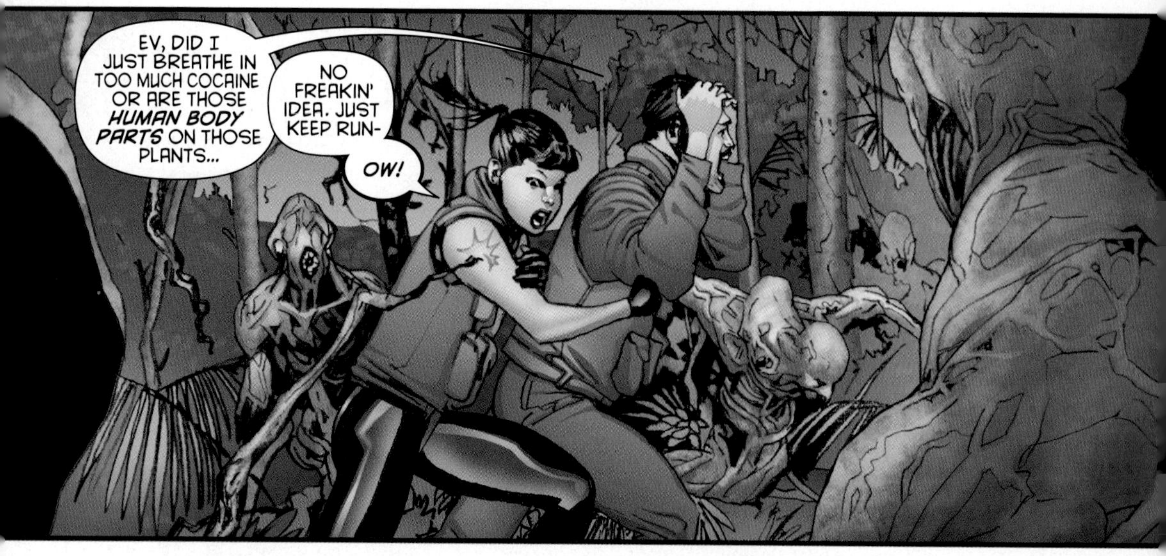
EV, DID I JUST BREATHE IN TOO MUCH COCAINE OR ARE THOSE *HUMAN BODY PARTS* ON THOSE PLANTS...
NO FREAKIN' IDEA. JUST KEEP RUN-
OW!

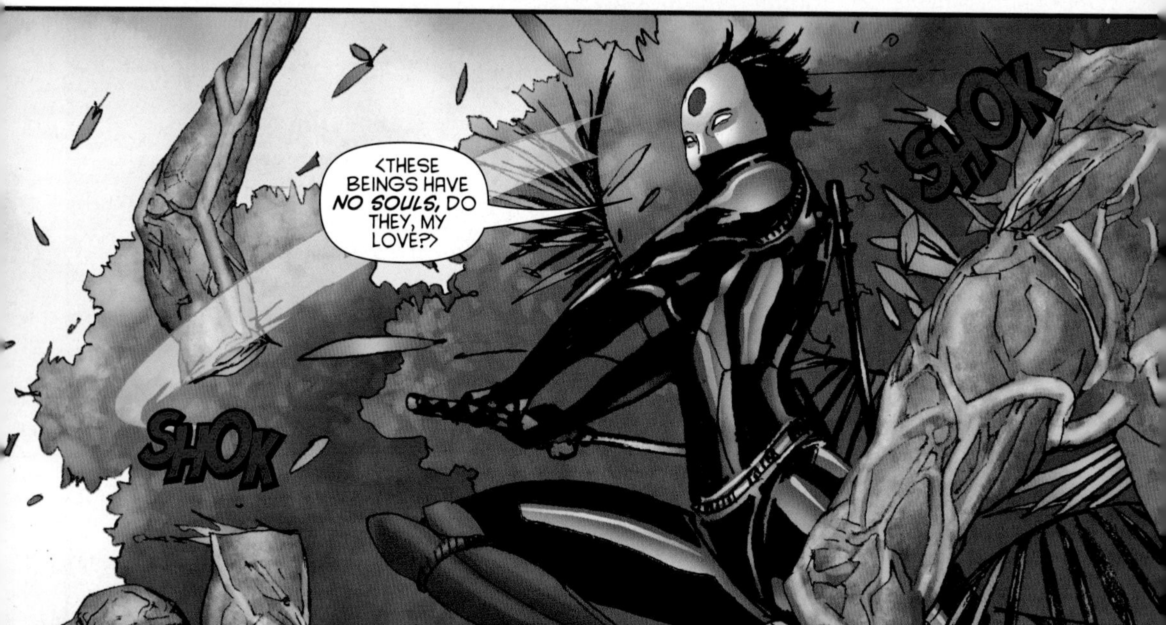
<THESE BEINGS HAVE *NO SOULS,* DO THEY, MY LOVE?>
SHOK
SHOK

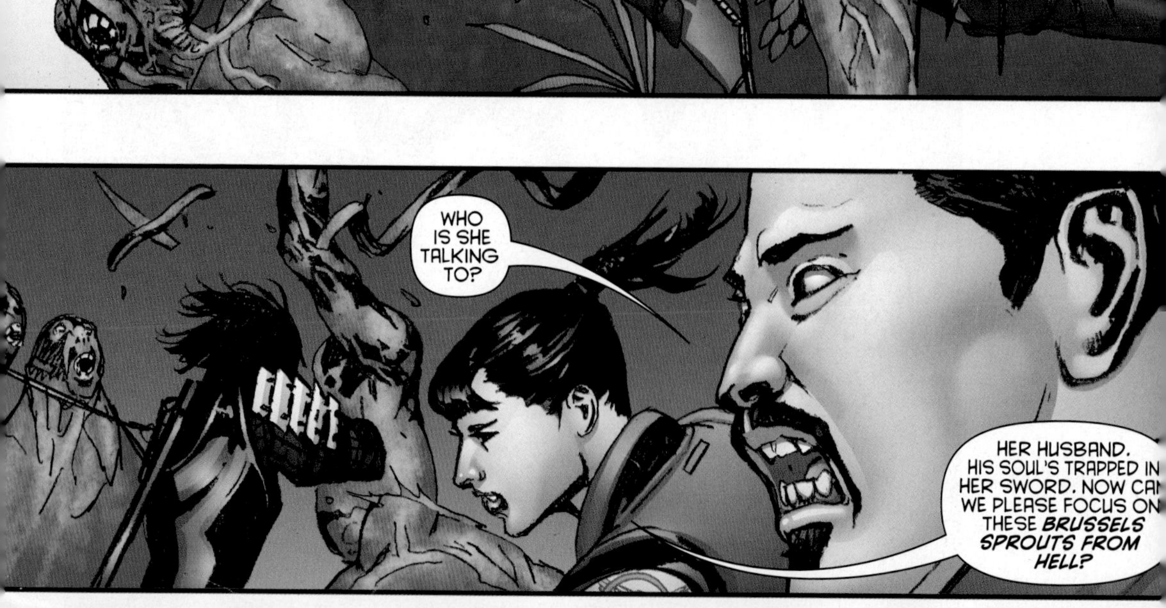
WHO IS SHE TALKING TO?
HER HUSBAND. HIS SOUL'S TRAPPED IN HER SWORD. NOW CAN WE PLEASE FOCUS ON THESE *BRUSSELS SPROUTS FROM HELL?*

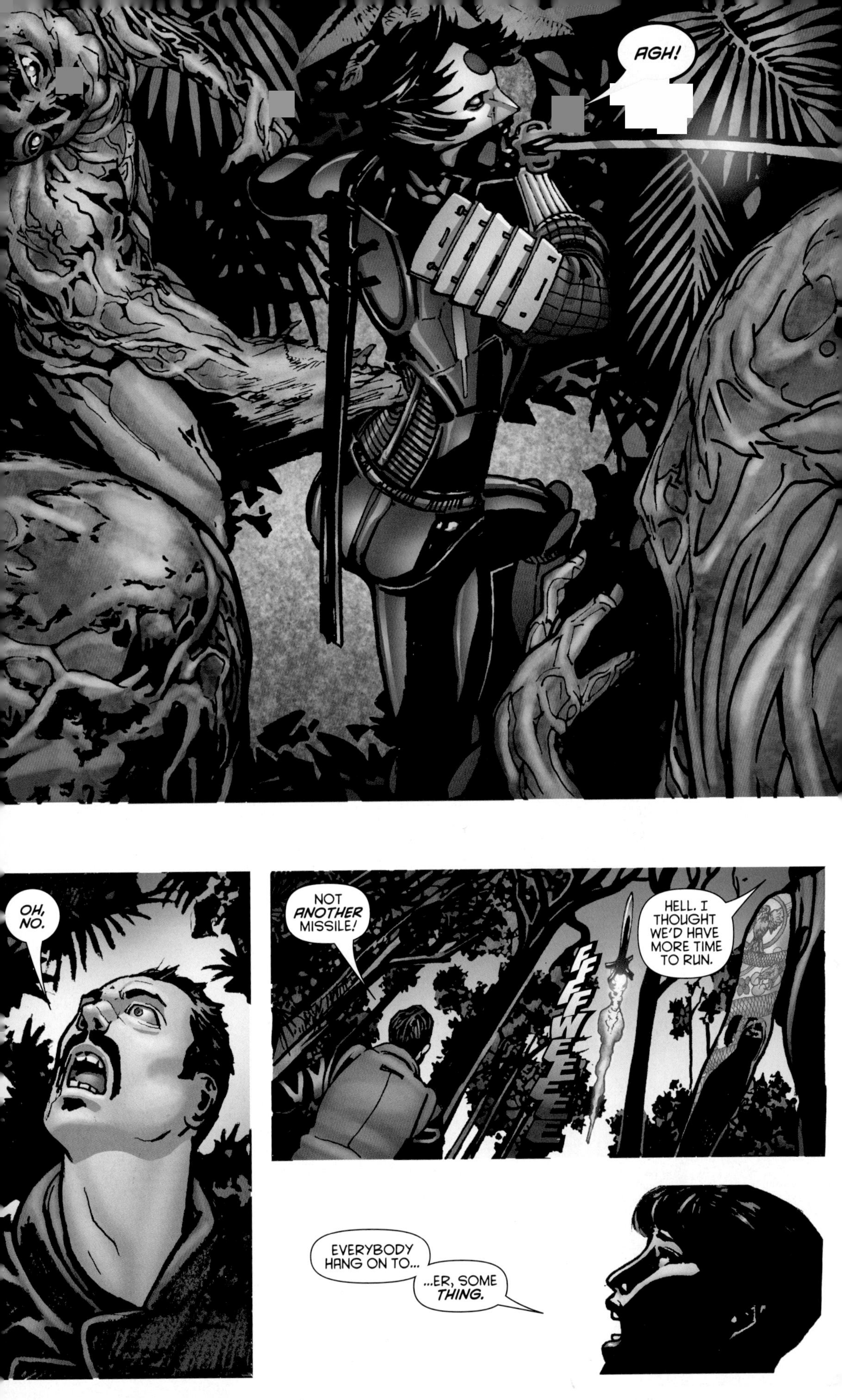
AGH!
OH, NO.
NOT ANOTHER MISSILE!
FFFWEEEE
HELL. I THOUGHT WE'D HAVE MORE TIME TO RUN.
EVERYBODY HANG ON TO...
...ER, SOME THING.

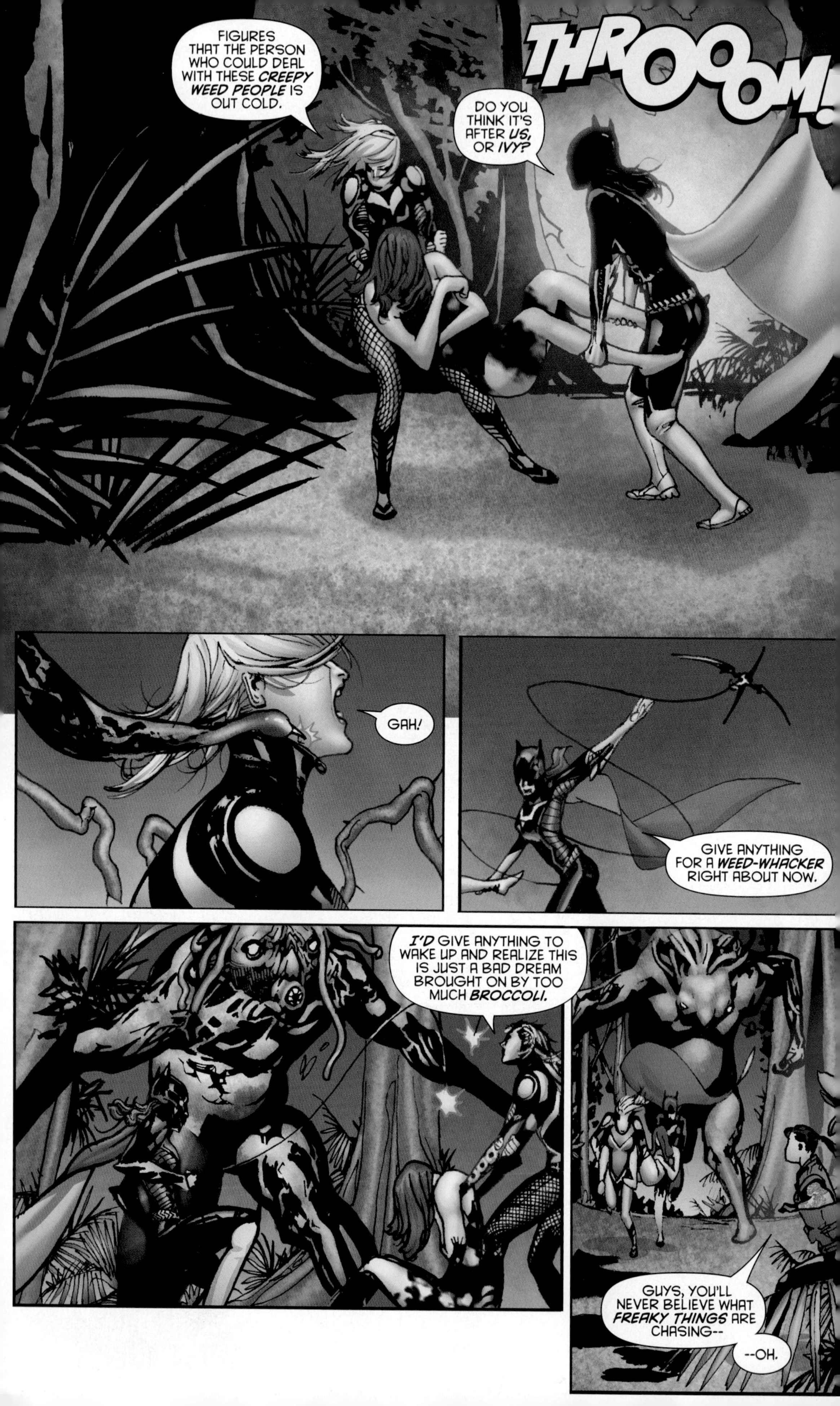

FIGURES THAT THE PERSON WHO COULD DEAL WITH THESE CREEPY WEED PEOPLE IS OUT COLD.
DO YOU THINK IT'S AFTER US, OR IVY?
THROOOOM!
GAH!
GIVE ANYTHING FOR A WEED-WHACKER RIGHT ABOUT NOW.
I'D GIVE ANYTHING TO WAKE UP AND REALIZE THIS IS JUST A BAD DREAM BROUGHT ON BY TOO MUCH BROCCOLI.
GUYS, YOU'LL NEVER BELIEVE WHAT FREAKY THINGS ARE CHASING--
--OH.

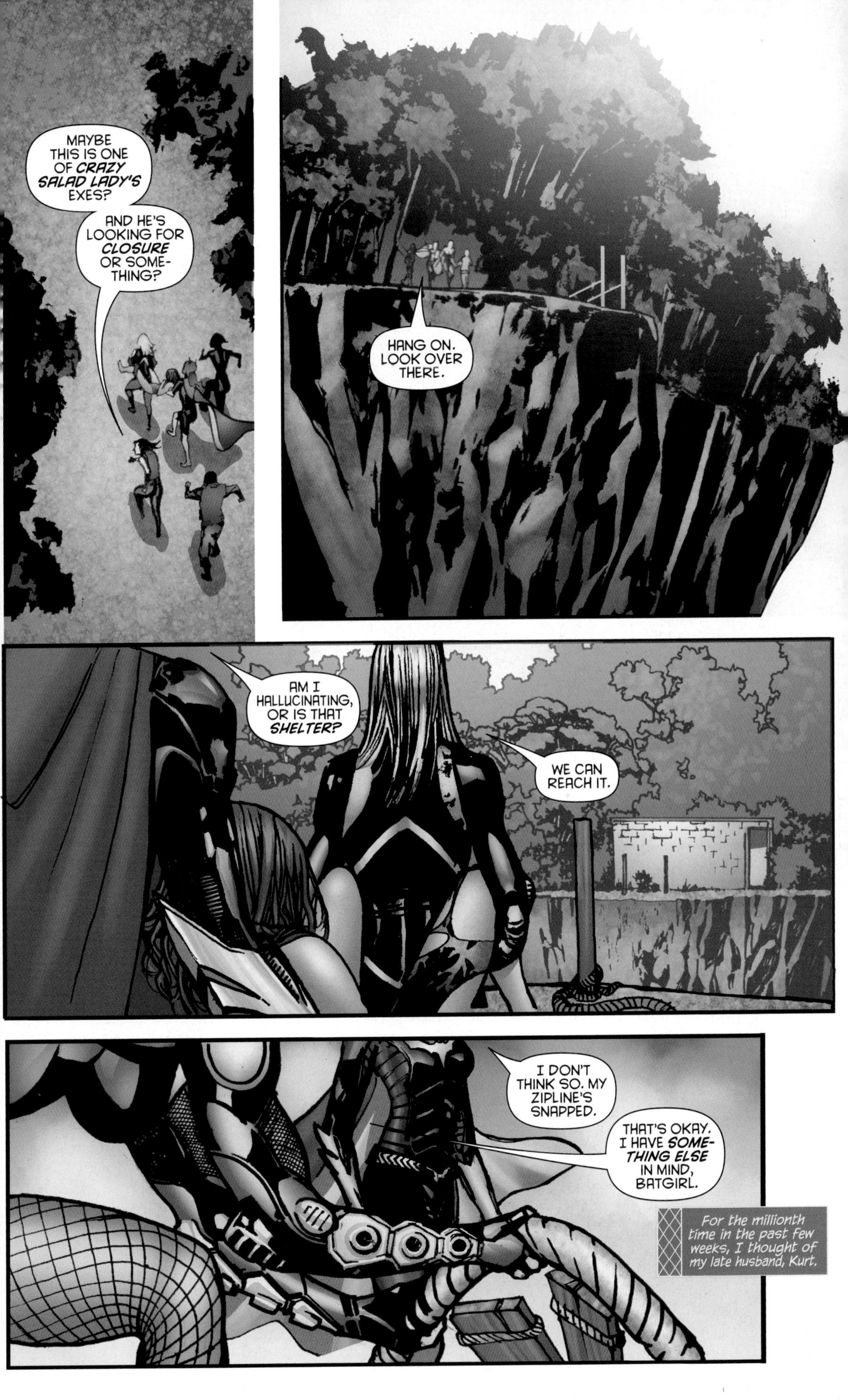
MAYBE THIS IS ONE OF CRAZY SALAD LADY'S EXES?
AND HE'S LOOKING FOR CLOSURE OR SOME-THING?
HANG ON. LOOK OVER THERE.
AM I HALLUCINATING, OR IS THAT SHELTER?
WE CAN REACH IT.
I DON'T THINK SO. MY ZIPLINE'S SNAPPED.
THAT'S OKAY. I HAVE SOME-THING ELSE IN MIND, BATGIRL.
For the millionth time in the past few weeks, I thought of my late husband, Kurt.

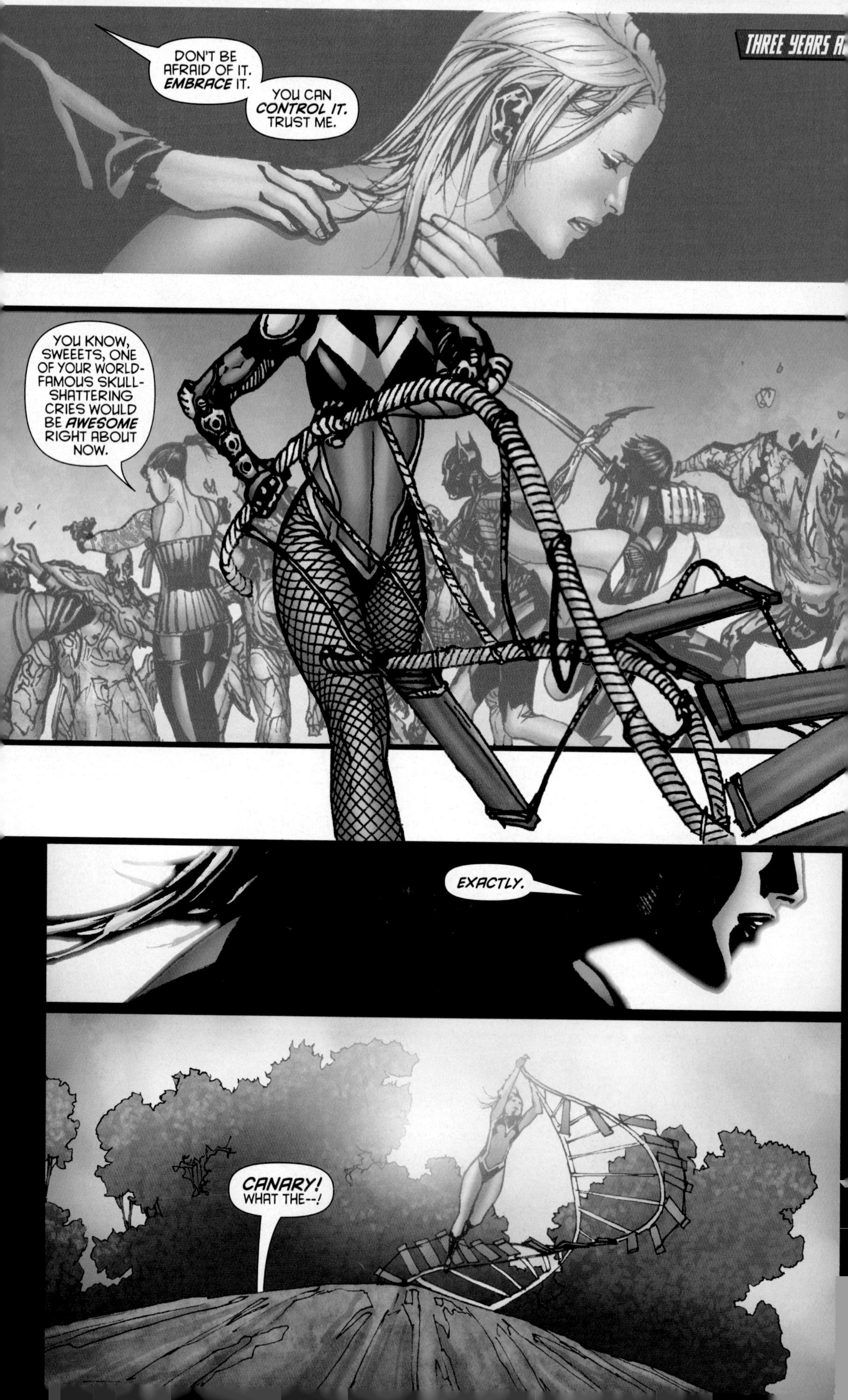
THREE YEARS A
DON'T BE AFRAID OF IT. EMBRACE IT.
YOU CAN CONTROL IT. TRUST ME.
YOU KNOW, SWEEETS, ONE OF YOUR WORLD-FAMOUS SKULL-SHATTERING CRIES WOULD BE AWESOME RIGHT ABOUT NOW.
EXACTLY.
CANARY! WHAT THE--!

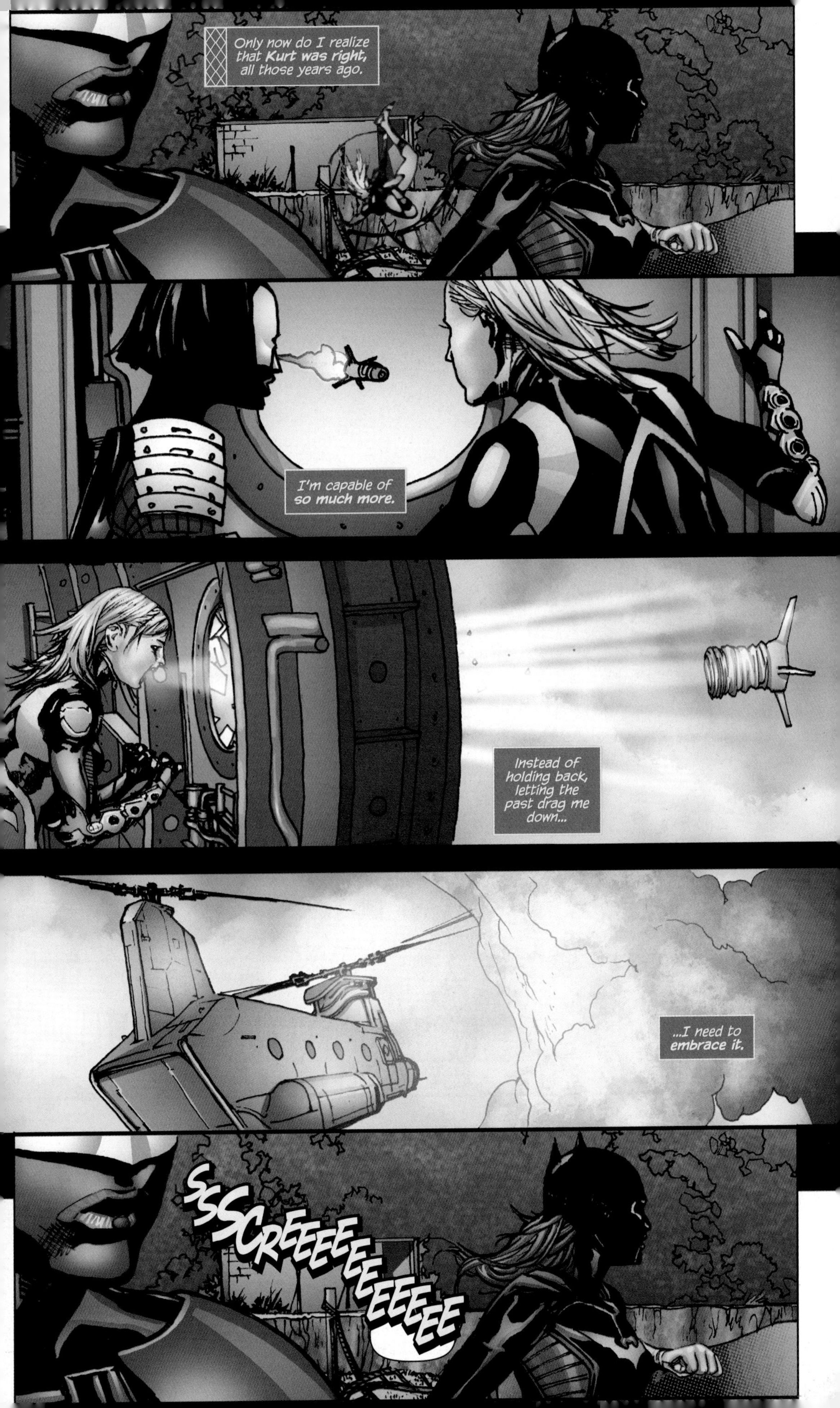
Only now do I realize that Kurt was right, all those years ago.
I'm capable of so much more.
Instead of holding back, letting the past drag me down...
...I need to embrace it.
SSSCREEEEEEEEEEEEEE

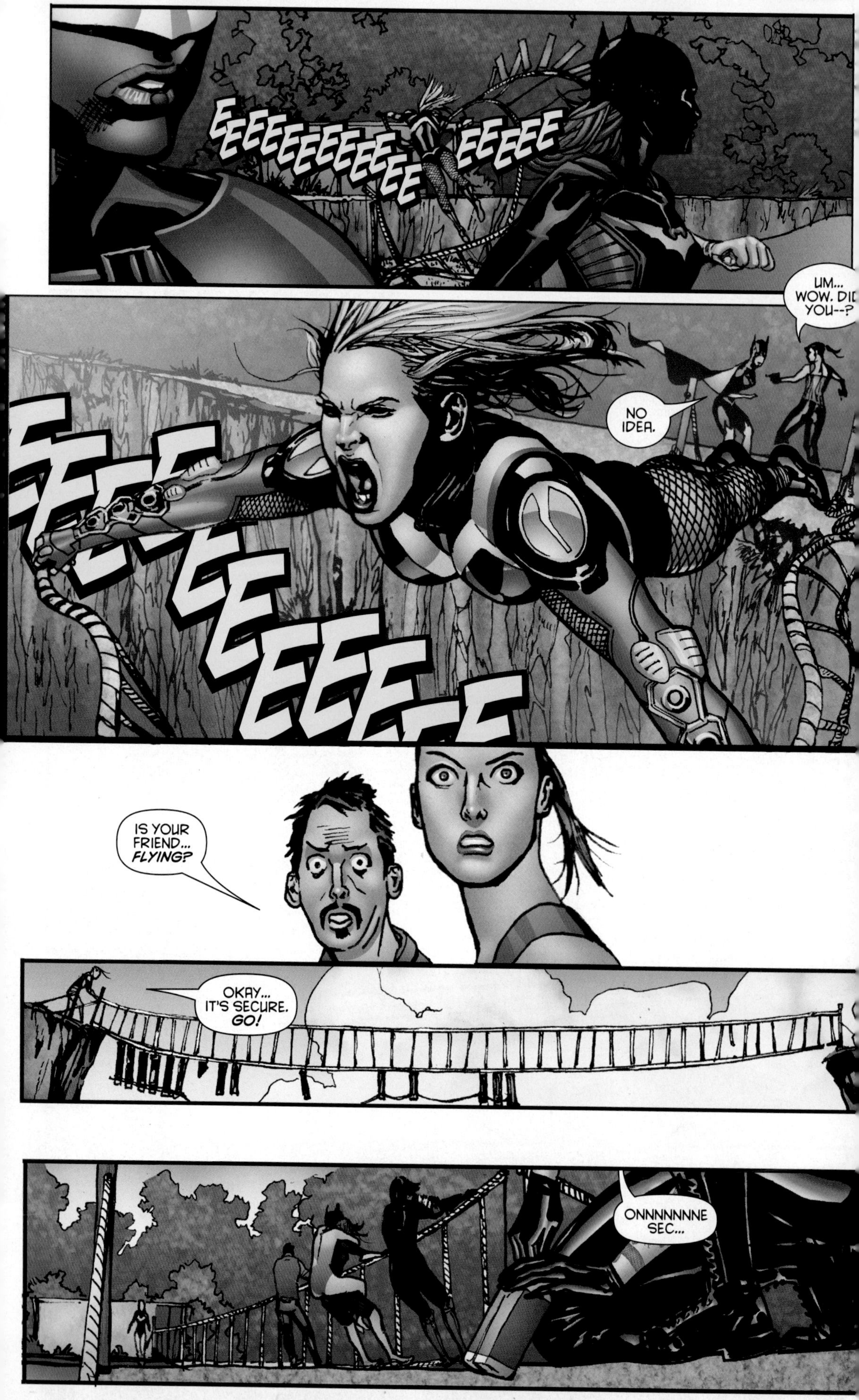

EEEEEEEEEEEEE EEEEE
UM... WOW. DID YOU--?
NO IDEA.
EEEEEEEEEEEEE
IS YOUR FRIEND... FLYING?
OKAY... IT'S SECURE. GO!
ONNNNNNNE SEC...

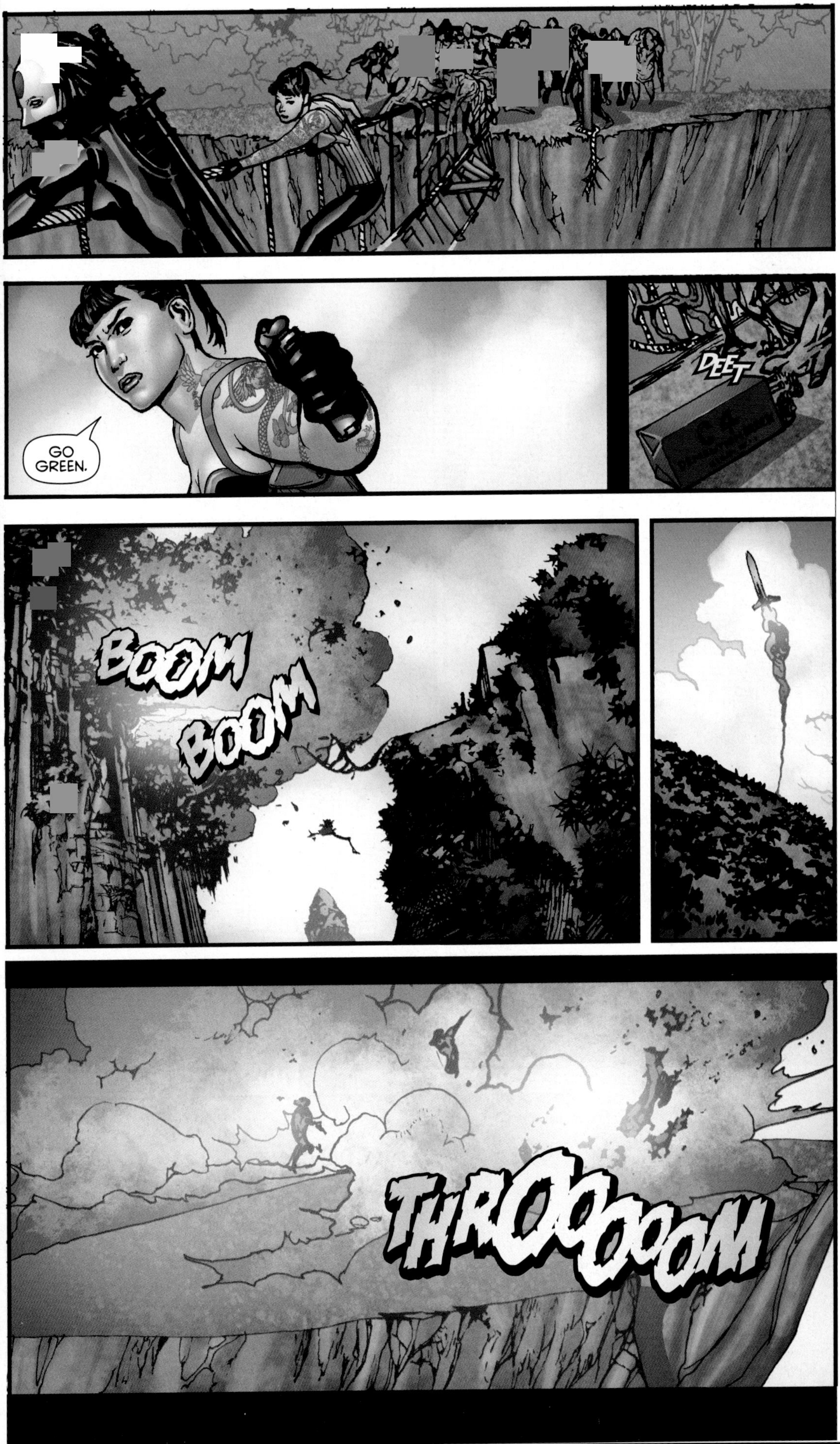
GO GREEN.
DEET
BOOM
BOOM
THROOOOOM

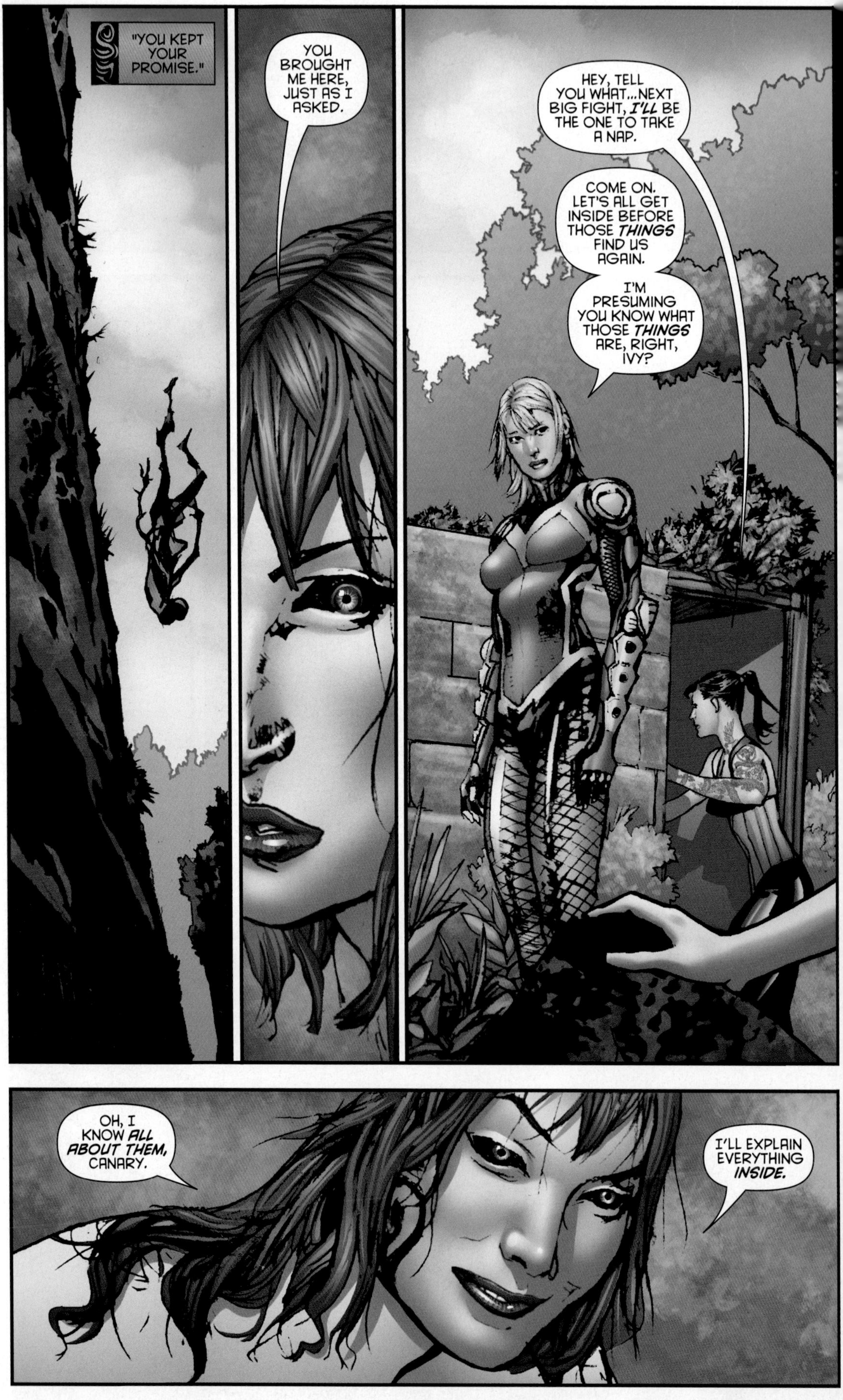
"YOU KEPT YOUR PROMISE."
YOU BROUGHT ME HERE, JUST AS I ASKED.
HEY, TELL YOU WHAT...NEXT BIG FIGHT, *I'LL* BE THE ONE TO TAKE A NAP.
COME ON. LET'S ALL GET INSIDE BEFORE THOSE *THINGS* FIND US AGAIN.
I'M PRESUMING YOU KNOW WHAT THOSE *THINGS* ARE, RIGHT, IVY?
OH, I KNOW *ALL ABOUT THEM,* CANARY.
I'LL EXPLAIN EVERYTHING *INSIDE.*

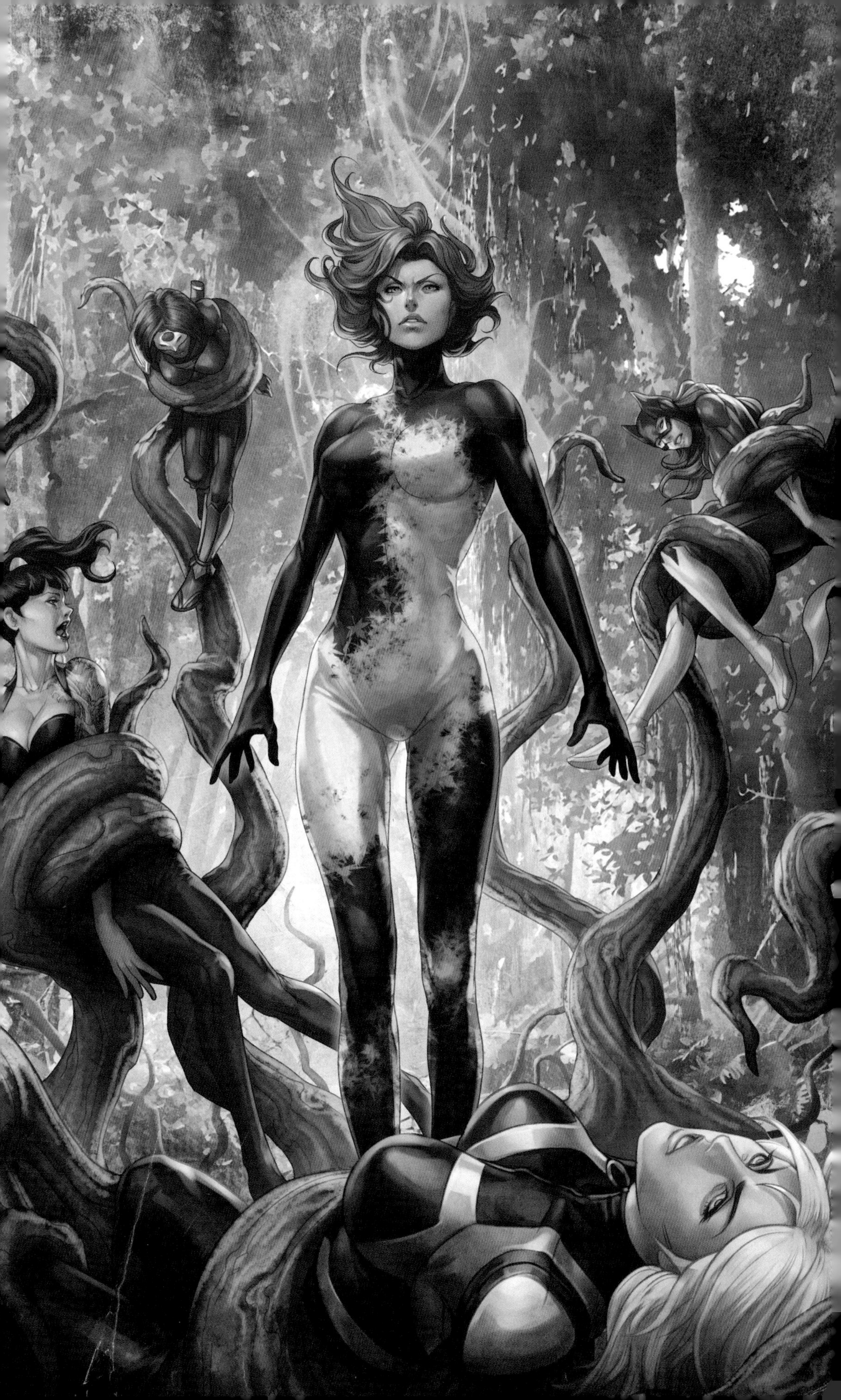

TANGLED UP INSIDE

DUANE SWIERCZYNSKI writer TRAVEL FOREMAN TIMOTHY GREEN II pencillers JEFF HUET JOSEPH SILVER inkers cover art by STANLEY "ARTGERM" L.

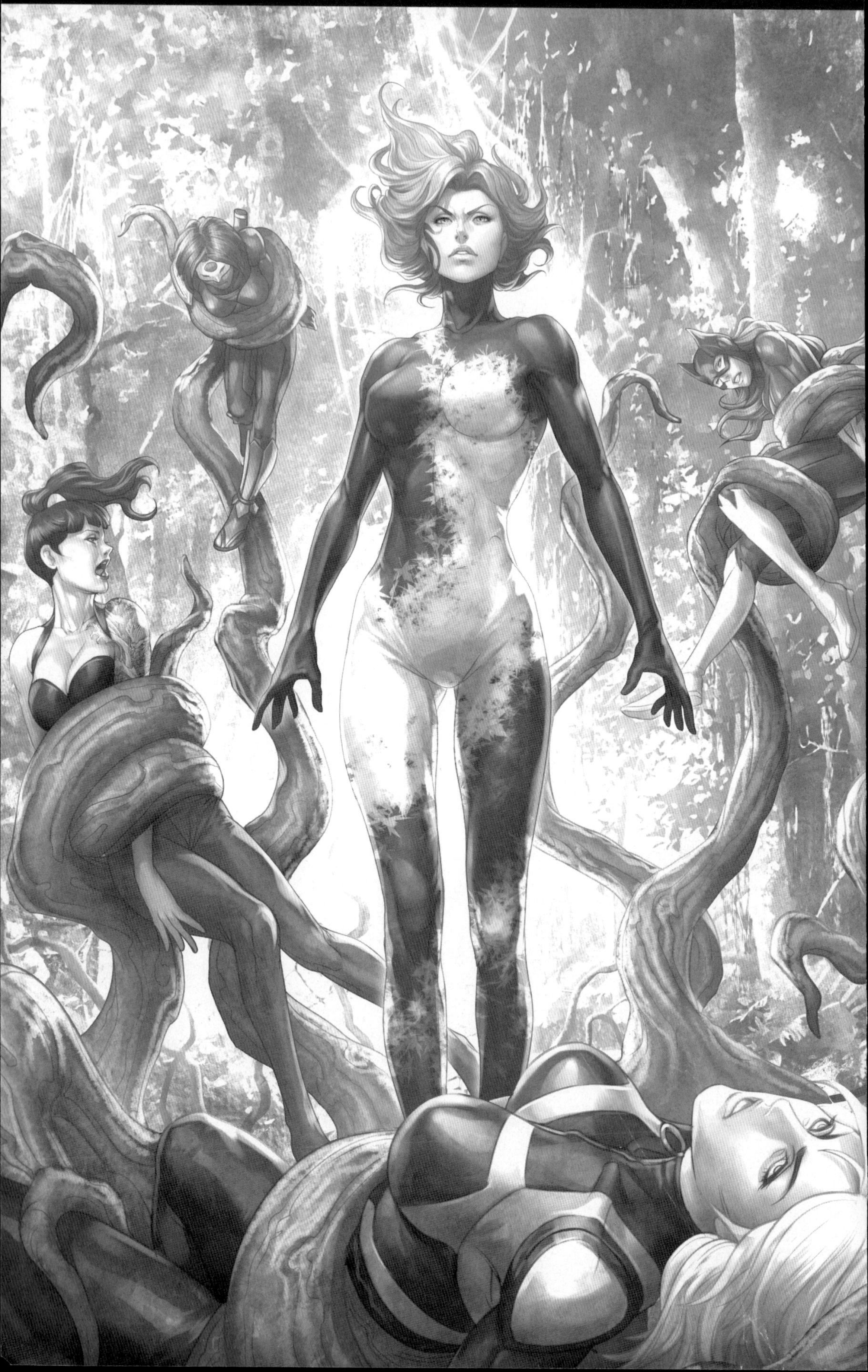

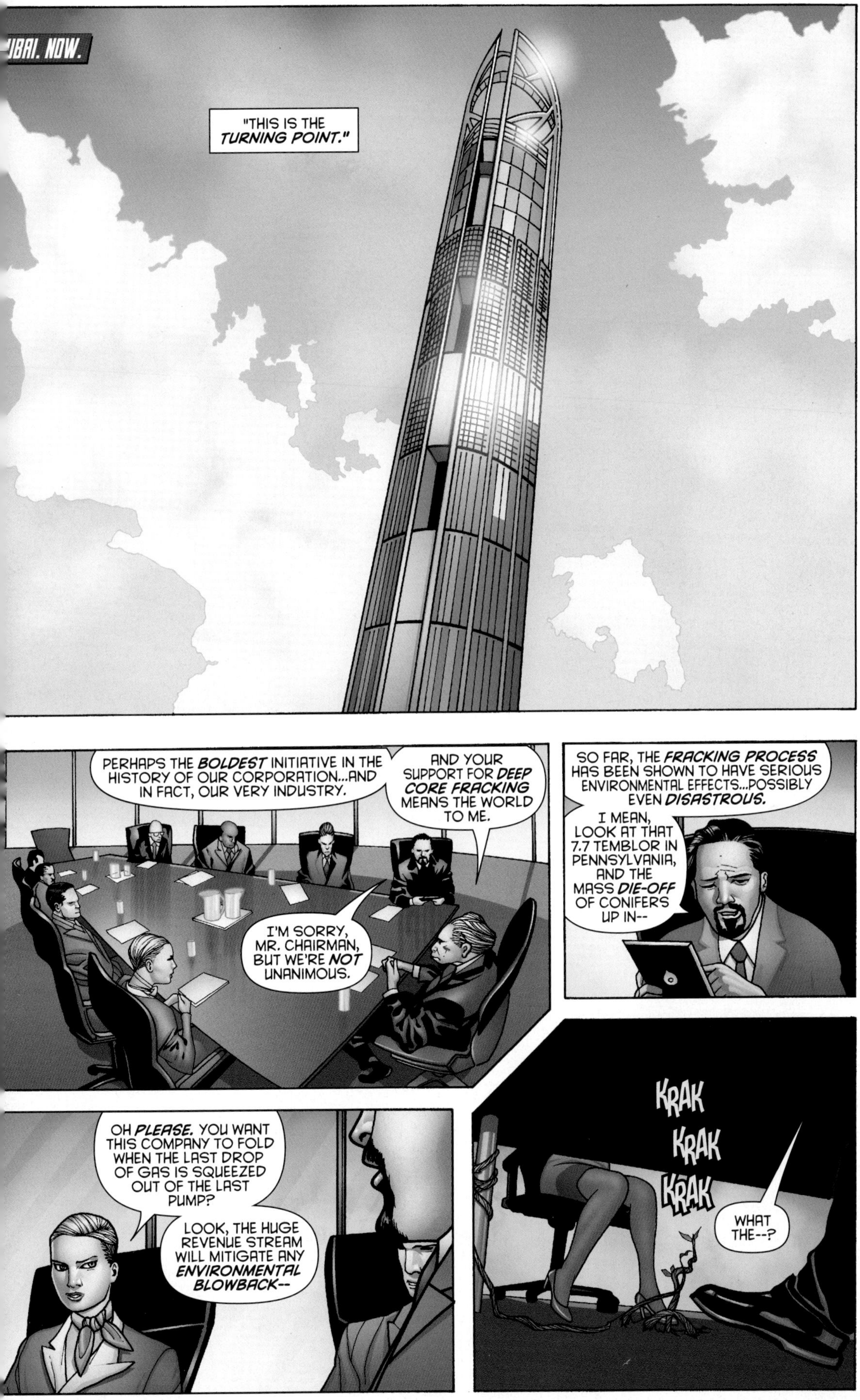
UBAI. NOW.
"THIS IS THE TURNING POINT."
PERHAPS THE BOLDEST INITIATIVE IN THE HISTORY OF OUR CORPORATION...AND IN FACT, OUR VERY INDUSTRY.
AND YOUR SUPPORT FOR DEEP CORE FRACKING MEANS THE WORLD TO ME.
I'M SORRY, MR. CHAIRMAN, BUT WE'RE NOT UNANIMOUS.
SO FAR, THE FRACKING PROCESS HAS BEEN SHOWN TO HAVE SERIOUS ENVIRONMENTAL EFFECTS...POSSIBLY EVEN DISASTROUS.
I MEAN, LOOK AT THAT 7.7 TEMBLOR IN PENNSYLVANIA, AND THE MASS DIE-OFF OF CONIFERS UP IN--
OH PLEASE. YOU WANT THIS COMPANY TO FOLD WHEN THE LAST DROP OF GAS IS SQUEEZED OUT OF THE LAST PUMP?
LOOK, THE HUGE REVENUE STREAM WILL MITIGATE ANY ENVIRONMENTAL BLOWBACK--
KRAK
KRAK
KRAK
WHAT THE--?

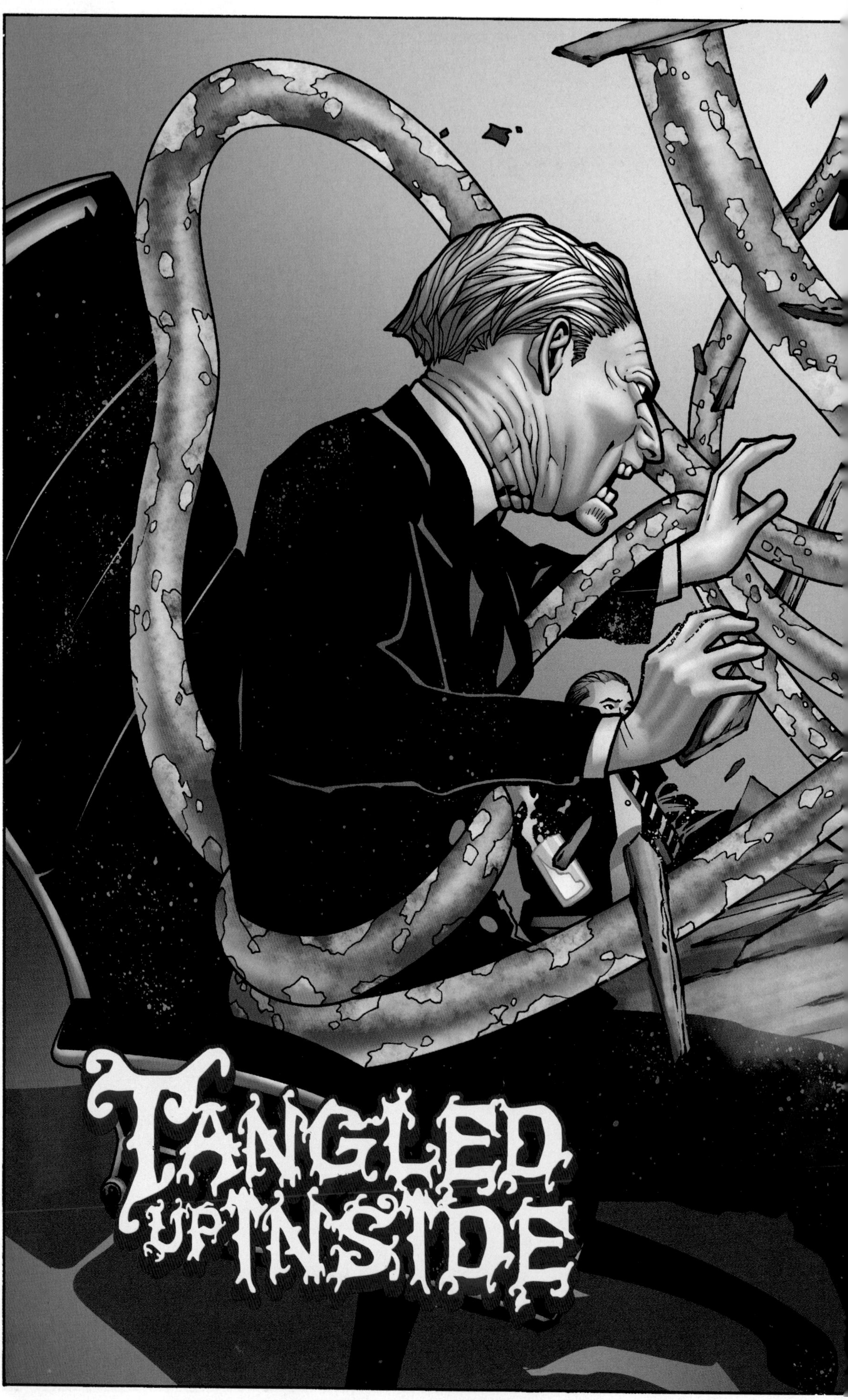
TANGLED
UP INSIDE

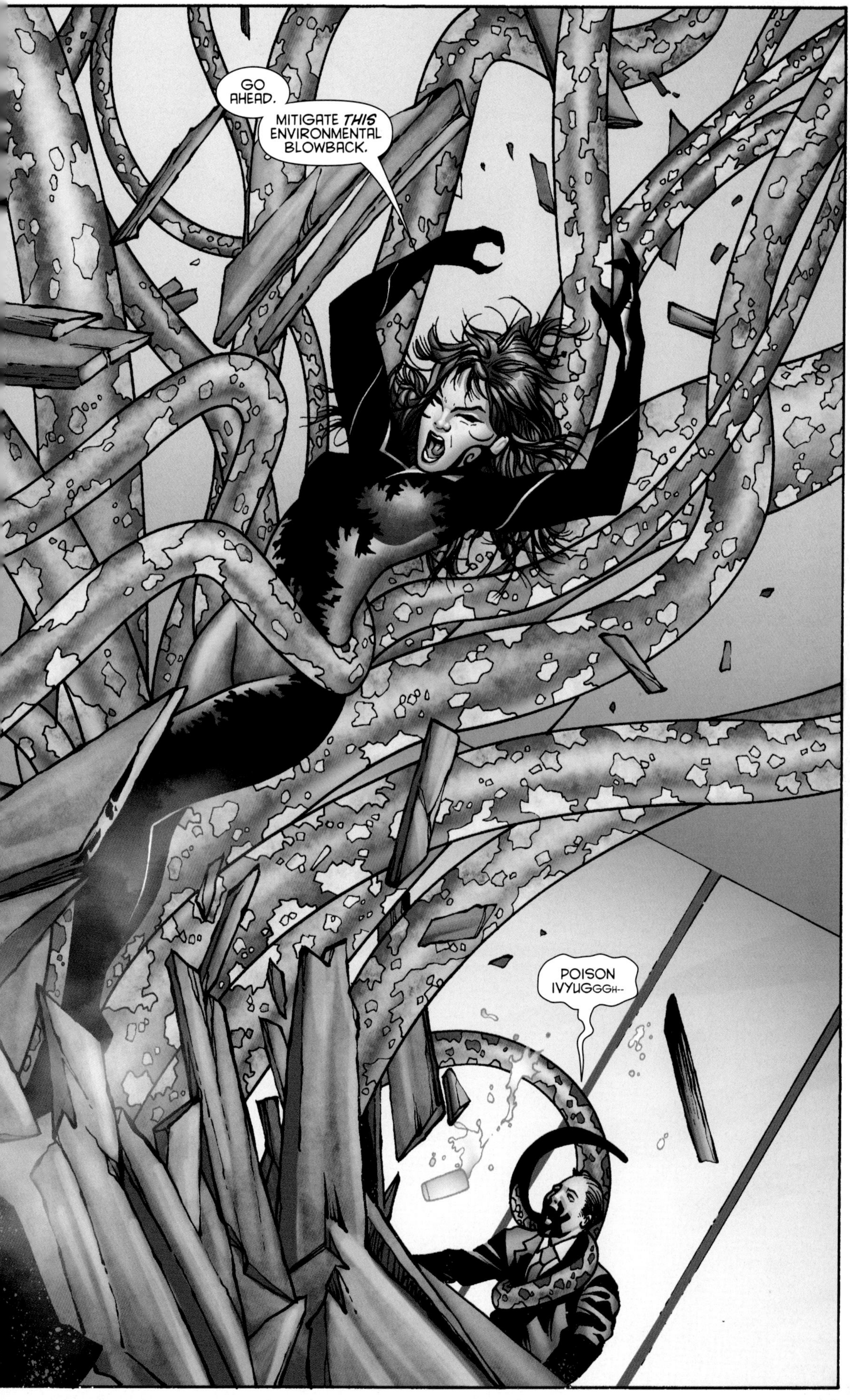
GO AHEAD.
MITIGATE THIS ENVIRONMENTAL BLOWBACK.
POISON IVYUGGGH--

THE AMAZON. ONE WEEK AGO.

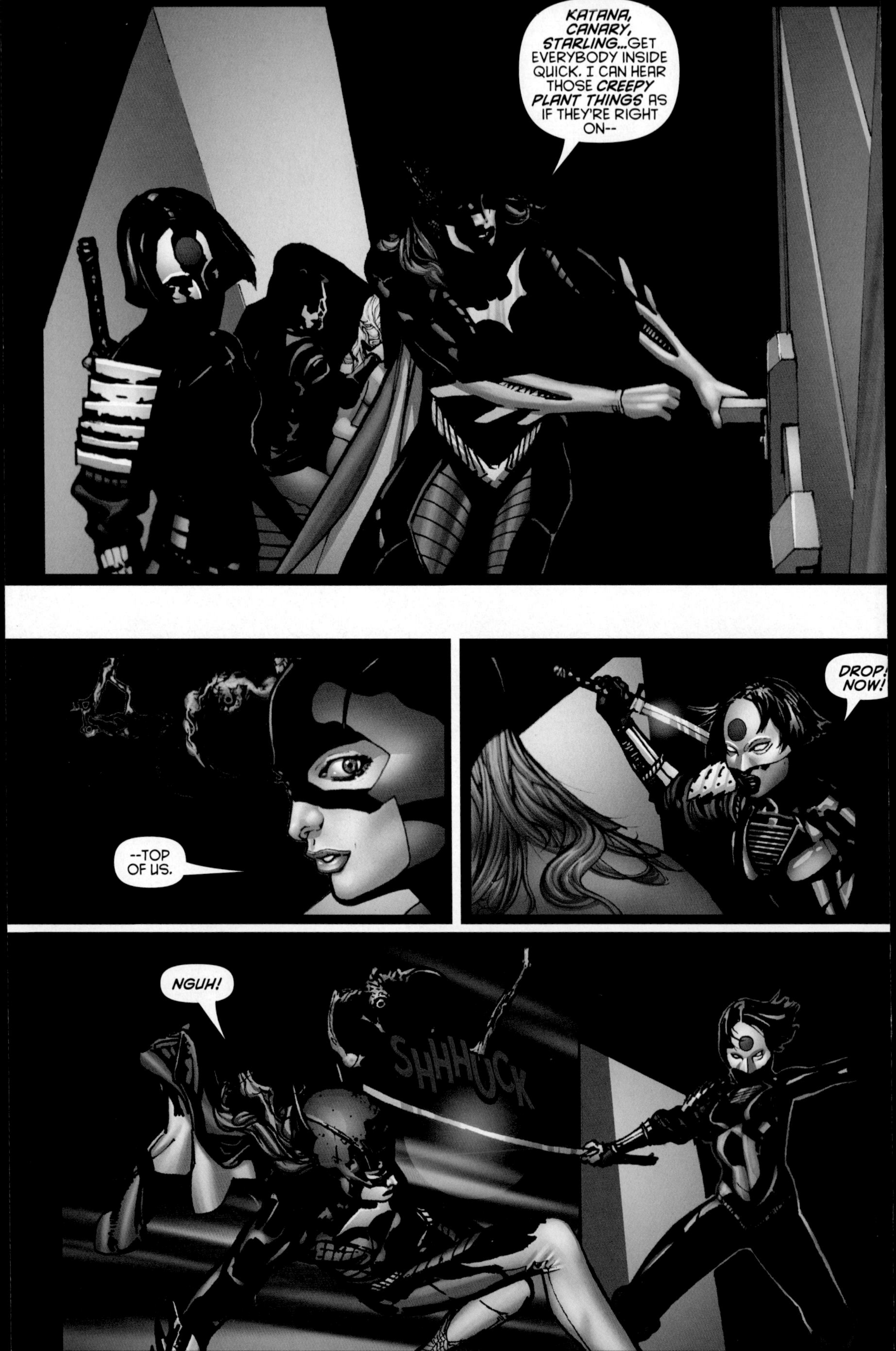
KATANA, CANARY, STARLING...GET EVERYBODY INSIDE QUICK. I CAN HEAR THOSE CREEPY PLANT THINGS AS IF THEY'RE RIGHT ON--
--TOP OF US.
DROP! NOW!
NGUH!
SHHHUCK

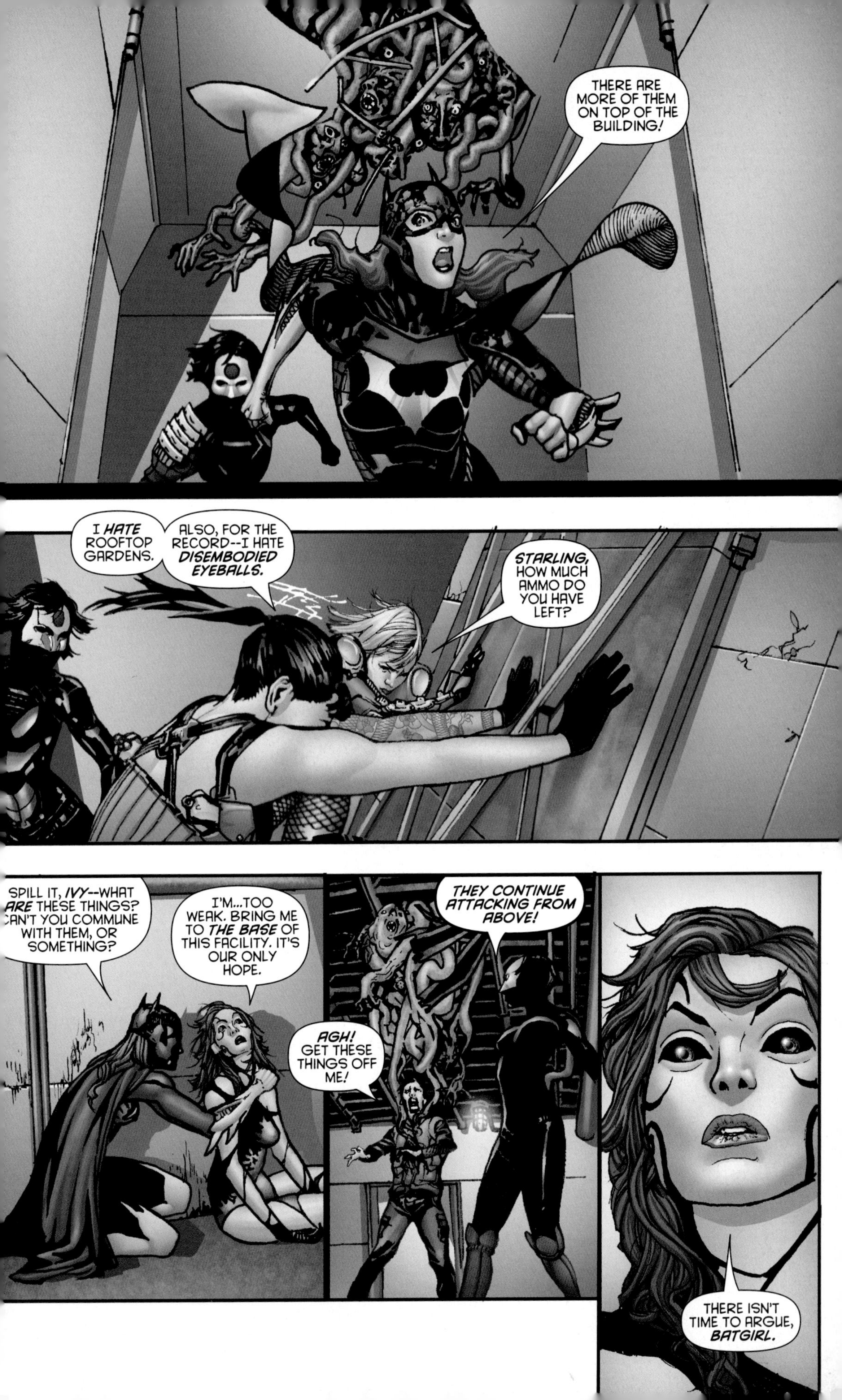
THERE ARE MORE OF THEM ON TOP OF THE BUILDING!
I HATE ROOFTOP GARDENS.
ALSO, FOR THE RECORD--I HATE DISEMBODIED EYEBALLS.
STARLING, HOW MUCH AMMO DO YOU HAVE LEFT?
SPILL IT, IVY--WHAT ARE THESE THINGS? CAN'T YOU COMMUNE WITH THEM, OR SOMETHING?
I'M...TOO WEAK. BRING ME TO THE BASE OF THIS FACILITY. IT'S OUR ONLY HOPE.
THEY CONTINUE ATTACKING FROM ABOVE!
AGH! GET THESE THINGS OFF ME!
THERE ISN'T TIME TO ARGUE, BATGIRL.

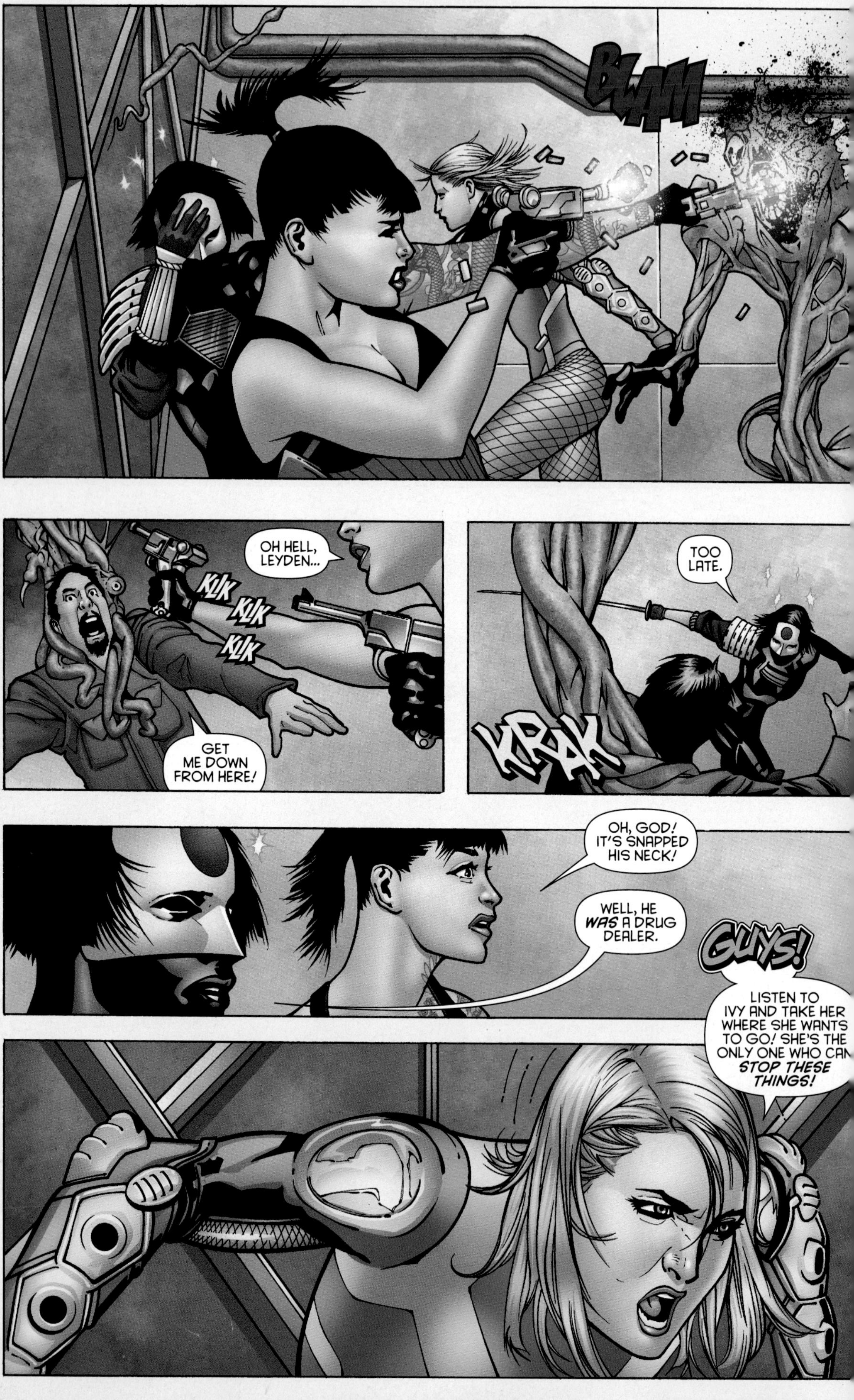
BLAM
OH HELL, LEYDEN...
KLIK KLIK KLIK
GET ME DOWN FROM HERE!
TOO LATE.
KRAK
OH, GOD! IT'S SNAPPED HIS NECK!
WELL, HE WAS A DRUG DEALER.
GUYS!
LISTEN TO IVY AND TAKE HER WHERE SHE WANTS TO GO! SHE'S THE ONLY ONE WHO CAN STOP THESE THINGS!

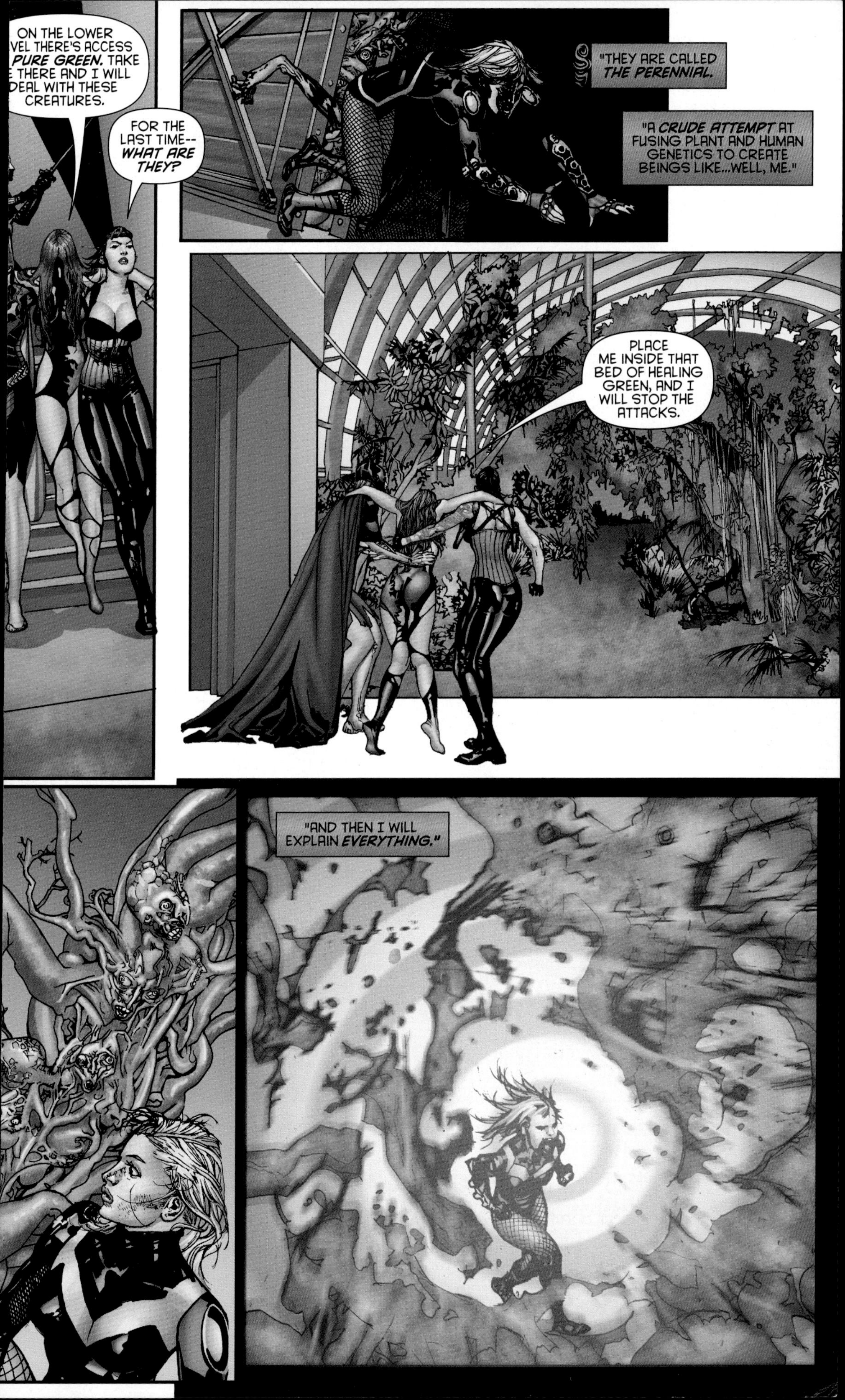
ON THE LOWER
VEL THERE'S ACCESS
PURE GREEN. TAKE
E THERE AND I WILL
DEAL WITH THESE
CREATURES.
FOR THE LAST TIME-- WHAT ARE THEY?
"THEY ARE CALLED THE PERENNIAL.
"A CRUDE ATTEMPT AT FUSING PLANT AND HUMAN GENETICS TO CREATE BEINGS LIKE...WELL, ME."
PLACE ME INSIDE THAT BED OF HEALING GREEN, AND I WILL STOP THE ATTACKS.
"AND THEN I WILL EXPLAIN EVERYTHING."

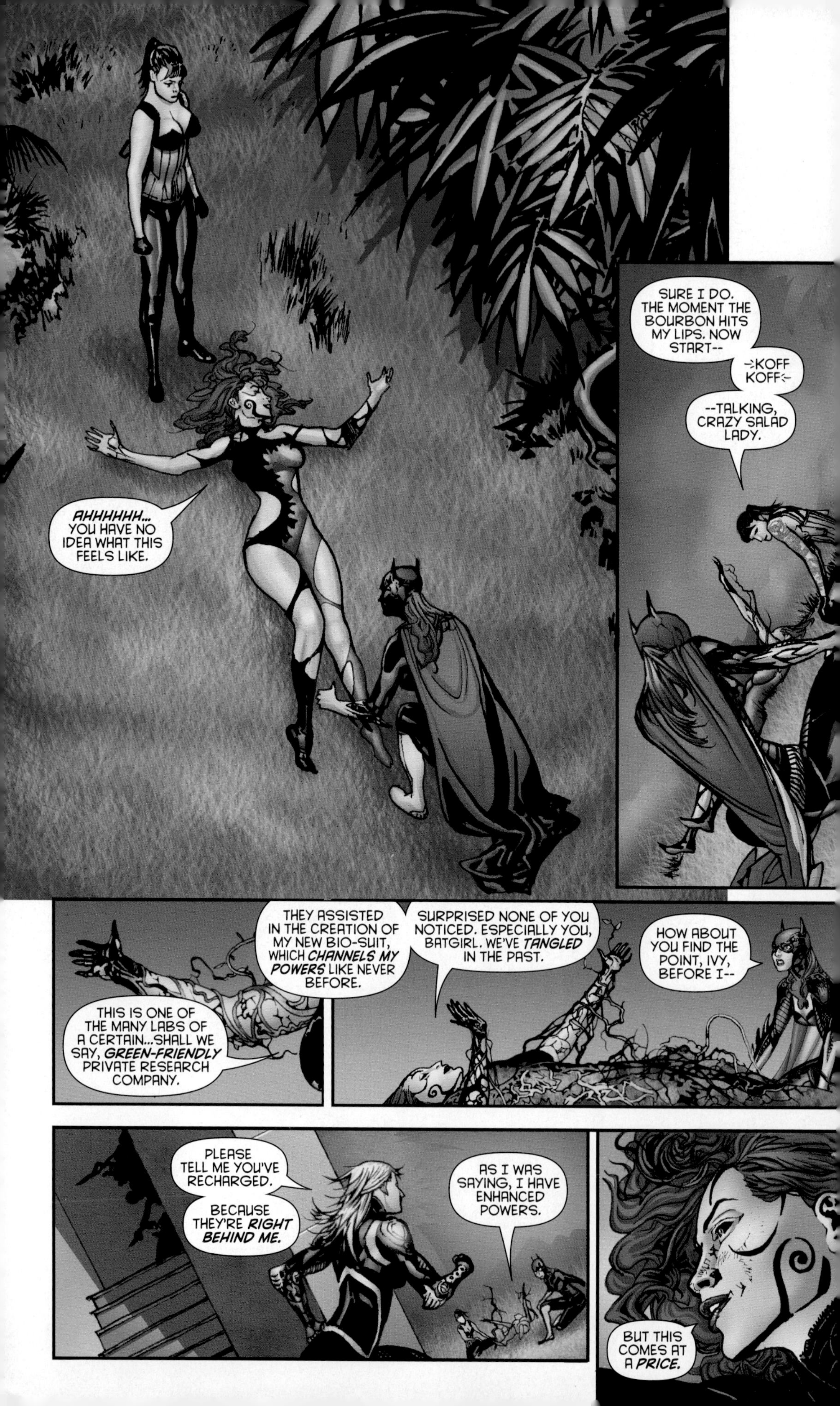
AHHHHHH... YOU HAVE NO IDEA WHAT THIS FEELS LIKE.
SURE I DO. THE MOMENT THE BOURBON HITS MY LIPS. NOW START--
KOFF KOFF
--TALKING, CRAZY SALAD LADY.
THEY ASSISTED IN THE CREATION OF MY NEW BIO-SUIT, WHICH CHANNELS MY POWERS LIKE NEVER BEFORE.
THIS IS ONE OF THE MANY LABS OF A CERTAIN...SHALL WE SAY, GREEN-FRIENDLY PRIVATE RESEARCH COMPANY.
SURPRISED NONE OF YOU NOTICED. ESPECIALLY YOU, BATGIRL. WE'VE TANGLED IN THE PAST.
HOW ABOUT YOU FIND THE POINT, IVY, BEFORE I--
PLEASE TELL ME YOU'VE RECHARGED.
BECAUSE THEY'RE RIGHT BEHIND ME.
AS I WAS SAYING, I HAVE ENHANCED POWERS.
BUT THIS COMES AT A PRICE.

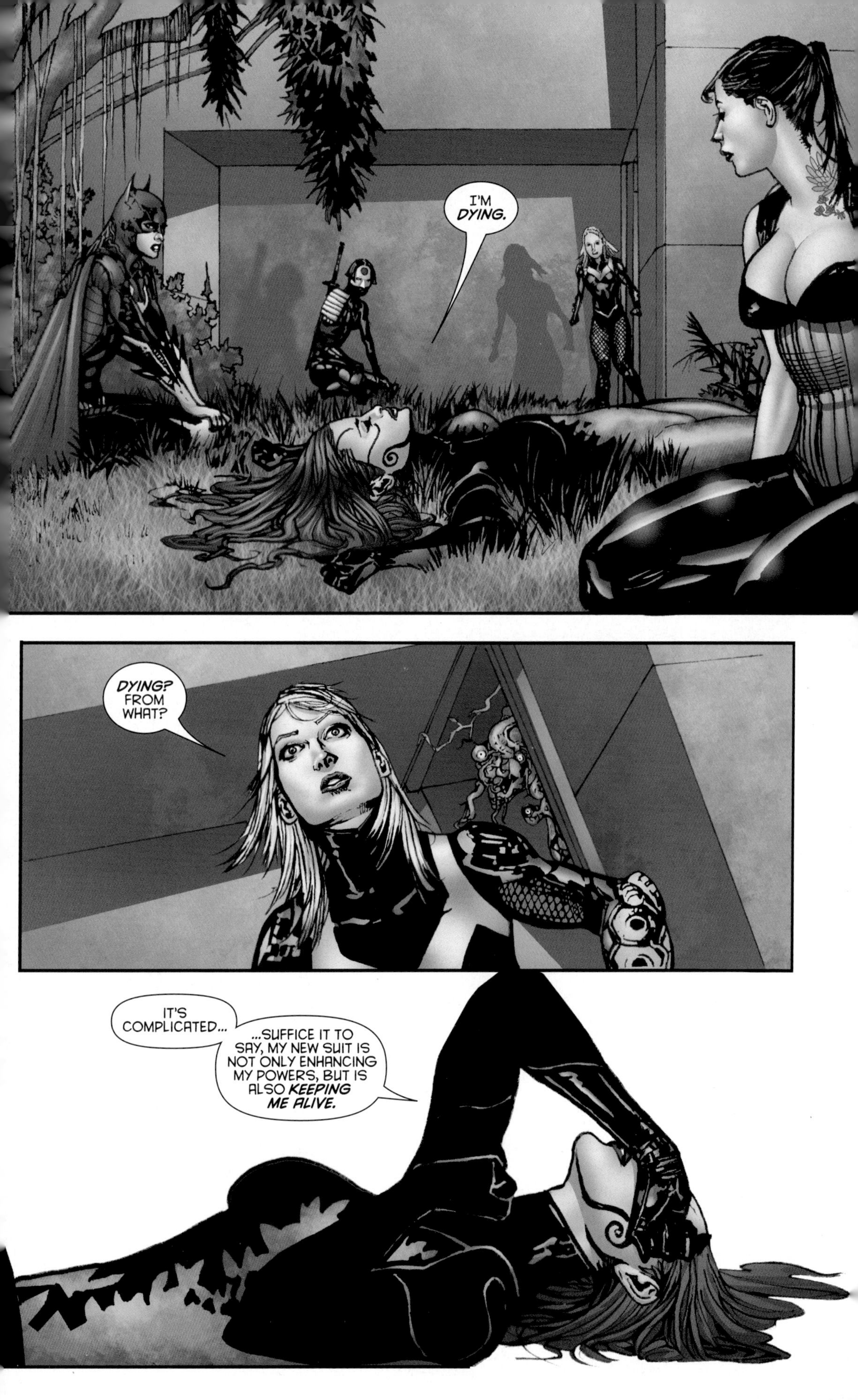
I'M *DYING.*
DYING? FROM WHAT?
IT'S COMPLICATED...
...SUFFICE IT TO SAY, MY NEW SUIT IS NOT ONLY ENHANCING MY POWERS, BUT IS ALSO *KEEPING ME ALIVE.*

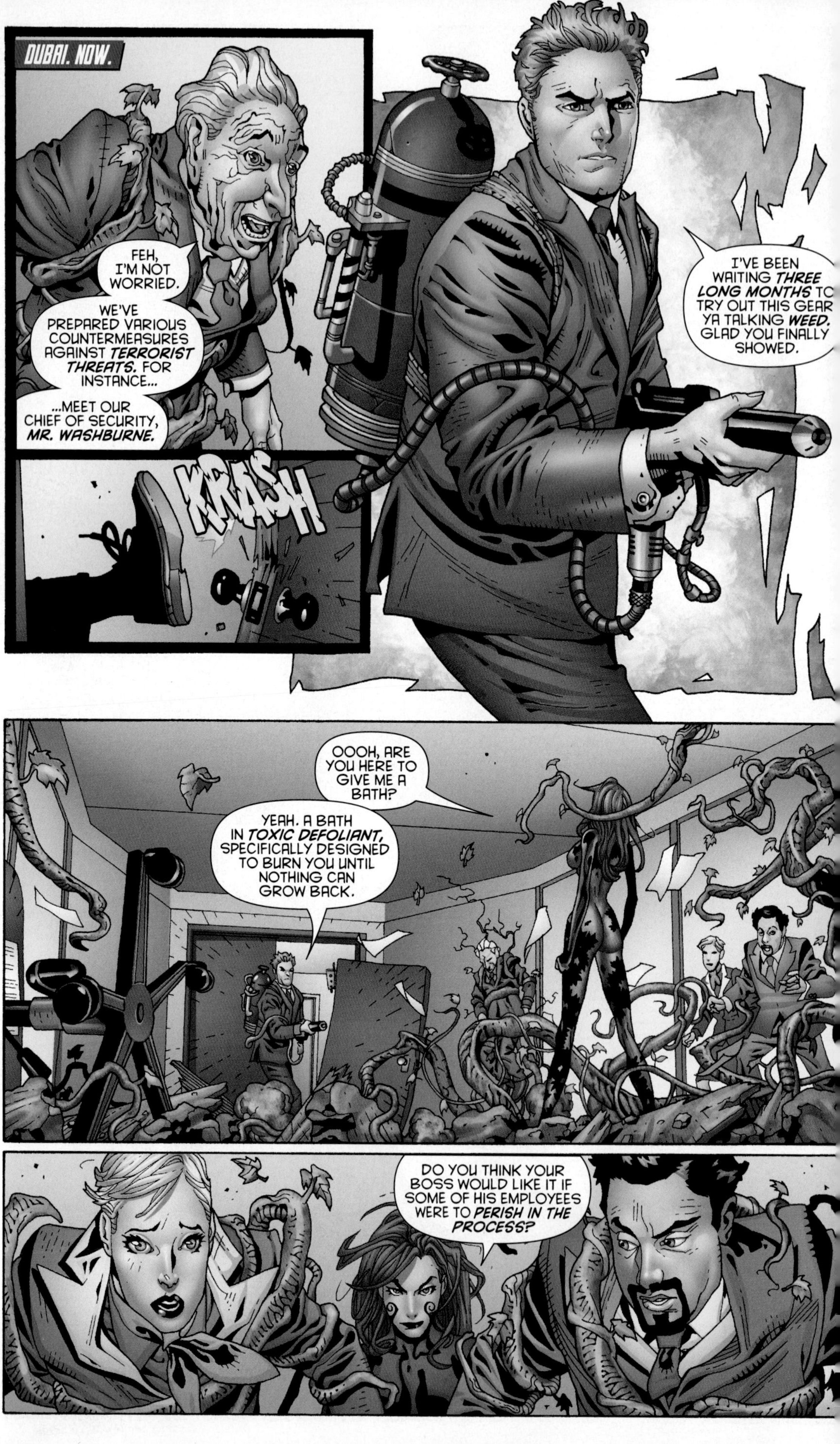
DUBAI. NOW.
FEH, I'M NOT WORRIED.
WE'VE PREPARED VARIOUS COUNTERMEASURES AGAINST *TERRORIST THREATS.* FOR INSTANCE...
...MEET OUR CHIEF OF SECURITY, *MR. WASHBURNE.*
KRASH
I'VE BEEN WAITING *THREE LONG MONTHS* TO TRY OUT THIS GEAR YA TALKING *WEED.* GLAD YOU FINALLY SHOWED.
OOOH, ARE YOU HERE TO GIVE ME A BATH?
YEAH. A BATH IN *TOXIC DEFOLIANT,* SPECIFICALLY DESIGNED TO BURN YOU UNTIL NOTHING CAN GROW BACK.
DO YOU THINK YOUR BOSS WOULD LIKE IT IF SOME OF HIS EMPLOYEES WERE TO *PERISH IN THE PROCESS?*

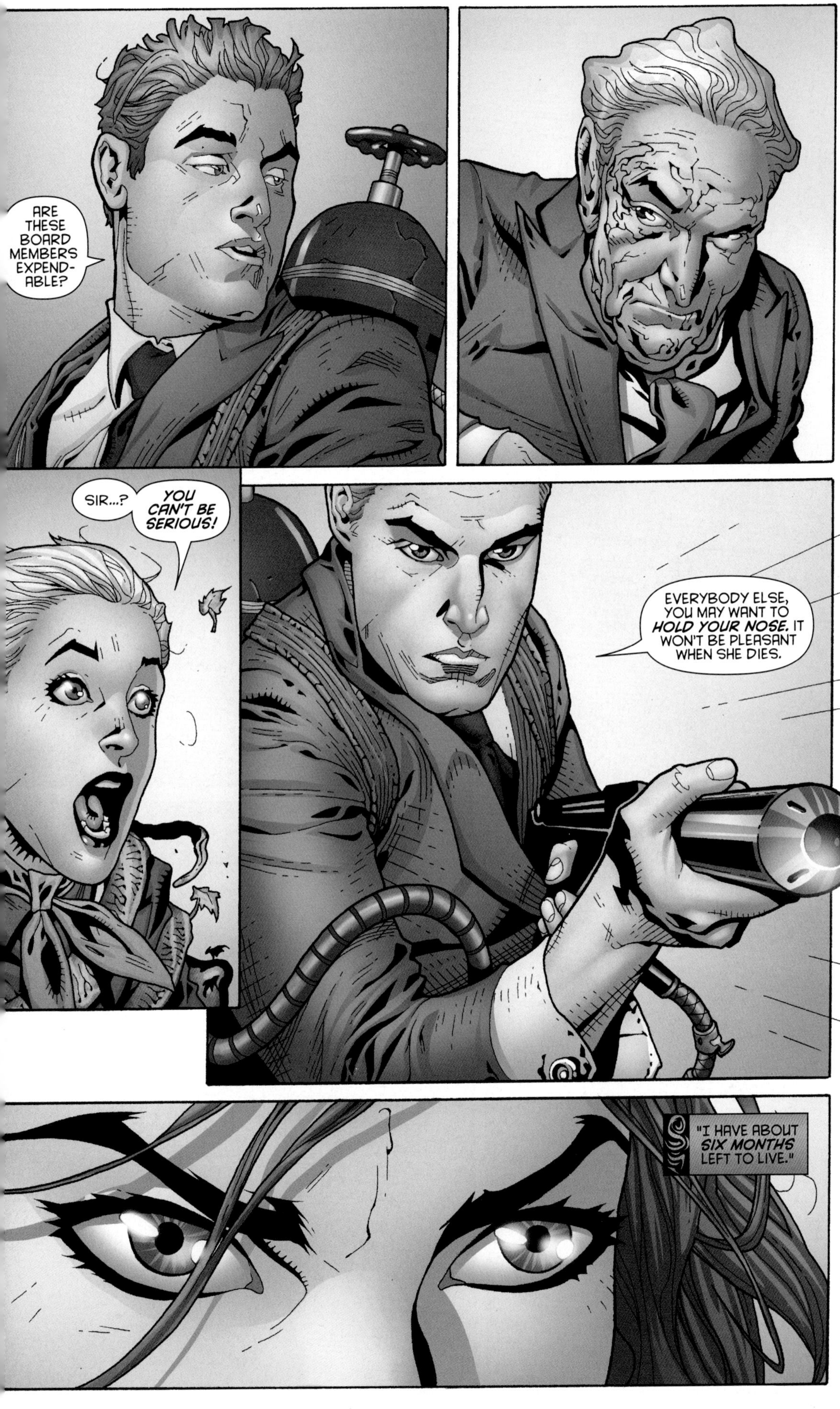
ARE THESE BOARD MEMBERS EXPEND-ABLE?
SIR...?
YOU CAN'T BE SERIOUS!
EVERYBODY ELSE, YOU MAY WANT TO HOLD YOUR NOSE. IT WON'T BE PLEASANT WHEN SHE DIES.
"I HAVE ABOUT SIX MONTHS LEFT TO LIVE."

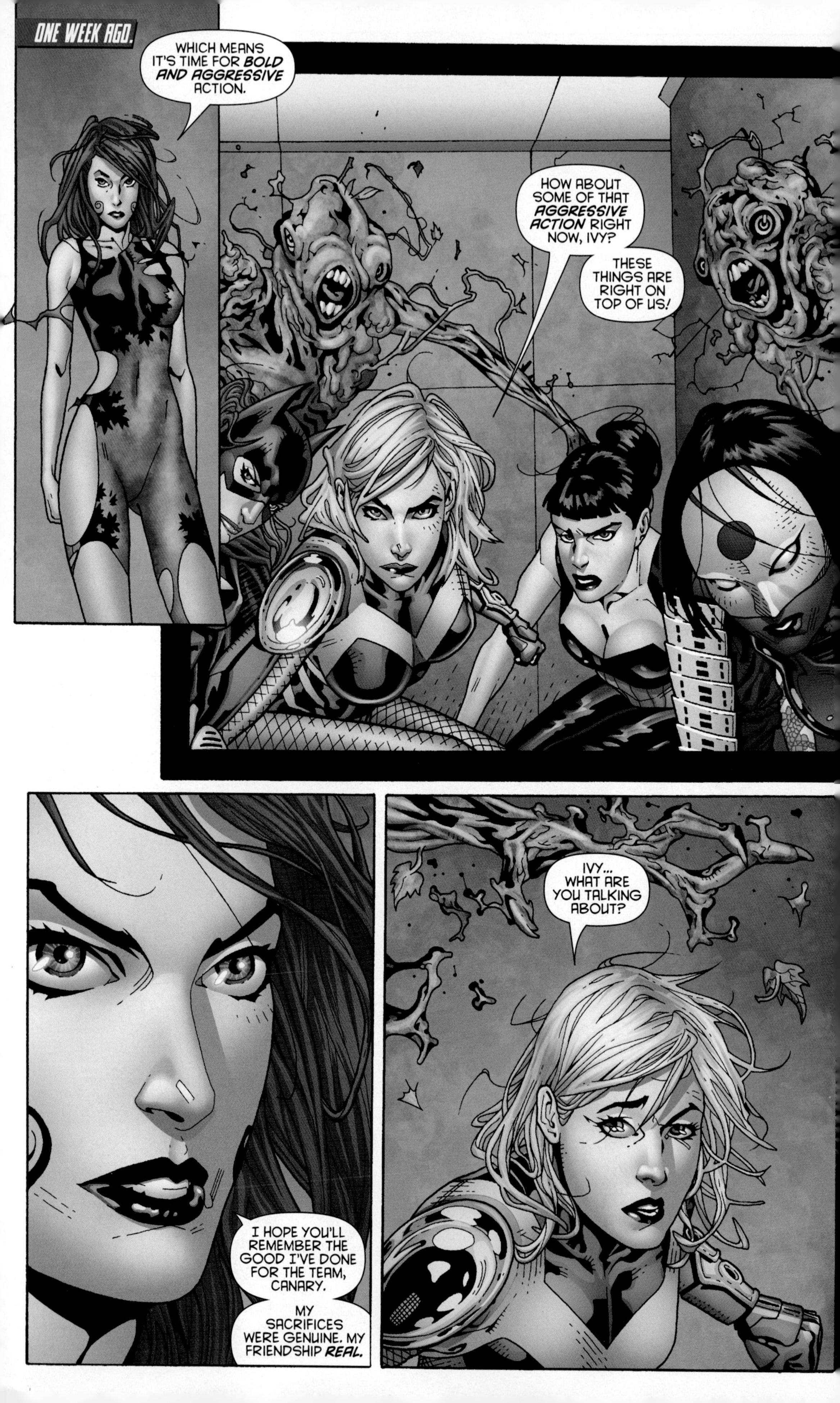
ONE WEEK AGO.
WHICH MEANS IT'S TIME FOR BOLD AND AGGRESSIVE ACTION.
HOW ABOUT SOME OF THAT AGGRESSIVE ACTION RIGHT NOW, IVY?
THESE THINGS ARE RIGHT ON TOP OF US!
I HOPE YOU'LL REMEMBER THE GOOD I'VE DONE FOR THE TEAM, CANARY.
MY SACRIFICES WERE GENUINE. MY FRIENDSHIP REAL.
IVY... WHAT ARE YOU TALKING ABOUT?

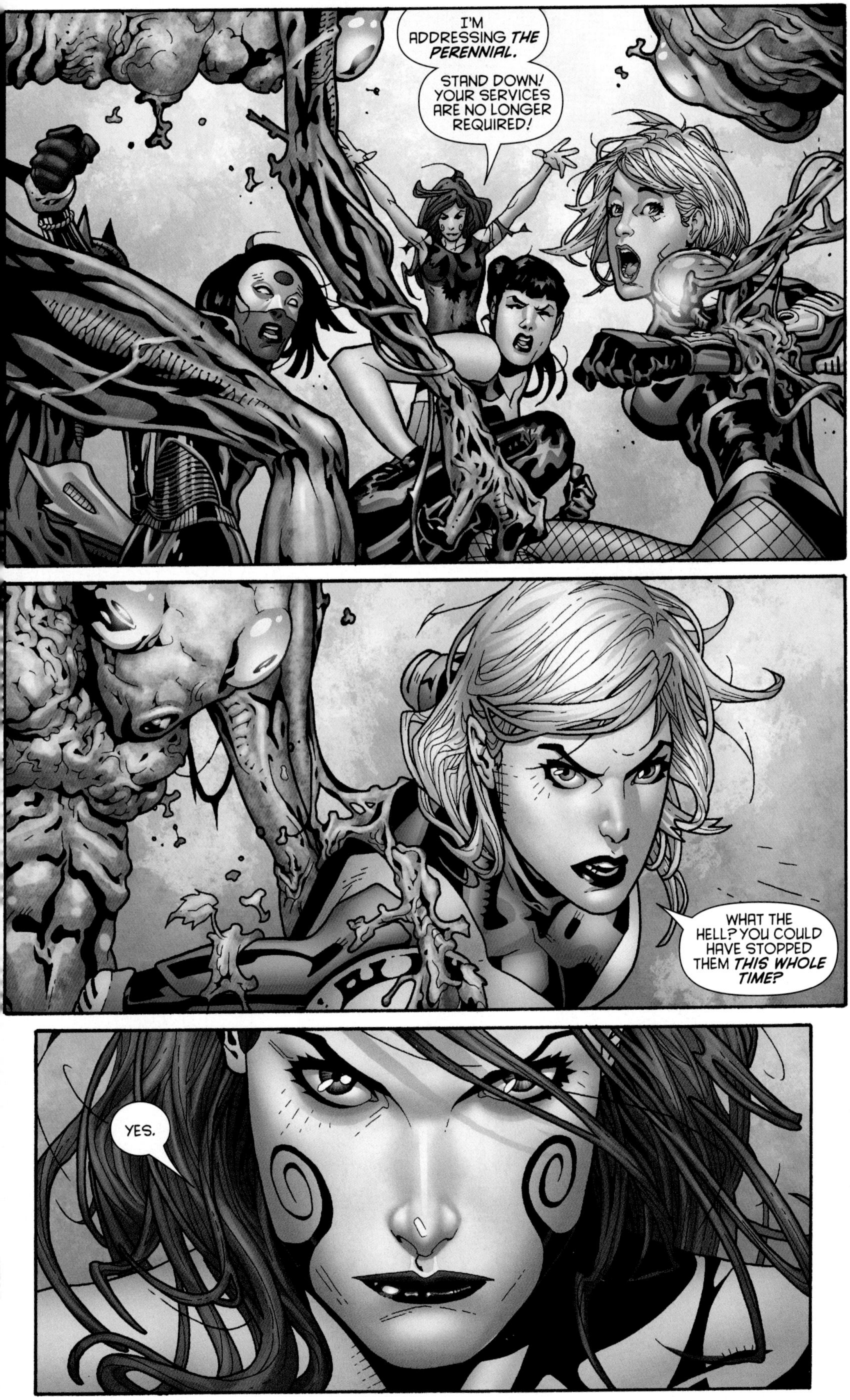
I'M ADDRESSING THE PERENNIAL.
STAND DOWN! YOUR SERVICES ARE NO LONGER REQUIRED!
WHAT THE HELL? YOU COULD HAVE STOPPED THEM THIS WHOLE TIME?
YES.

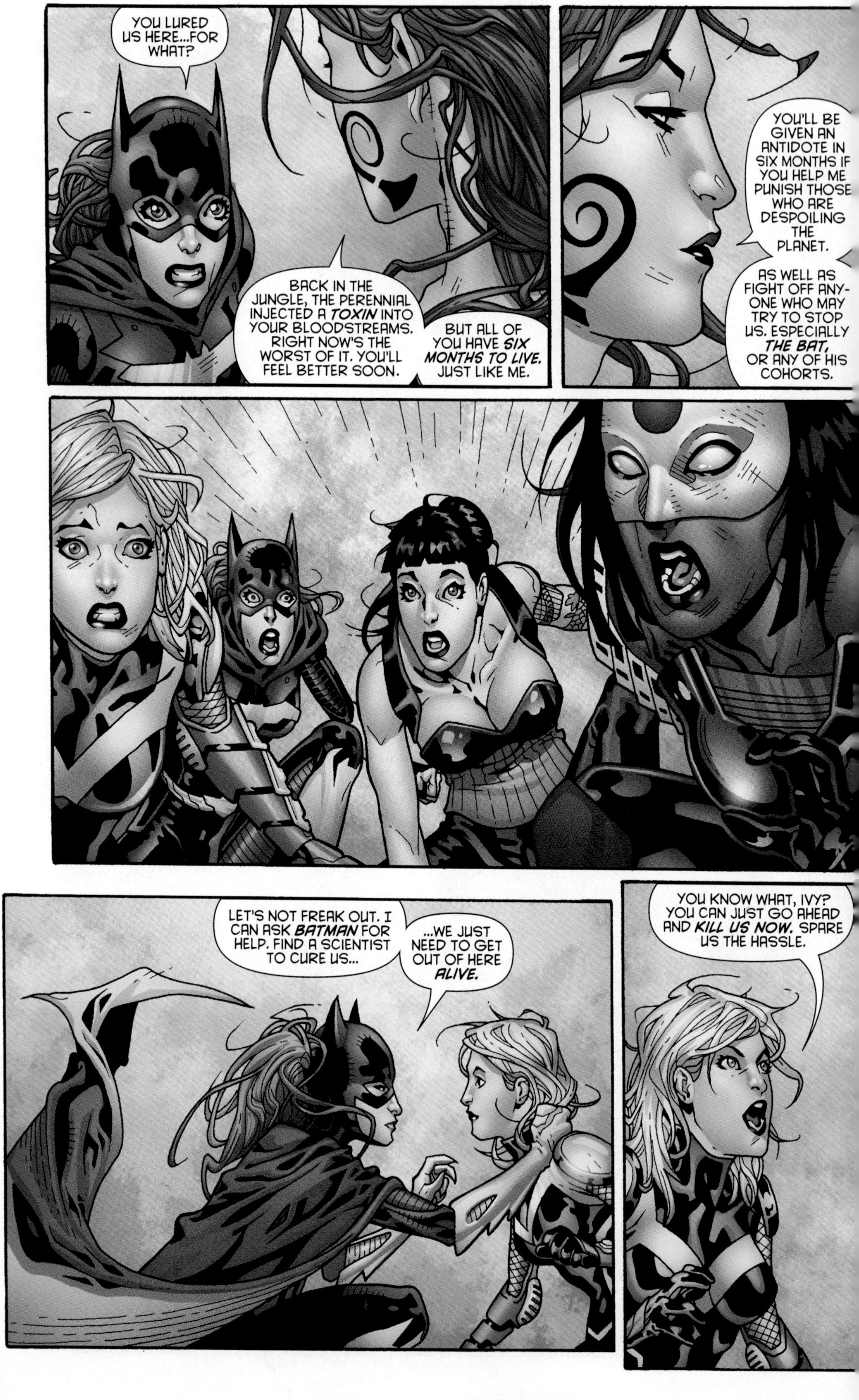
YOU LURED US HERE...FOR WHAT?
BACK IN THE JUNGLE, THE PERENNIAL INJECTED A TOXIN INTO YOUR BLOODSTREAMS. RIGHT NOW'S THE WORST OF IT. YOU'LL FEEL BETTER SOON.
BUT ALL OF YOU HAVE SIX MONTHS TO LIVE. JUST LIKE ME.
YOU'LL BE GIVEN AN ANTIDOTE IN SIX MONTHS IF YOU HELP ME PUNISH THOSE WHO ARE DESPOILING THE PLANET.
AS WELL AS FIGHT OFF ANY-ONE WHO MAY TRY TO STOP US. ESPECIALLY THE BAT, OR ANY OF HIS COHORTS.
LET'S NOT FREAK OUT. I CAN ASK BATMAN FOR HELP. FIND A SCIENTIST TO CURE US...
...WE JUST NEED TO GET OUT OF HERE ALIVE.
YOU KNOW WHAT, IVY? YOU CAN JUST GO AHEAD AND KILL US NOW. SPARE US THE HASSLE.

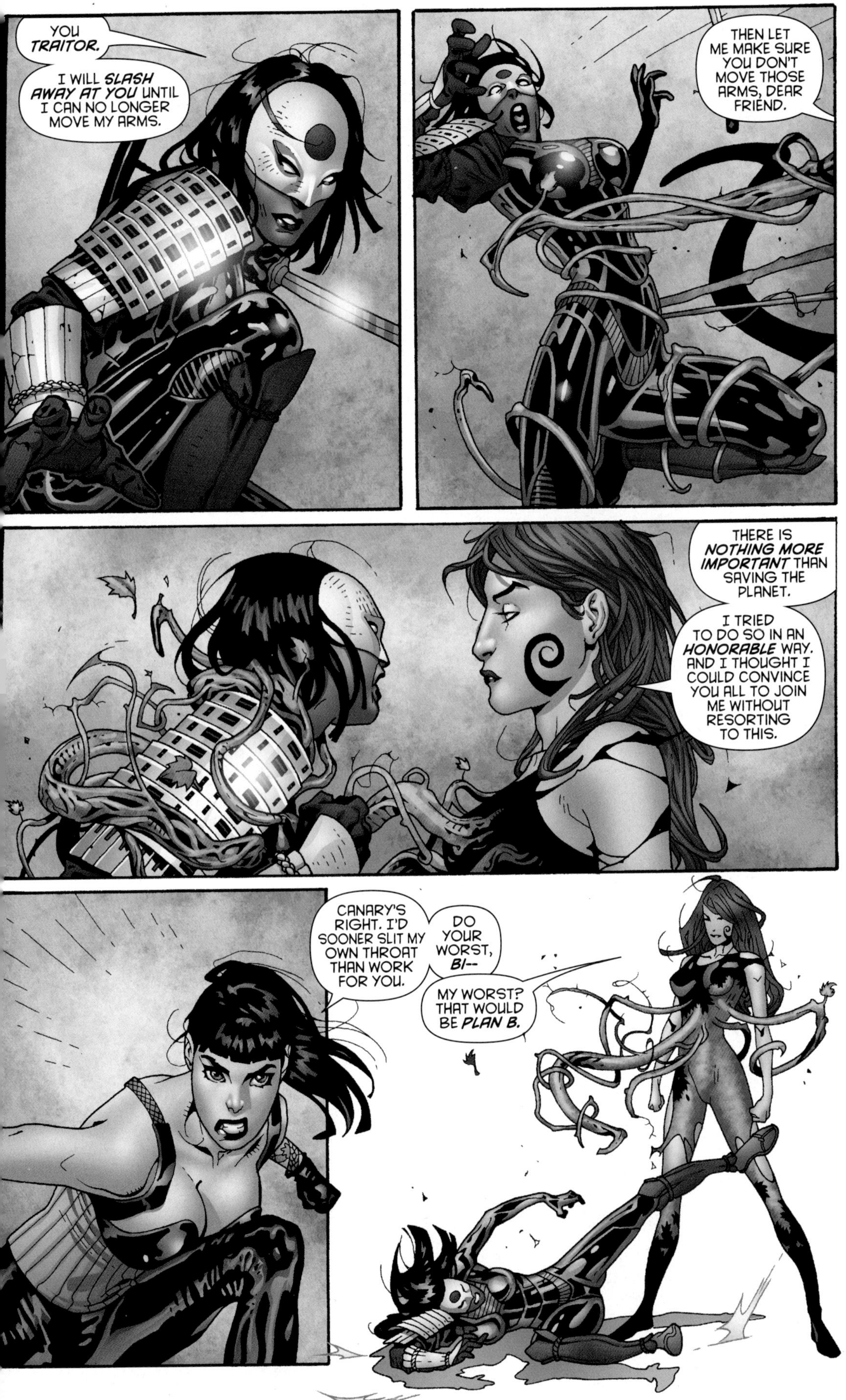
YOU TRAITOR.
I WILL SLASH AWAY AT YOU UNTIL I CAN NO LONGER MOVE MY ARMS.
THEN LET ME MAKE SURE YOU DON'T MOVE THOSE ARMS, DEAR FRIEND.
THERE IS NOTHING MORE IMPORTANT THAN SAVING THE PLANET.
I TRIED TO DO SO IN AN HONORABLE WAY. AND I THOUGHT I COULD CONVINCE YOU ALL TO JOIN ME WITHOUT RESORTING TO THIS.
CANARY'S RIGHT. I'D SOONER SLIT MY OWN THROAT THAN WORK FOR YOU.
DO YOUR WORST, BI--
MY WORST? THAT WOULD BE PLAN B.

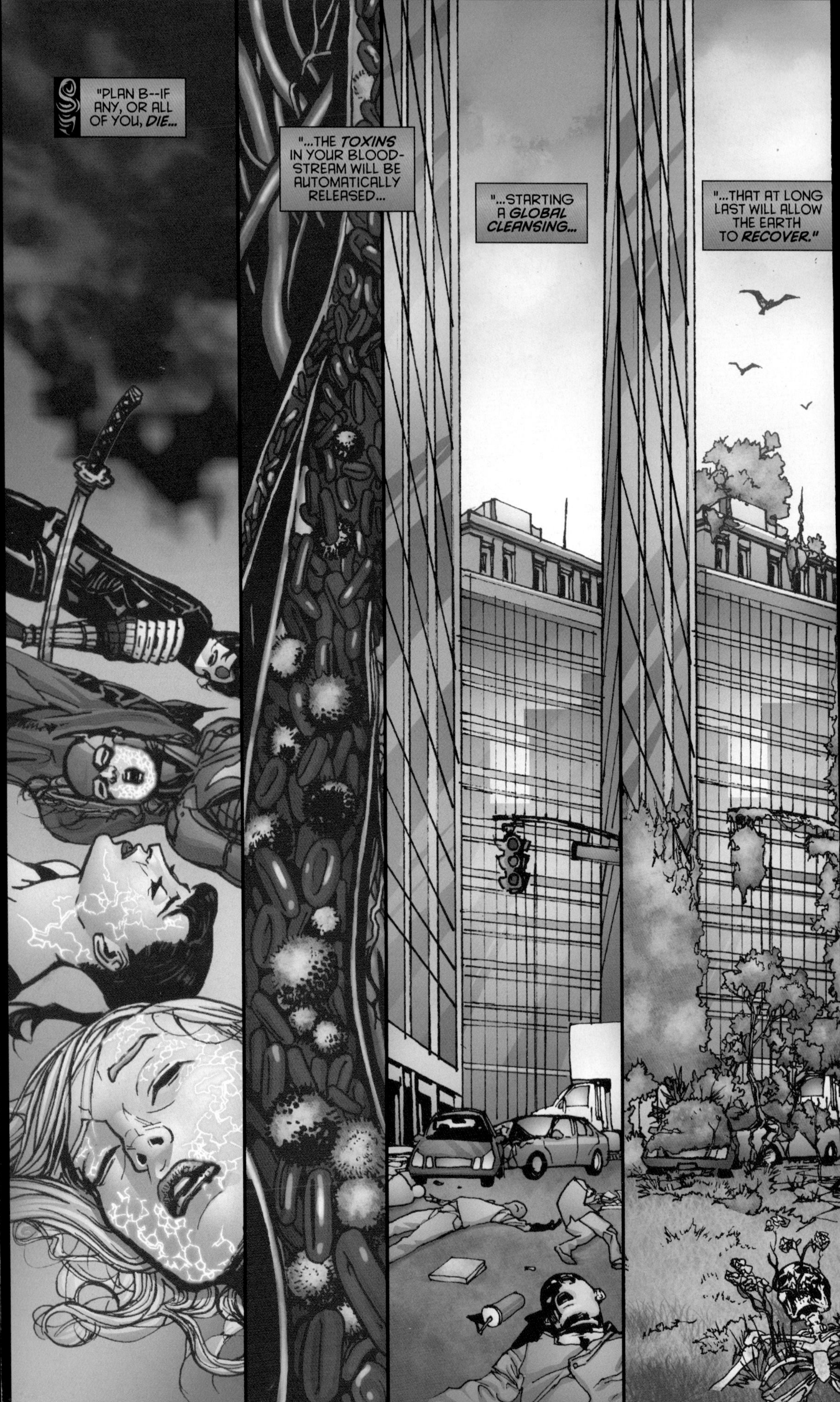
"PLAN B--IF ANY, OR ALL OF YOU, *DIE*...
"...THE *TOXINS* IN YOUR BLOOD-STREAM WILL BE AUTOMATICALLY RELEASED...
"...STARTING A *GLOBAL CLEANSING*...
"...THAT AT LONG LAST WILL ALLOW THE EARTH TO *RECOVER*."

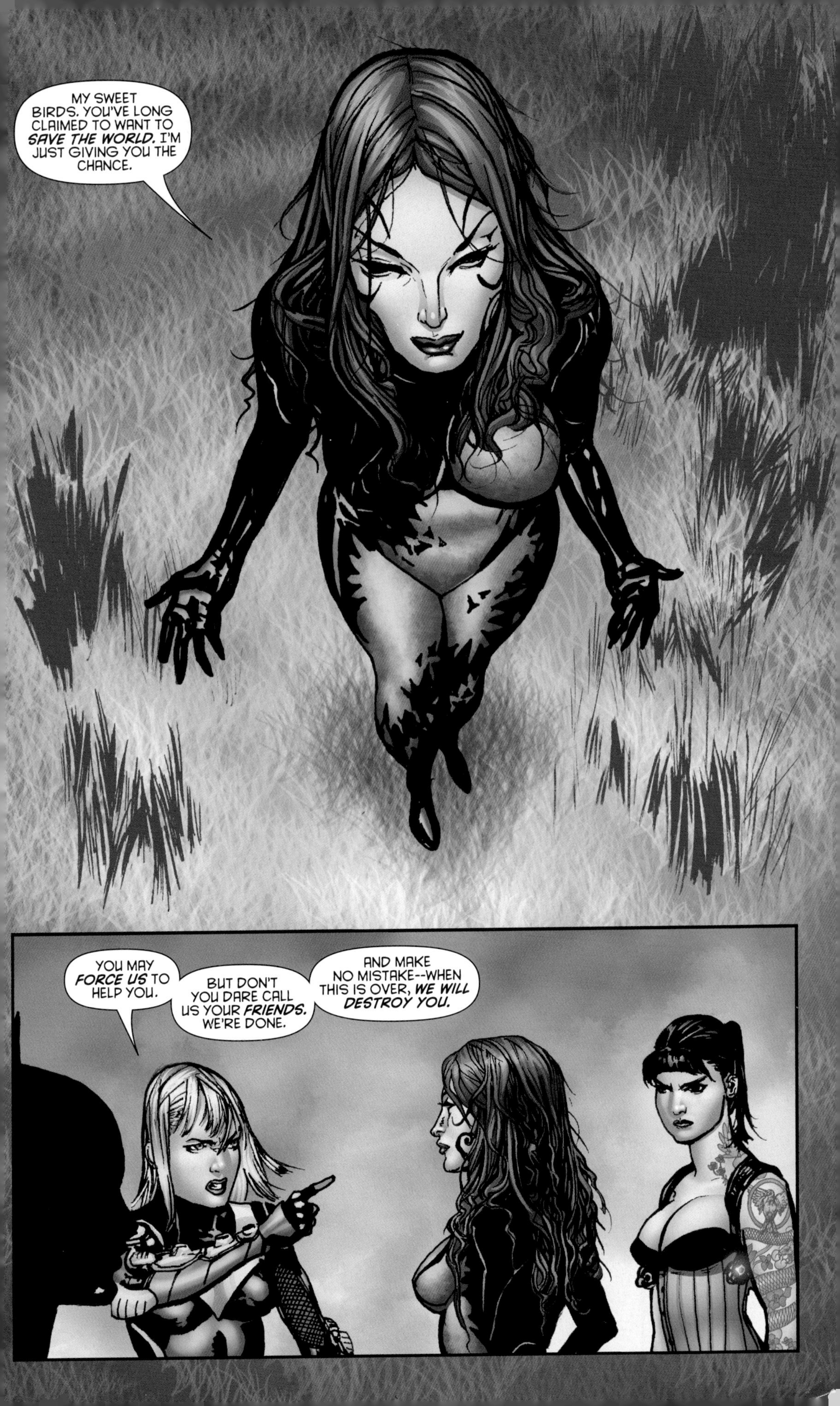
MY SWEET BIRDS. YOU'VE LONG CLAIMED TO WANT TO **SAVE THE WORLD.** I'M JUST GIVING YOU THE CHANCE.
YOU MAY **FORCE US** TO HELP YOU.
BUT DON'T YOU DARE CALL US YOUR **FRIENDS.** WE'RE DONE.
AND MAKE NO MISTAKE--WHEN THIS IS OVER, **WE WILL DESTROY YOU.**

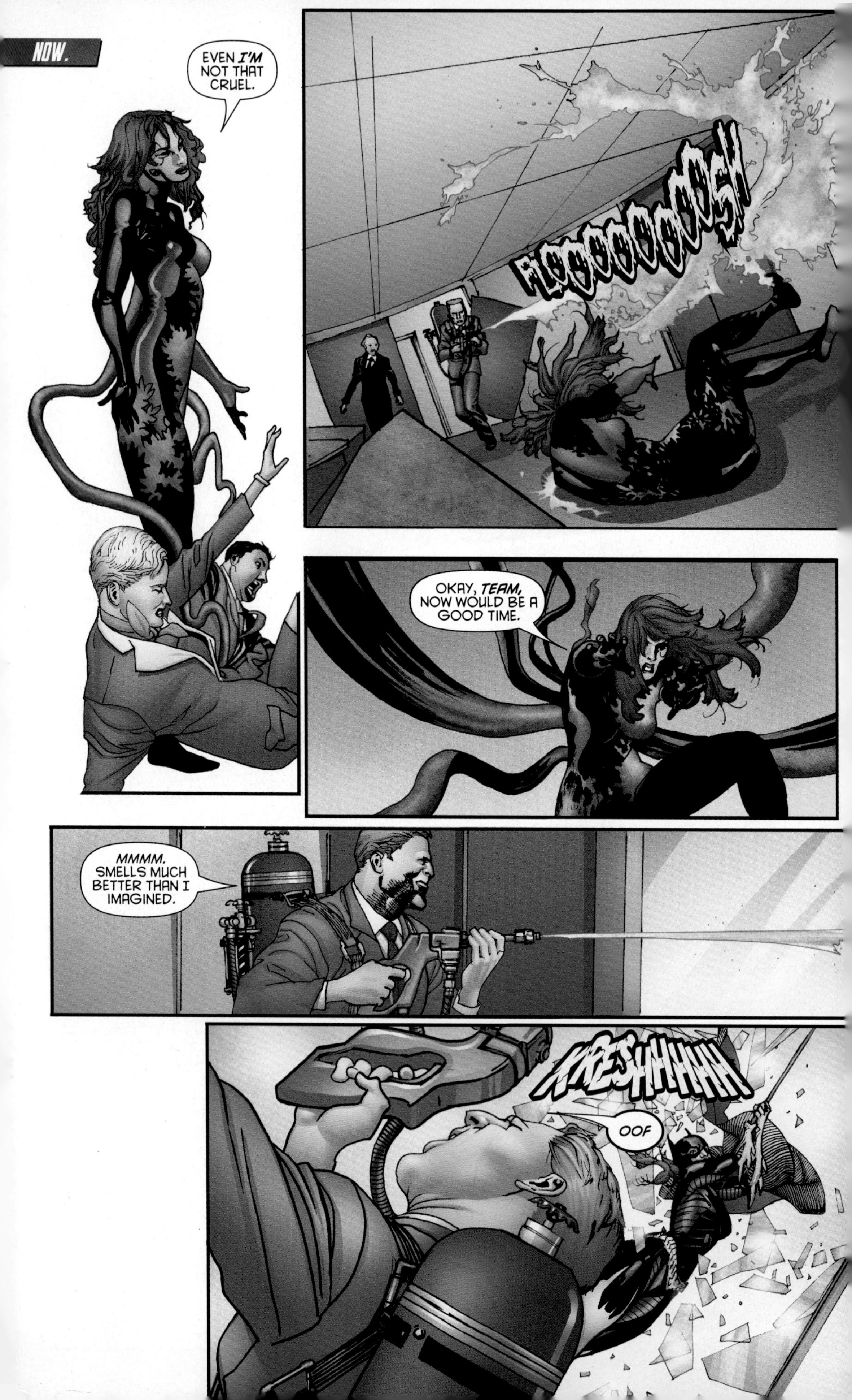
NOW.
EVEN I'M NOT THAT CRUEL.
FLOOOOOOOOOSH
OKAY, TEAM, NOW WOULD BE A GOOD TIME.
MMMM. SMELLS MUCH BETTER THAN I IMAGINED.
KRESHHHHHH
OOF

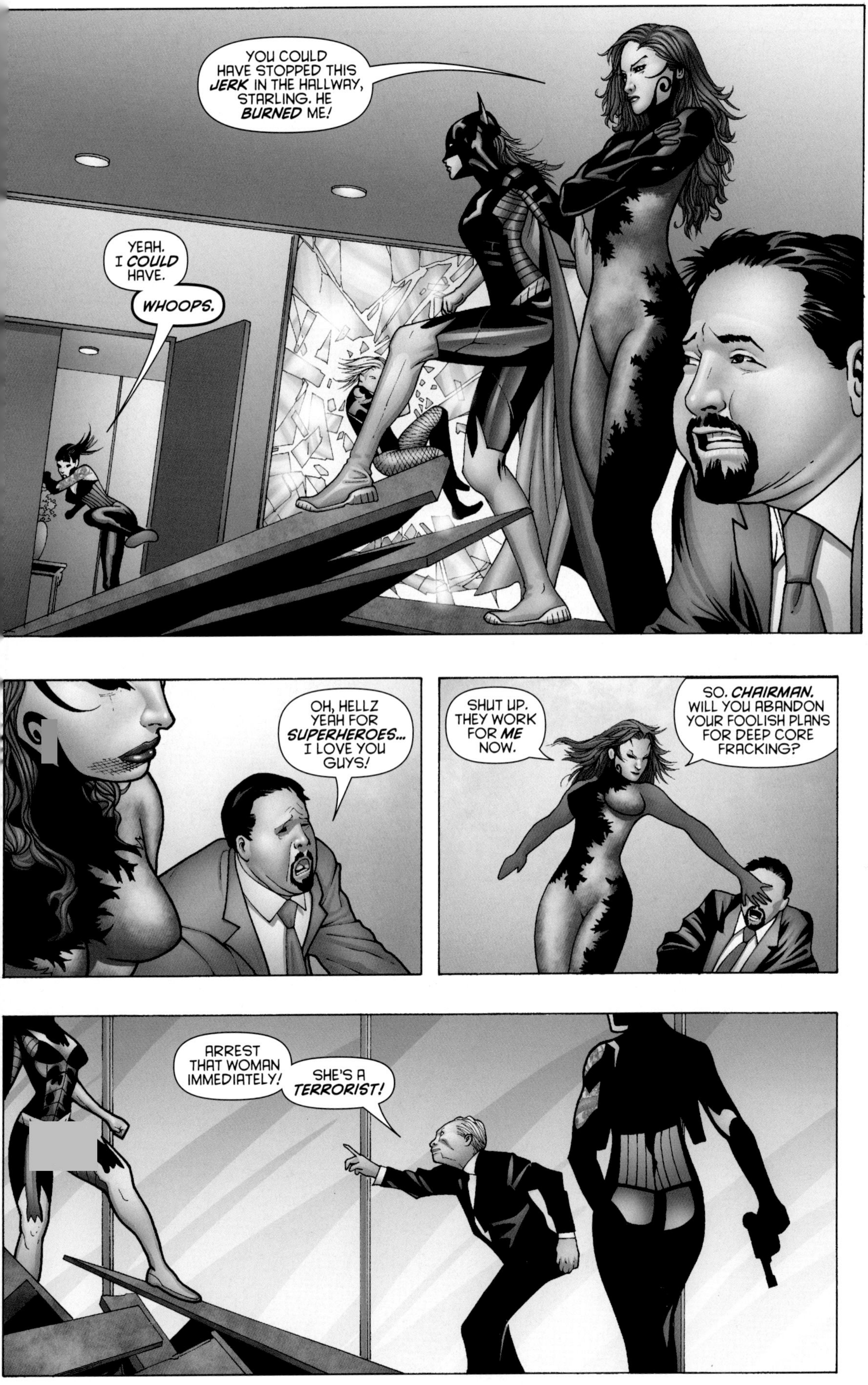
YOU COULD HAVE STOPPED THIS JERK IN THE HALLWAY, STARLING. HE BURNED ME!
YEAH. I COULD HAVE.
WHOOPS.
OH, HELLZ YEAH FOR SUPERHEROES... I LOVE YOU GUYS!
SHUT UP. THEY WORK FOR ME NOW.
SO. CHAIRMAN. WILL YOU ABANDON YOUR FOOLISH PLANS FOR DEEP CORE FRACKING?
ARREST THAT WOMAN IMMEDIATELY!
SHE'S A TERRORIST!

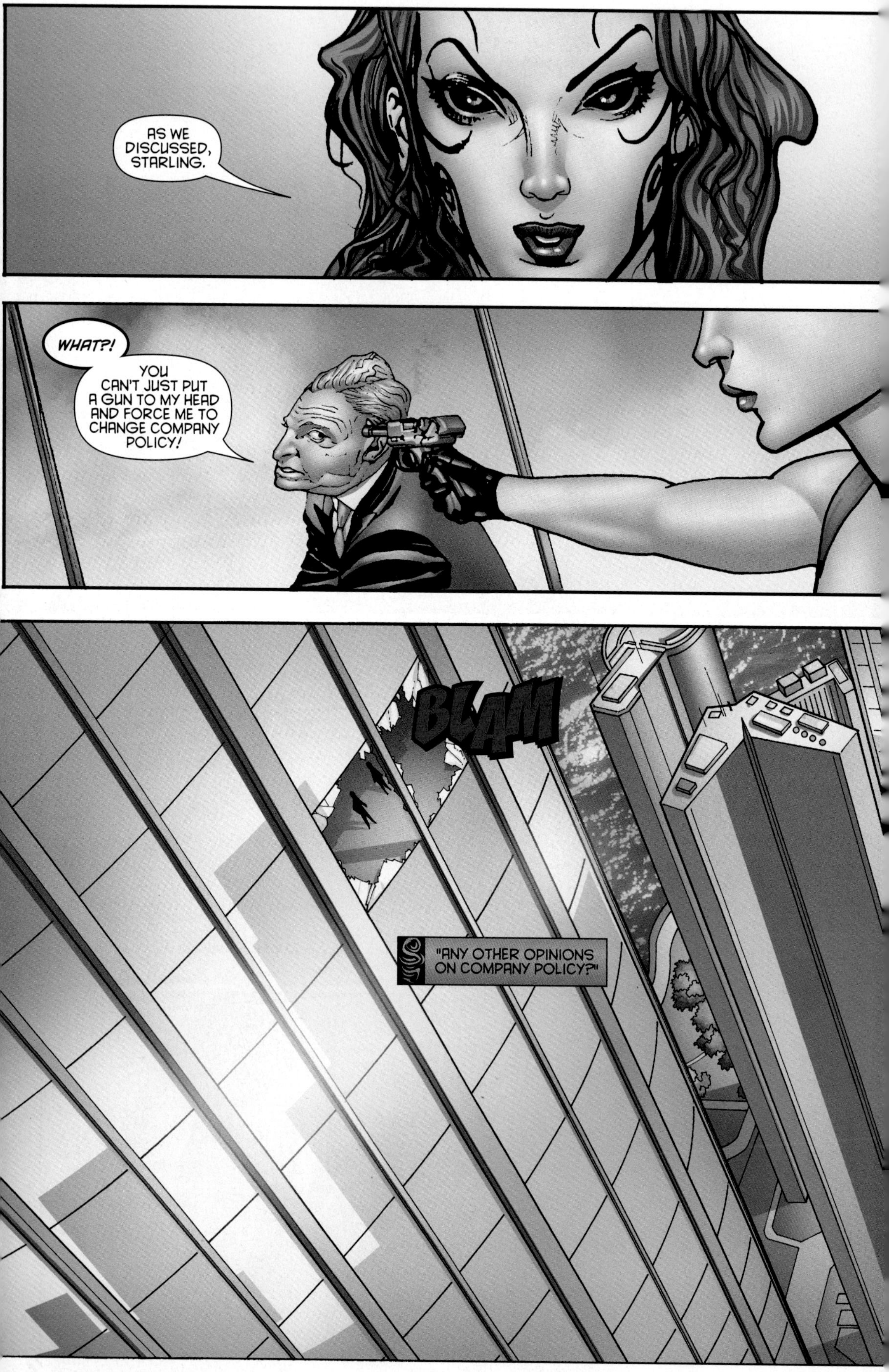
AS WE DISCUSSED, STARLING.
WHAT?!
YOU CAN'T JUST PUT A GUN TO MY HEAD AND FORCE ME TO CHANGE COMPANY POLICY!
BLAM
"ANY OTHER OPINIONS ON COMPANY POLICY?"

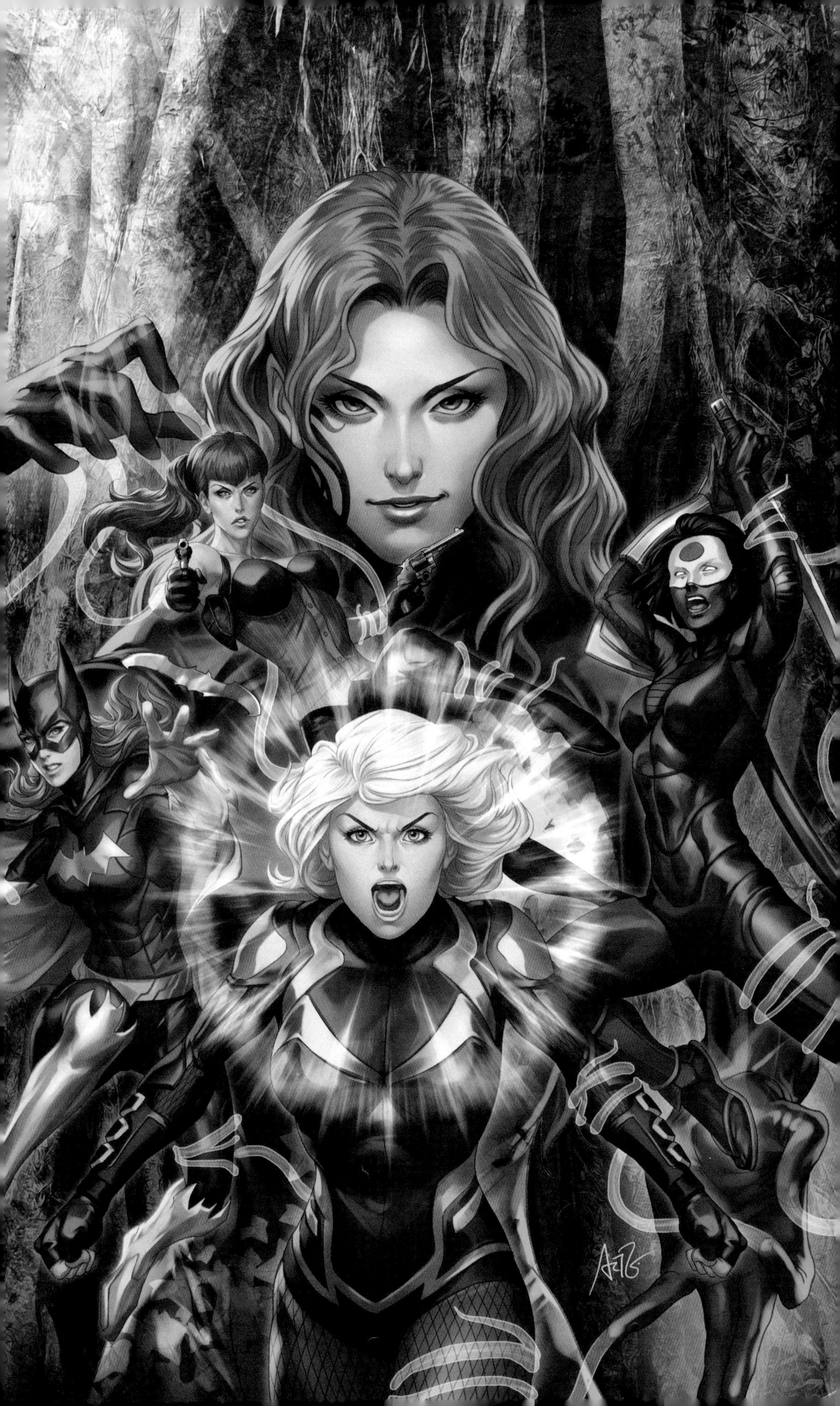

HEARTBREAK AND VINE

DUANE SWIERCZYNSKI writer **CLIFF RICHARDS** artist cover art by **STANLEY "ARTGERM" LAU**

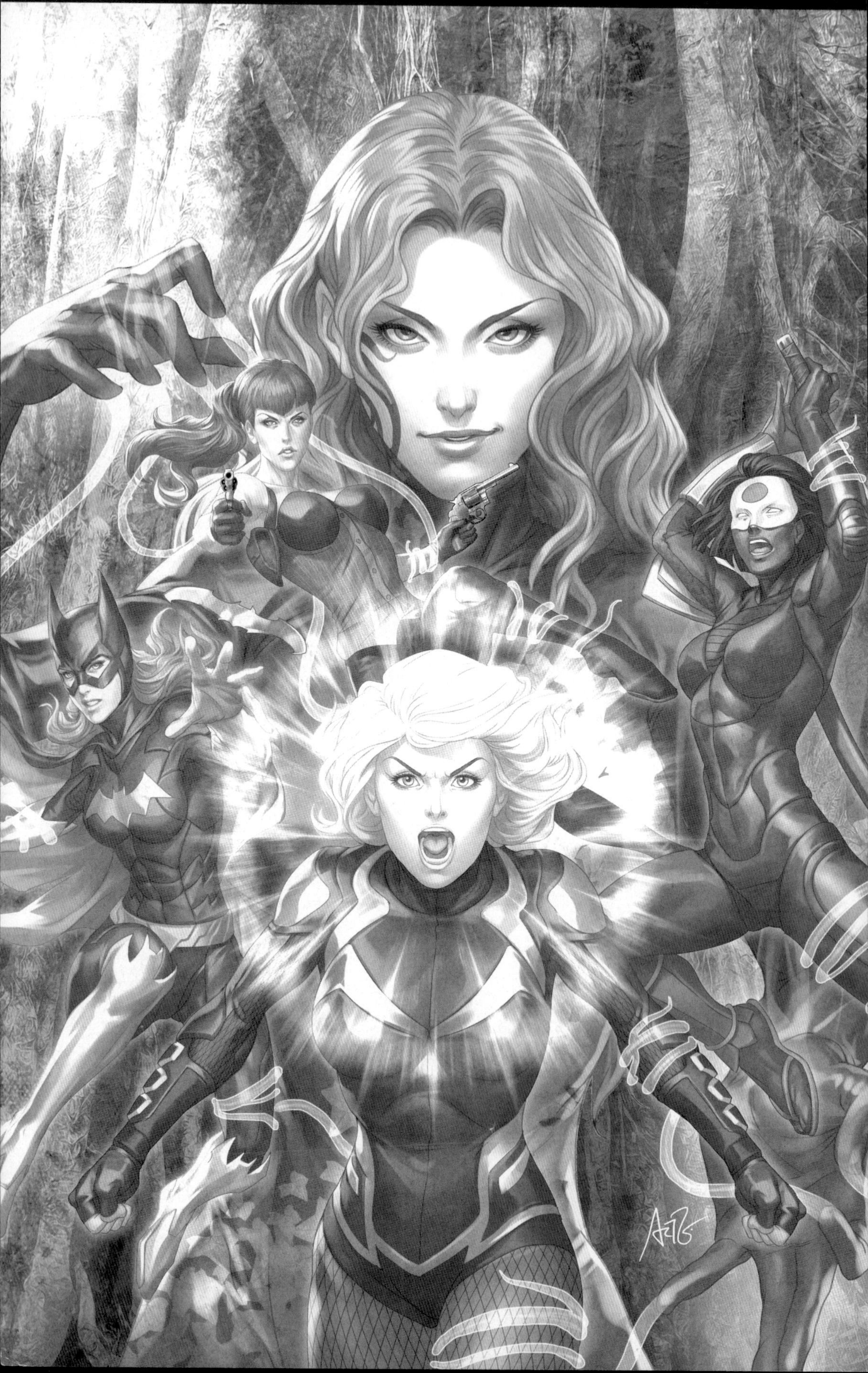

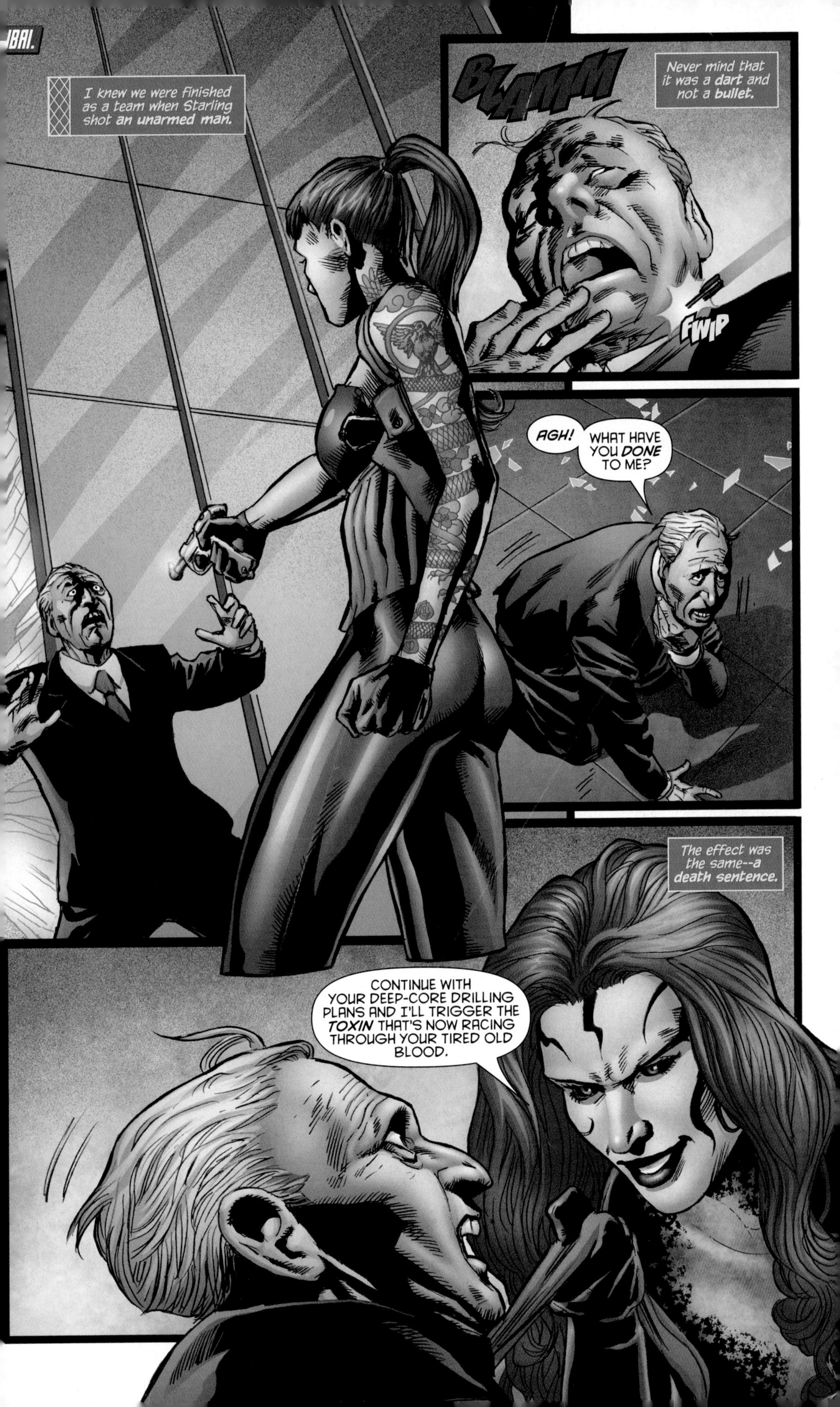

IBAI.
I knew we were finished as a team when Starling shot an unarmed man.
BLAMM
Never mind that it was a dart and not a bullet.
FWIP
AGH!
WHAT HAVE YOU DONE TO ME?
The effect was the same--a death sentence.
CONTINUE WITH YOUR DEEP-CORE DRILLING PLANS AND I'LL TRIGGER THE TOXIN THAT'S NOW RACING THROUGH YOUR TIRED OLD BLOOD.

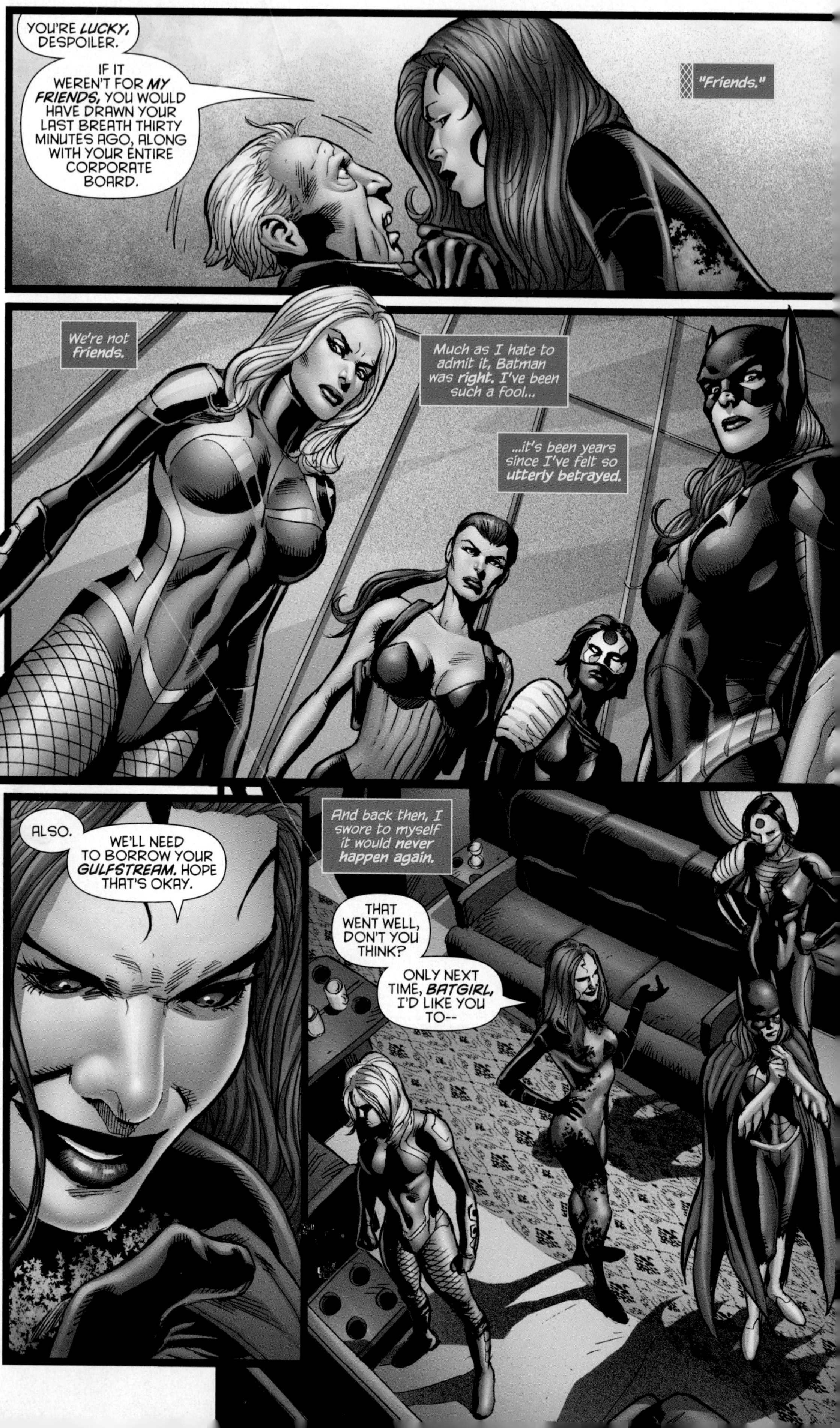
YOU'RE LUCKY, DESPOILER.
IF IT WEREN'T FOR MY FRIENDS, YOU WOULD HAVE DRAWN YOUR LAST BREATH THIRTY MINUTES AGO, ALONG WITH YOUR ENTIRE CORPORATE BOARD.
"Friends."
We're not friends.
Much as I hate to admit it, Batman was right. I've been such a fool...
...it's been years since I've felt so utterly betrayed.
ALSO.
WE'LL NEED TO BORROW YOUR GULFSTREAM. HOPE THAT'S OKAY.
And back then, I swore to myself it would never happen again.
THAT WENT WELL, DON'T YOU THINK?
ONLY NEXT TIME, BATGIRL, I'D LIKE YOU TO--

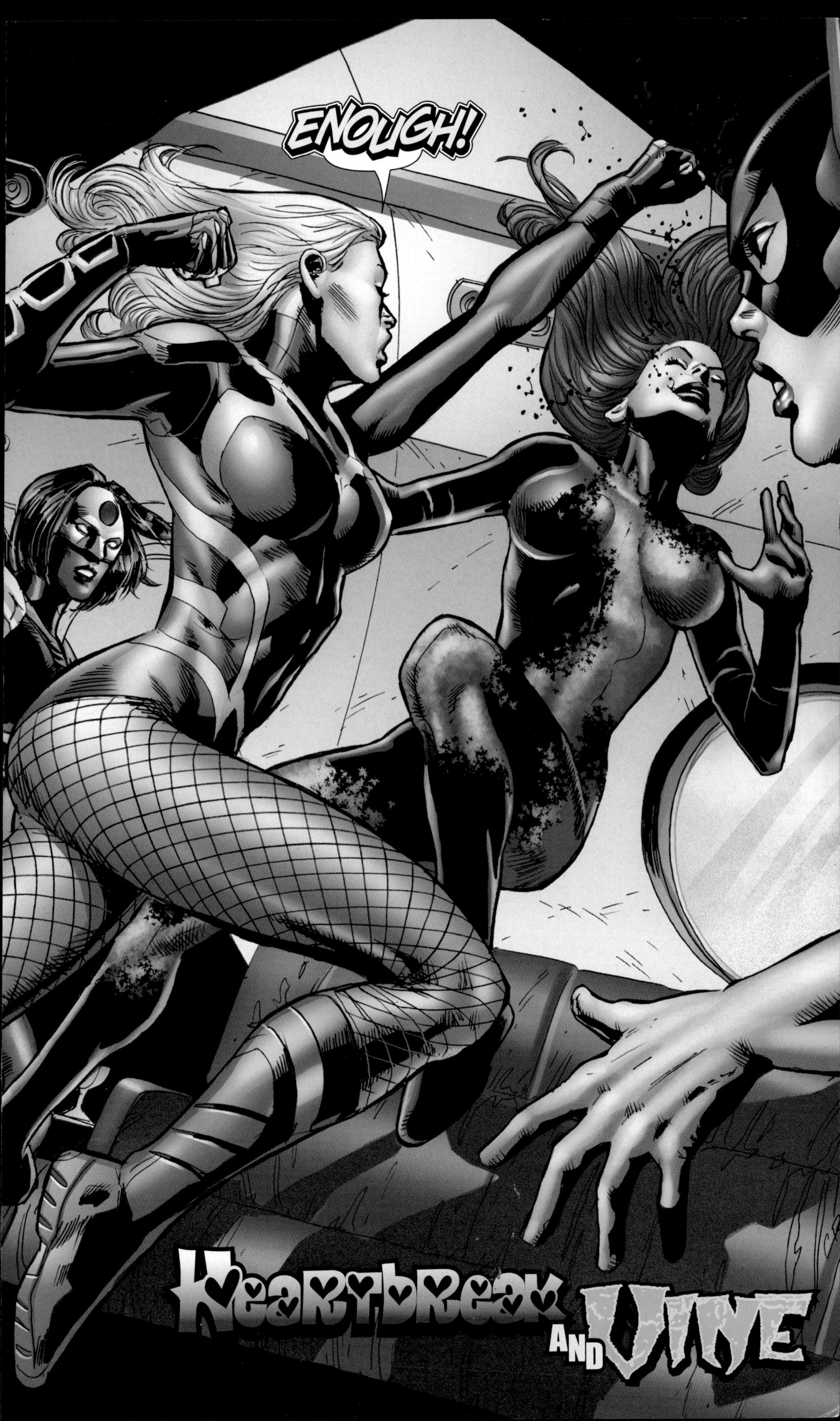
ENOUGH!
HEARTBREAK AND VINE

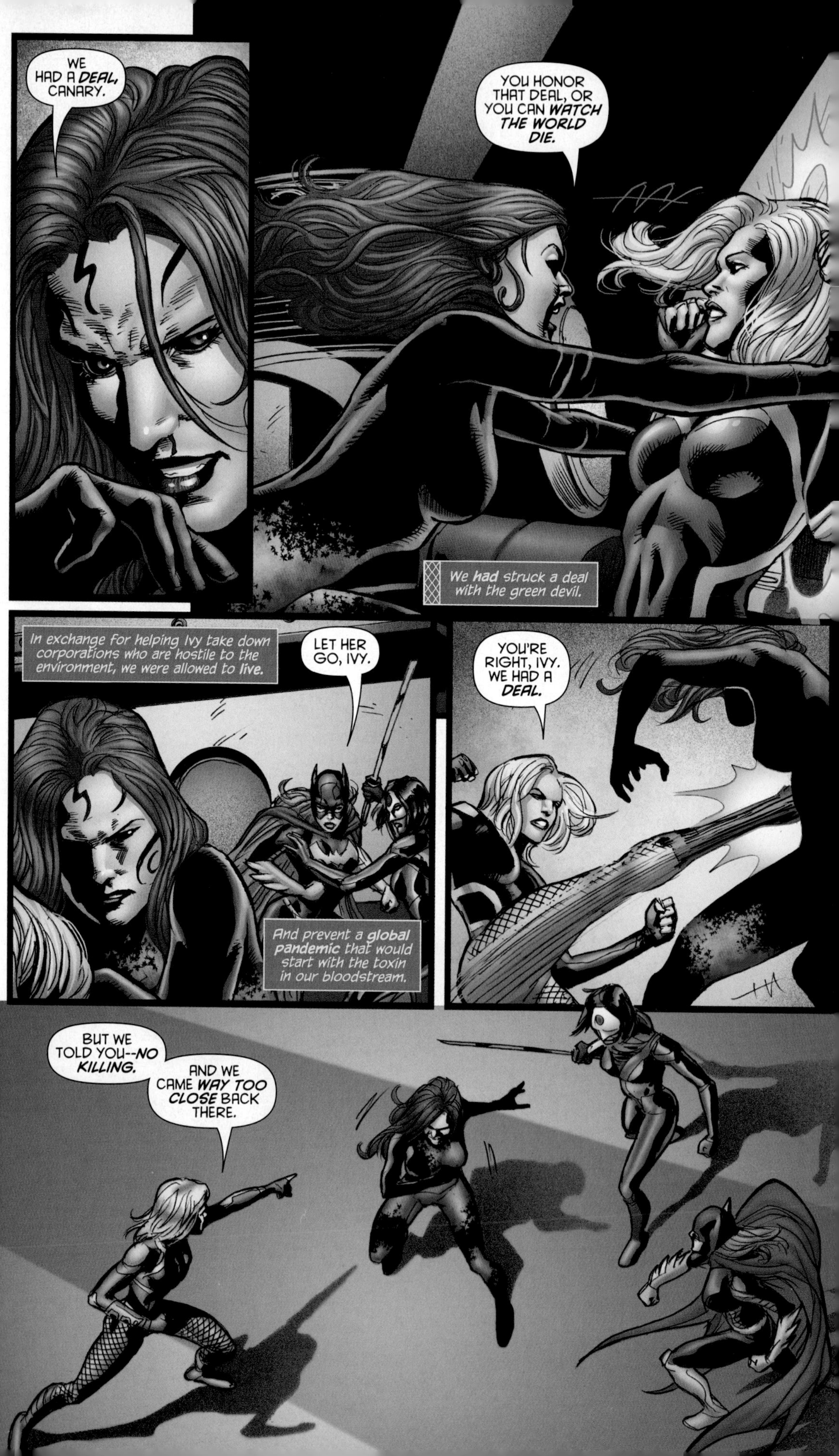
WE HAD A DEAL, CANARY.
YOU HONOR THAT DEAL, OR YOU CAN WATCH THE WORLD DIE.
We had struck a deal with the green devil.
In exchange for helping Ivy take down corporations who are hostile to the environment, we were allowed to live.
LET HER GO, IVY.
And prevent a global pandemic that would start with the toxin in our bloodstream.
YOU'RE RIGHT, IVY. WE HAD A DEAL.
BUT WE TOLD YOU--NO KILLING.
AND WE CAME WAY TOO CLOSE BACK THERE.

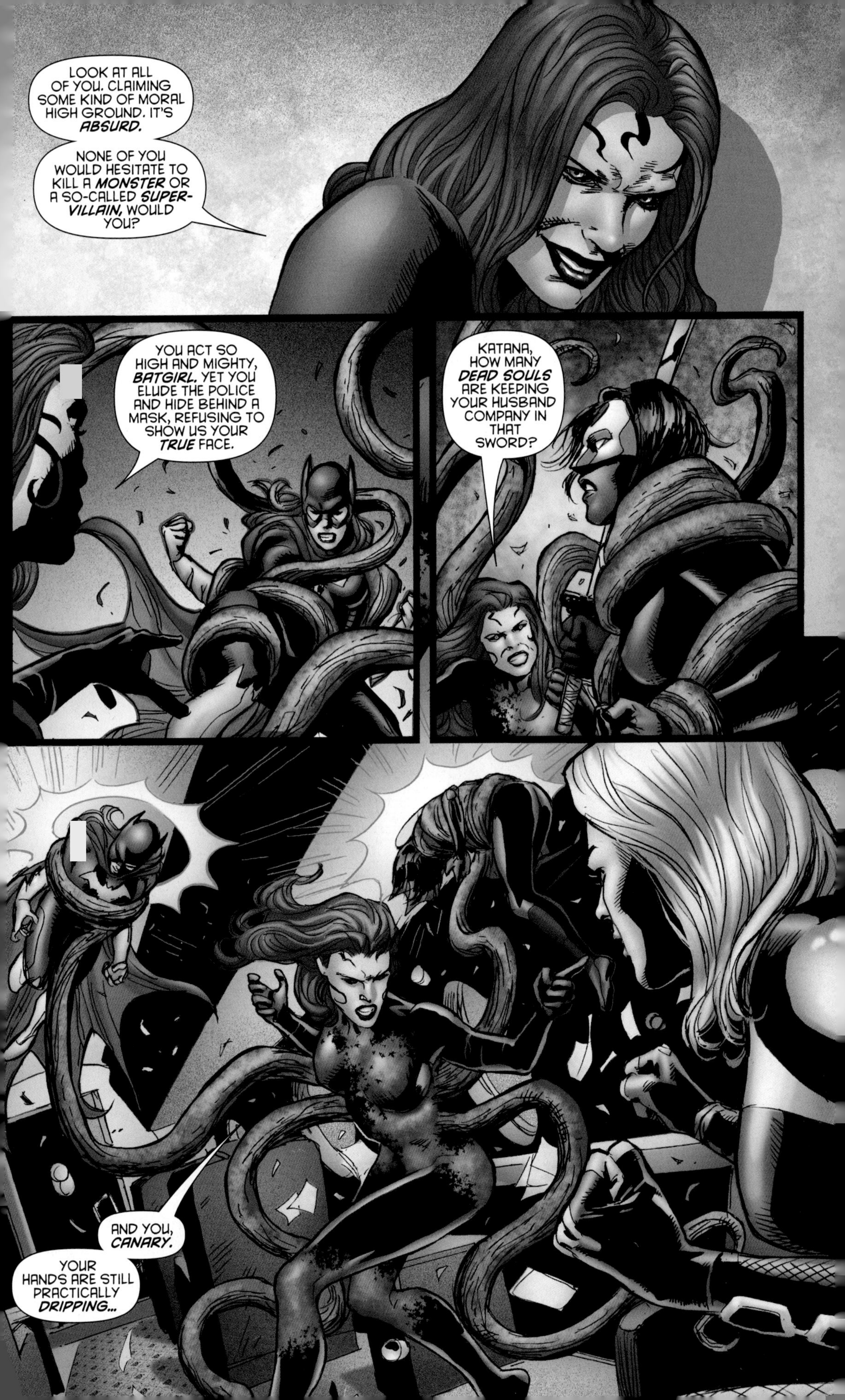
LOOK AT ALL OF YOU. CLAIMING SOME KIND OF MORAL HIGH GROUND. IT'S ABSURD.
NONE OF YOU WOULD HESITATE TO KILL A MONSTER OR A SO-CALLED SUPER-VILLAIN, WOULD YOU?
YOU ACT SO HIGH AND MIGHTY, BATGIRL. YET YOU ELUDE THE POLICE AND HIDE BEHIND A MASK, REFUSING TO SHOW US YOUR TRUE FACE.
KATANA, HOW MANY DEAD SOULS ARE KEEPING YOUR HUSBAND COMPANY IN THAT SWORD?
AND YOU, CANARY.
YOUR HANDS ARE STILL PRACTICALLY DRIPPING...

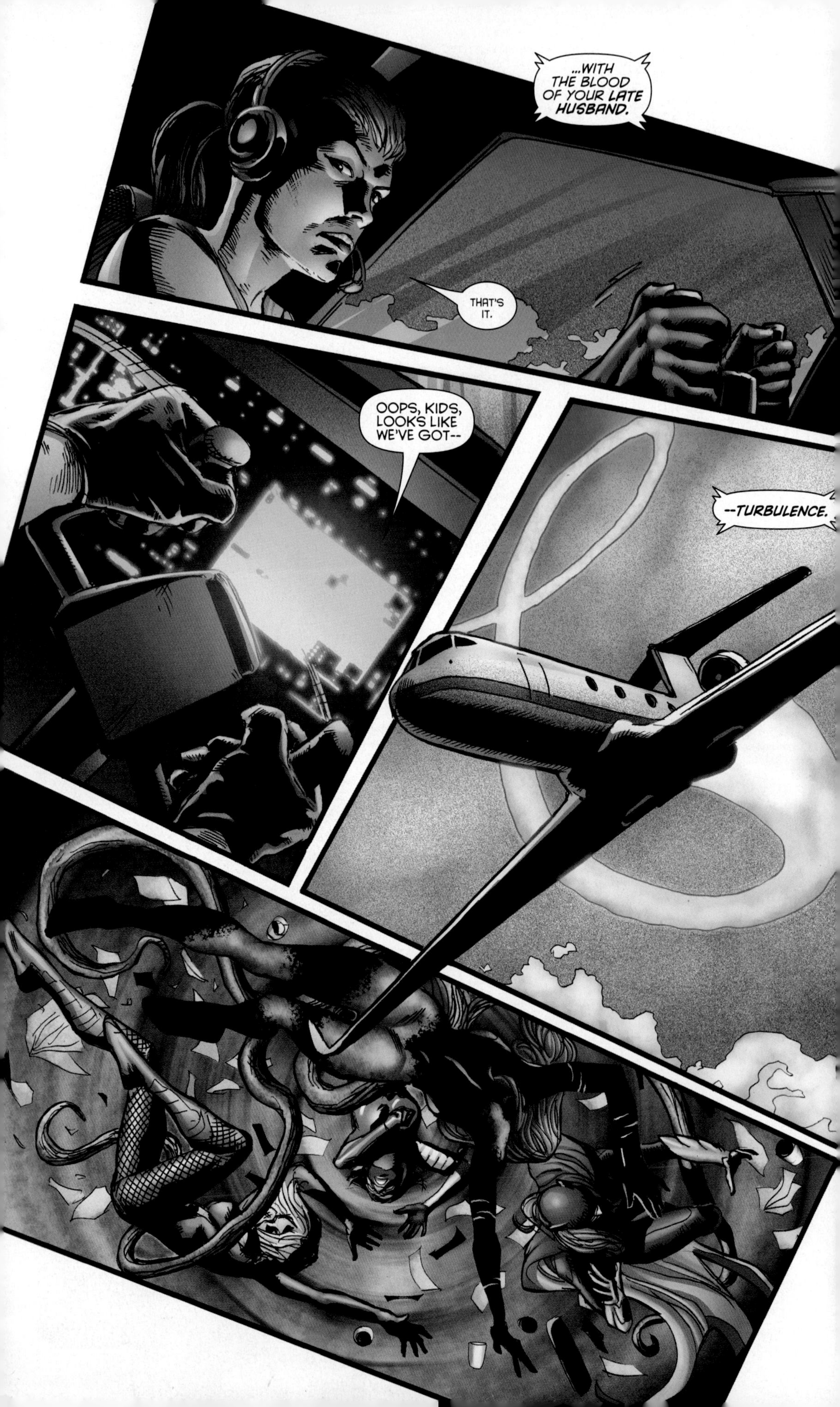
...WITH THE BLOOD OF YOUR LATE HUSBAND.
THAT'S IT.
OOPS, KIDS, LOOKS LIKE WE'VE GOT--
--TURBULENCE.

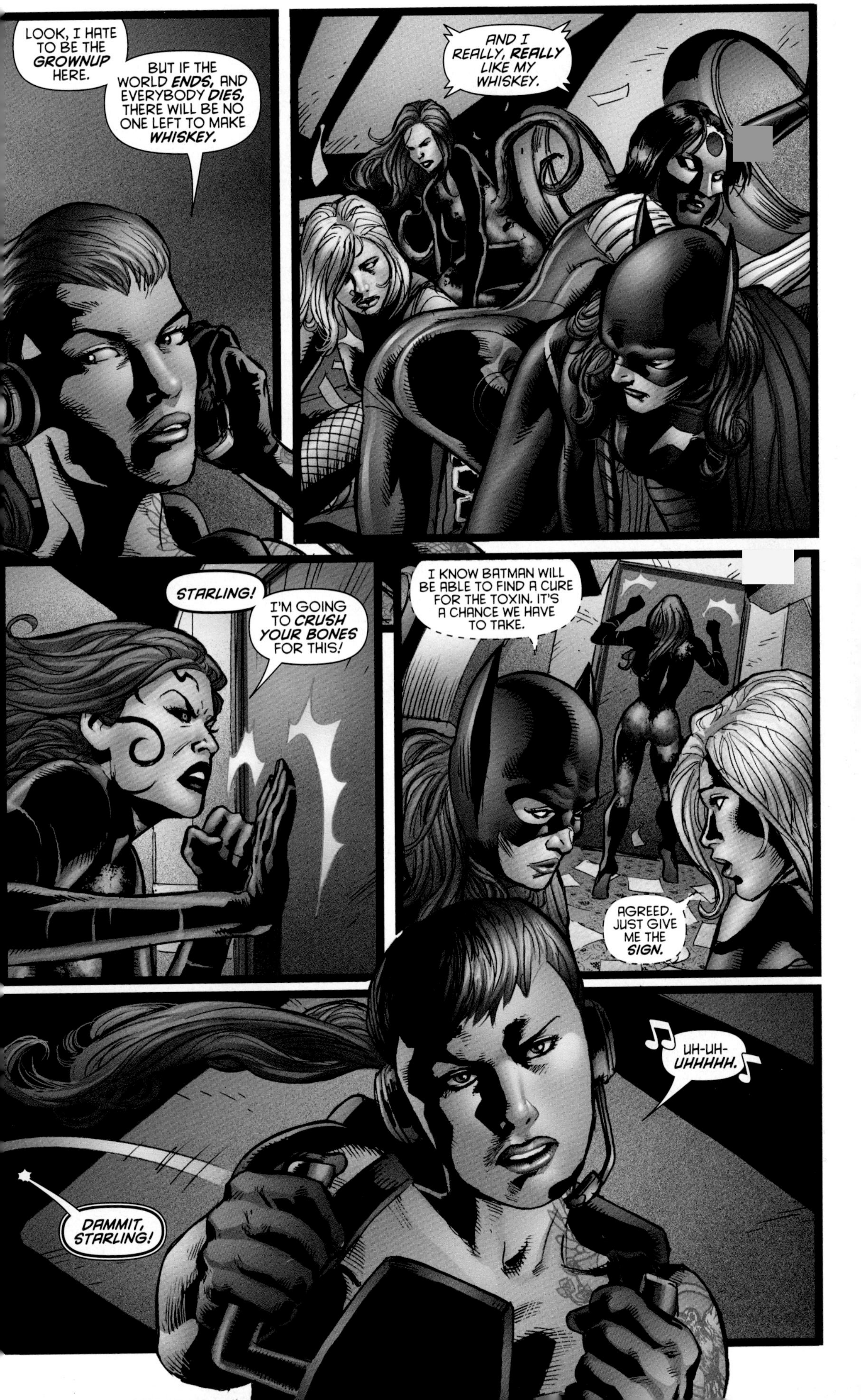

LOOK, I HATE TO BE THE GROWNUP HERE.
BUT IF THE WORLD ENDS, AND EVERYBODY DIES, THERE WILL BE NO ONE LEFT TO MAKE WHISKEY.
AND I REALLY, REALLY LIKE MY WHISKEY.
STARLING!
I'M GOING TO CRUSH YOUR BONES FOR THIS!
I KNOW BATMAN WILL BE ABLE TO FIND A CURE FOR THE TOXIN. IT'S A CHANCE WE HAVE TO TAKE.
AGREED. JUST GIVE ME THE SIGN.
UH-UH-UHHHHH.
DAMMIT, STARLING!

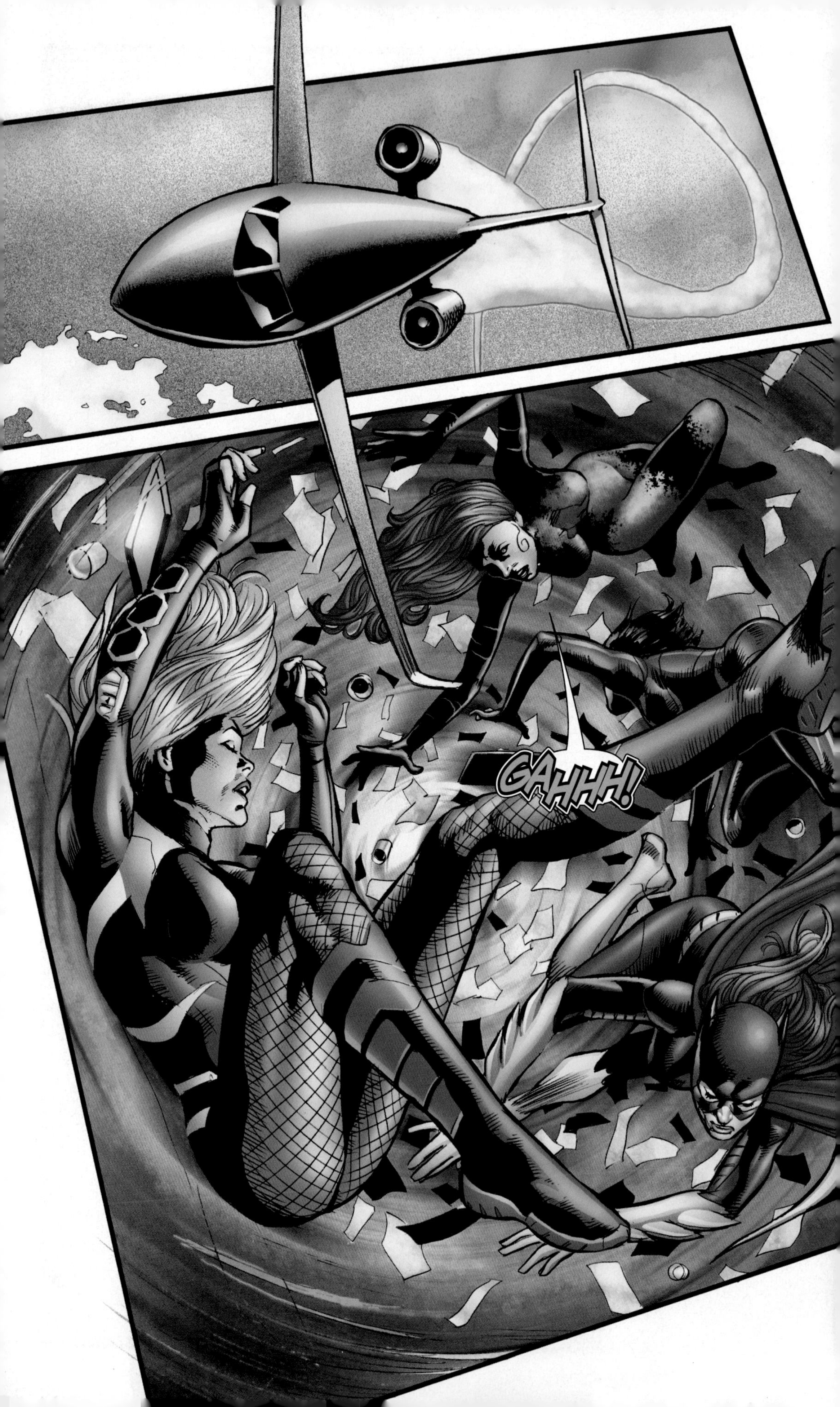
GAHHH!

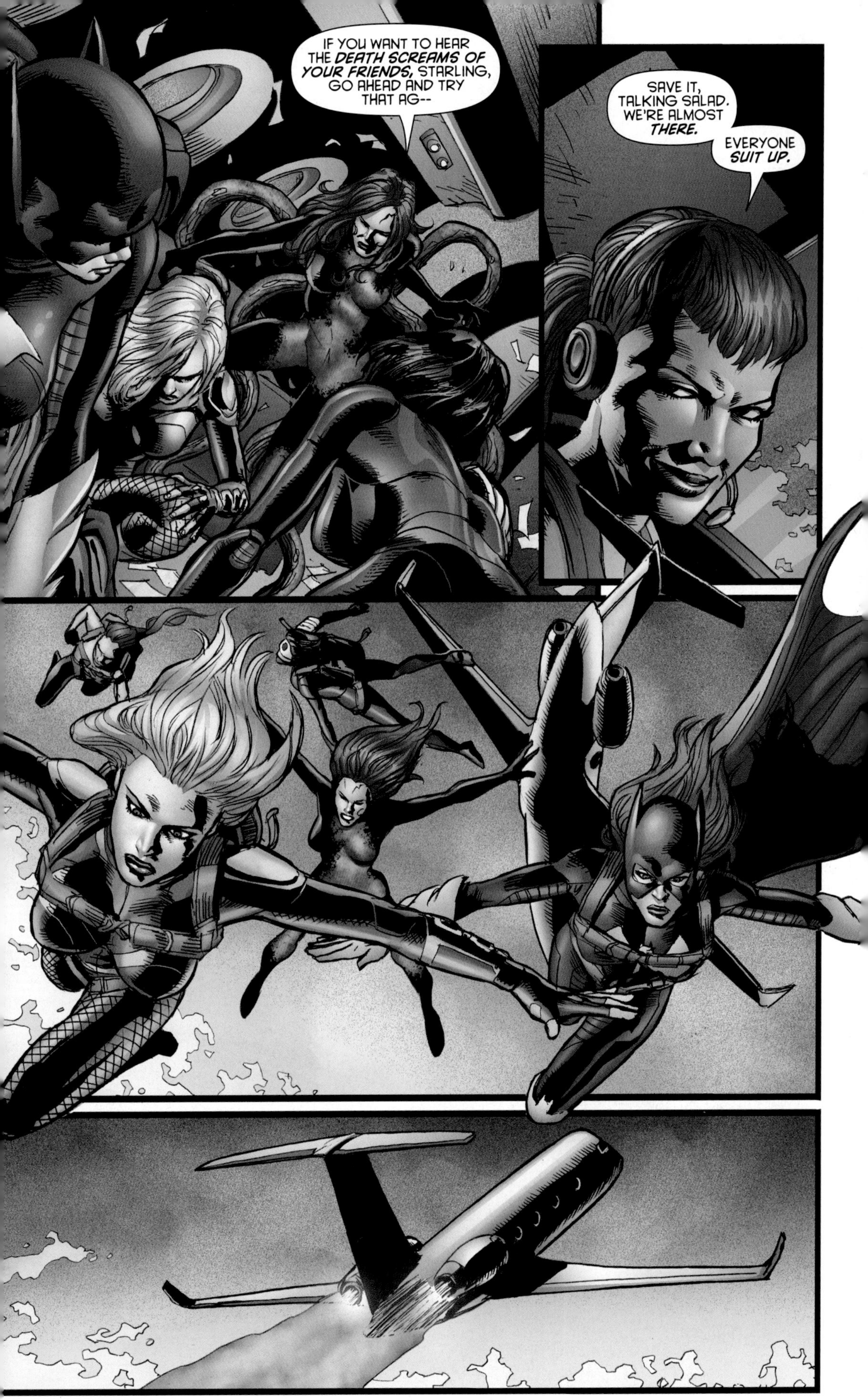

IF YOU WANT TO HEAR THE *DEATH SCREAMS OF YOUR FRIENDS,* STARLING, GO AHEAD AND TRY THAT AG--
SAVE IT, TALKING SALAD. WE'RE ALMOST *THERE.*
EVERYONE *SUIT UP.*

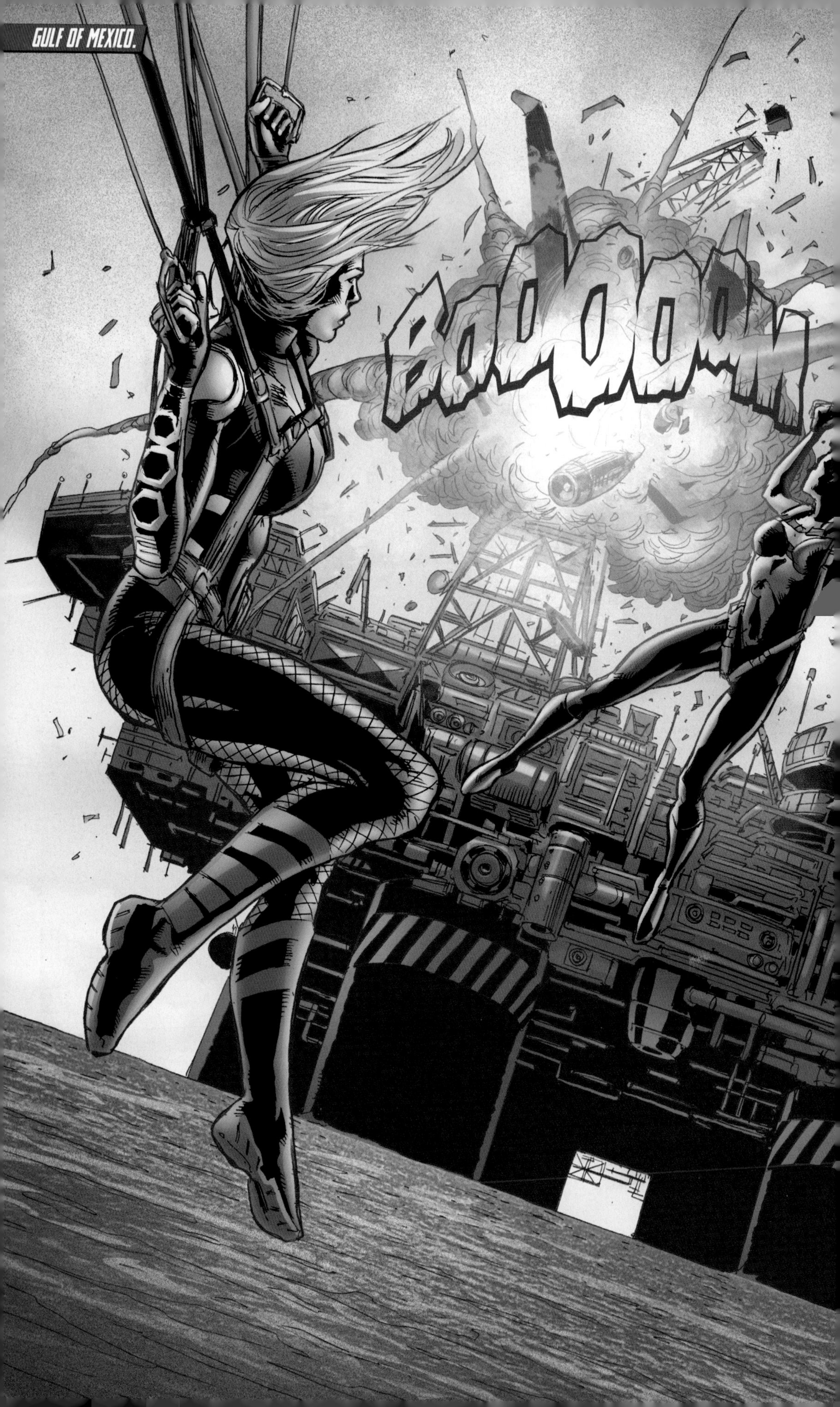
GULF OF MEXICO.

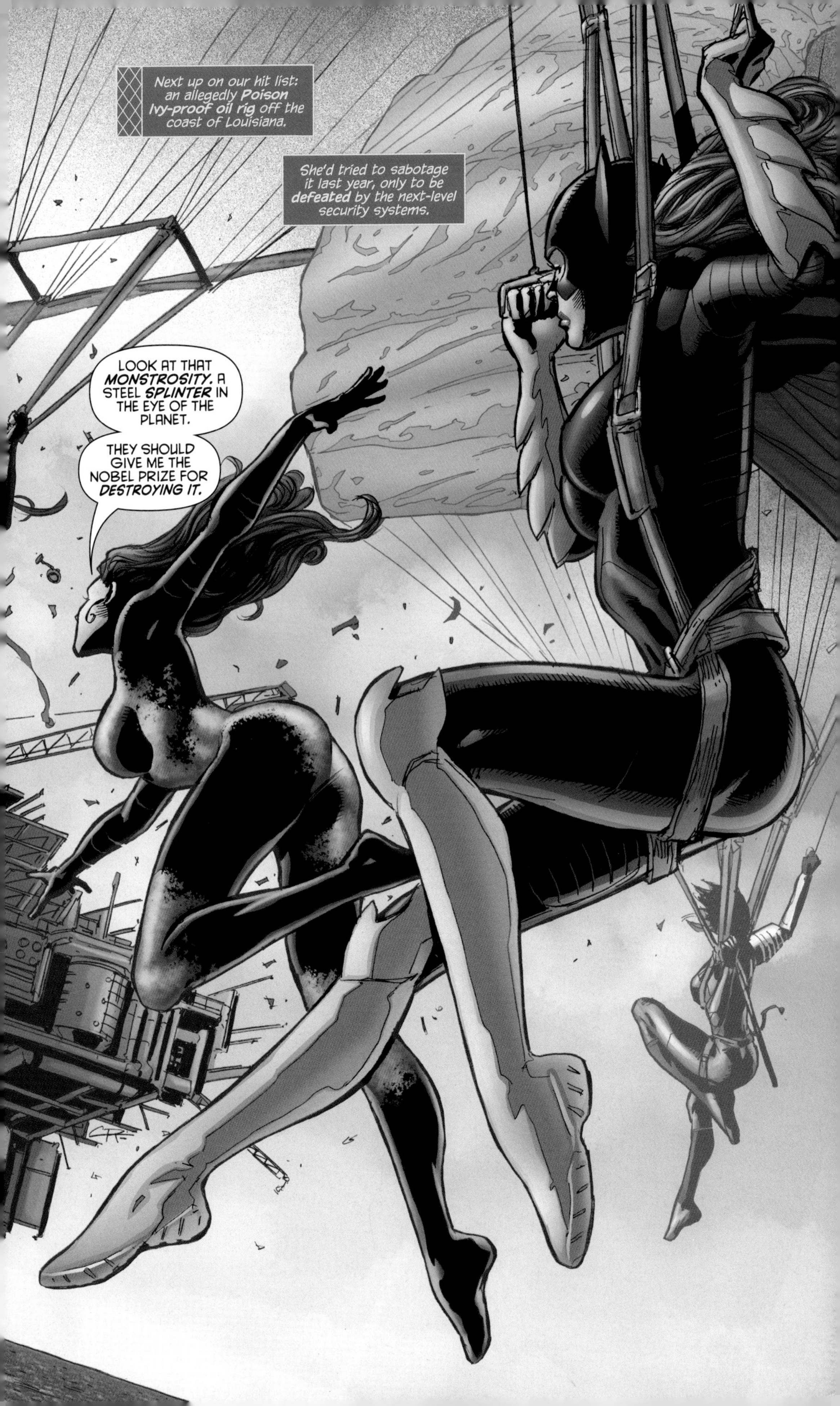

Next up on our hit list: an allegedly Poison Ivy-proof oil rig off the coast of Louisiana.
She'd tried to sabotage it last year, only to be defeated by the next-level security systems.
LOOK AT THAT MONSTROSITY. A STEEL SPLINTER IN THE EYE OF THE PLANET.
THEY SHOULD GIVE ME THE NOBEL PRIZE FOR DESTROYING IT.

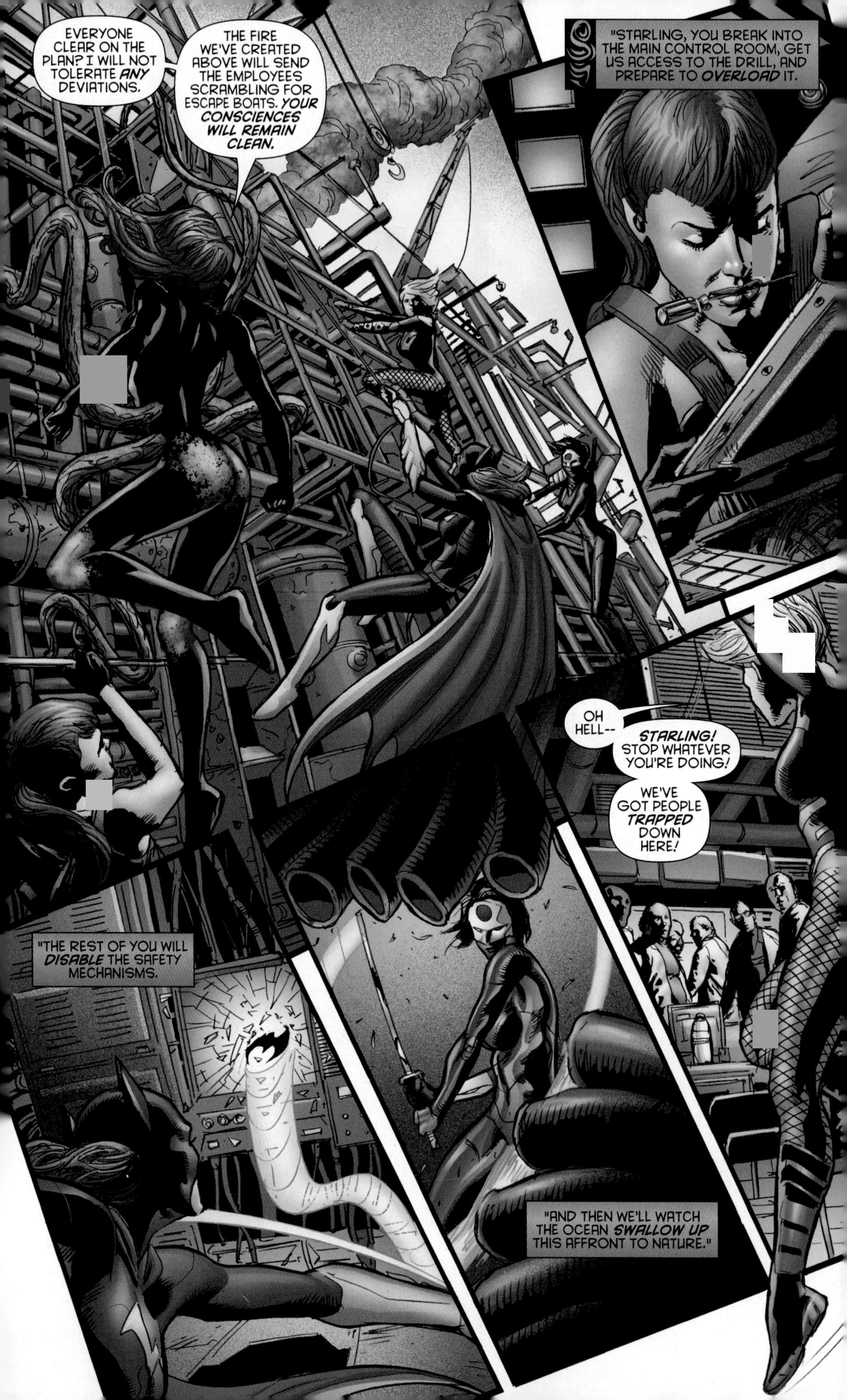
EVERYONE CLEAR ON THE PLAN? I WILL NOT TOLERATE ANY DEVIATIONS.
THE FIRE WE'VE CREATED ABOVE WILL SEND THE EMPLOYEES SCRAMBLING FOR ESCAPE BOATS. YOUR CONSCIENCES WILL REMAIN CLEAN.
"STARLING, YOU BREAK INTO THE MAIN CONTROL ROOM, GET US ACCESS TO THE DRILL, AND PREPARE TO OVERLOAD IT.
"THE REST OF YOU WILL DISABLE THE SAFETY MECHANISMS.
"AND THEN WE'LL WATCH THE OCEAN SWALLOW UP THIS AFFRONT TO NATURE."
OH HELL--
STARLING! STOP WHATEVER YOU'RE DOING!
WE'VE GOT PEOPLE TRAPPED DOWN HERE!

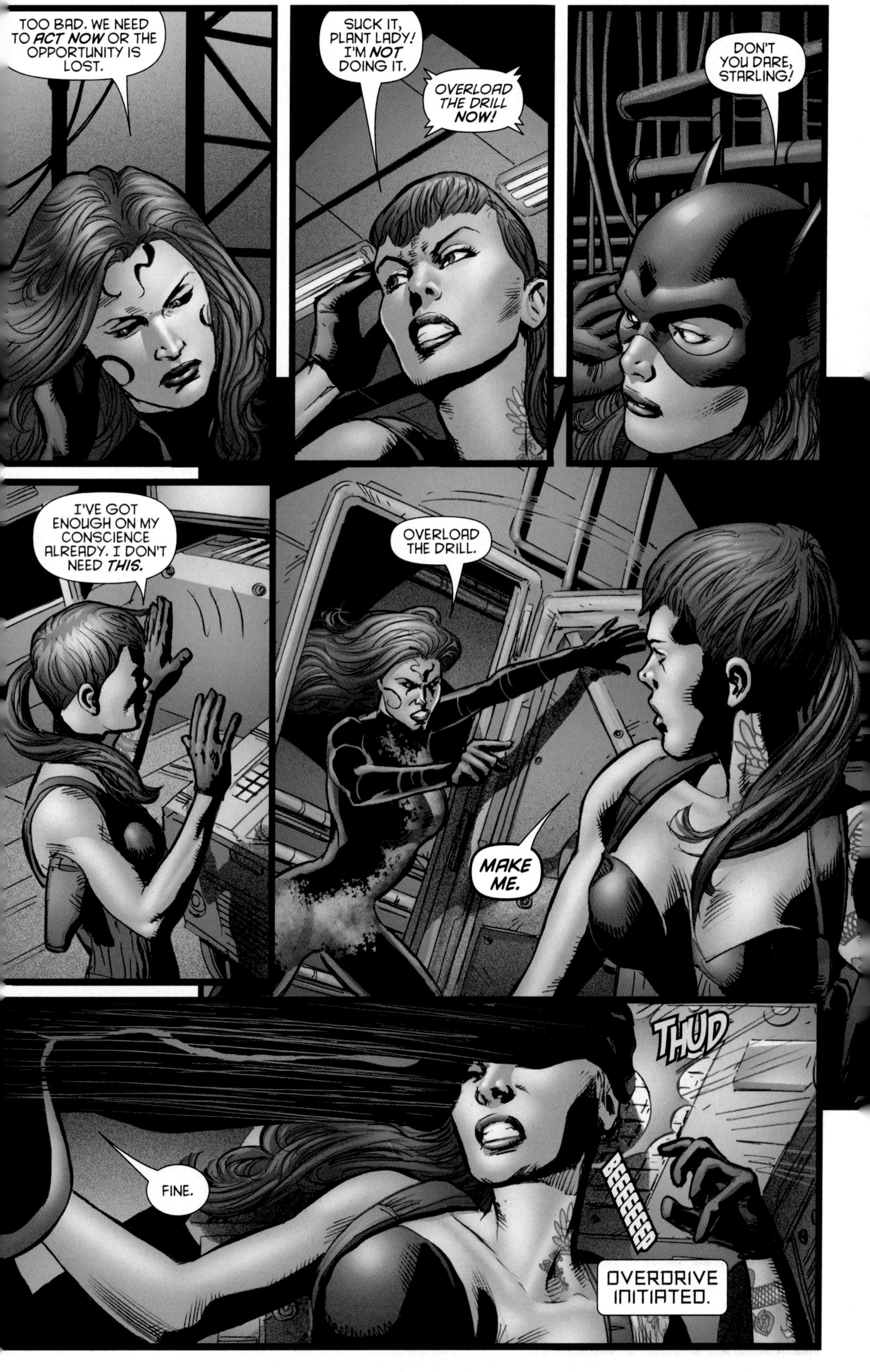

TOO BAD. WE NEED TO ACT NOW OR THE OPPORTUNITY IS LOST.
SUCK IT, PLANT LADY! I'M NOT DOING IT.
OVERLOAD THE DRILL NOW!
DON'T YOU DARE, STARLING!
I'VE GOT ENOUGH ON MY CONSCIENCE ALREADY. I DON'T NEED THIS.
OVERLOAD THE DRILL.
MAKE ME.
THUD
FINE.
BEEEEEEP
OVERDRIVE INITIATED.

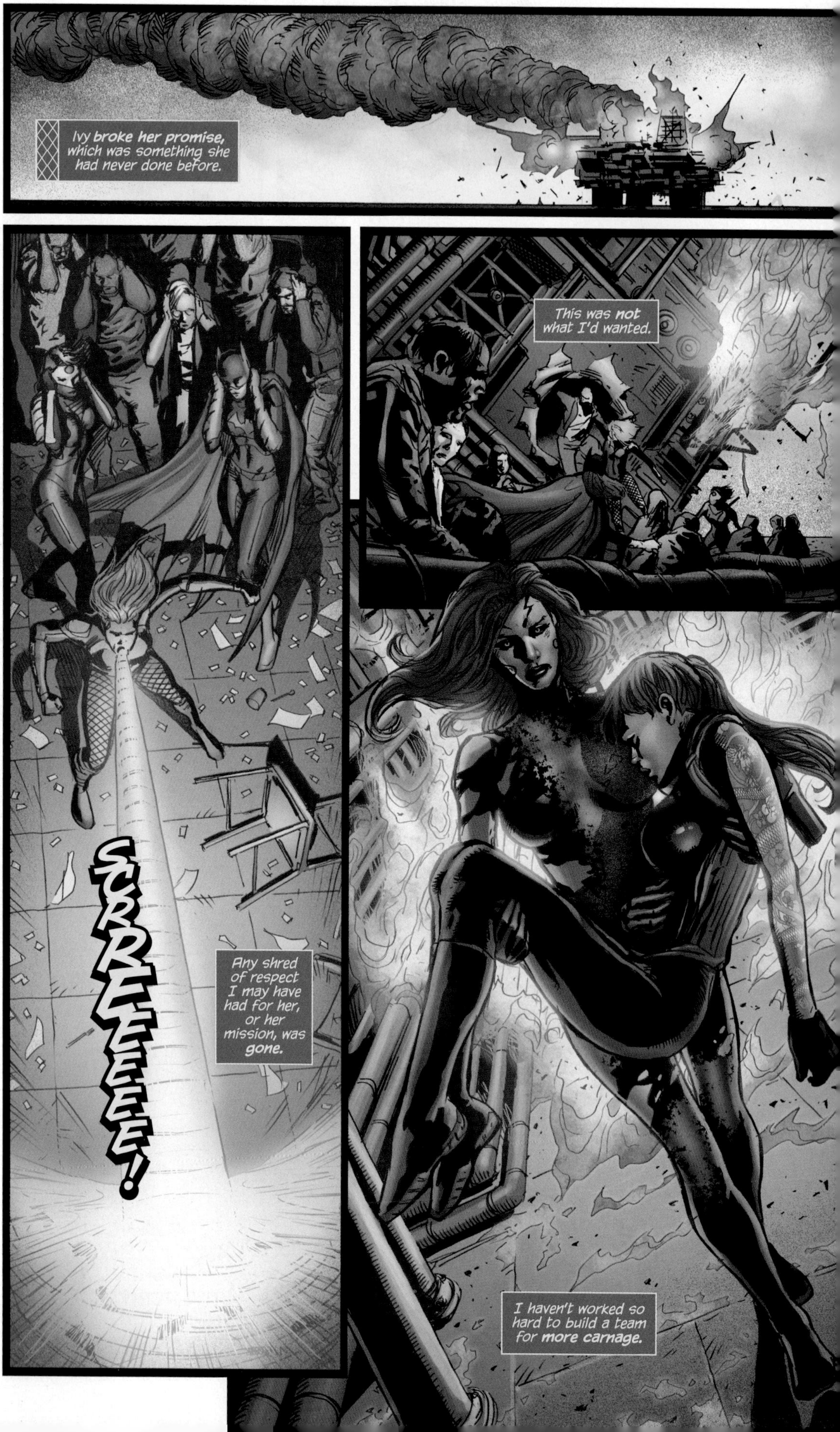
Ivy broke her promise, which was something she had never done before.
This was not what I'd wanted.
SCRREEEEE!
Any shred of respect I may have had for her, or her mission, was gone.
I haven't worked so hard to build a team for more carnage.

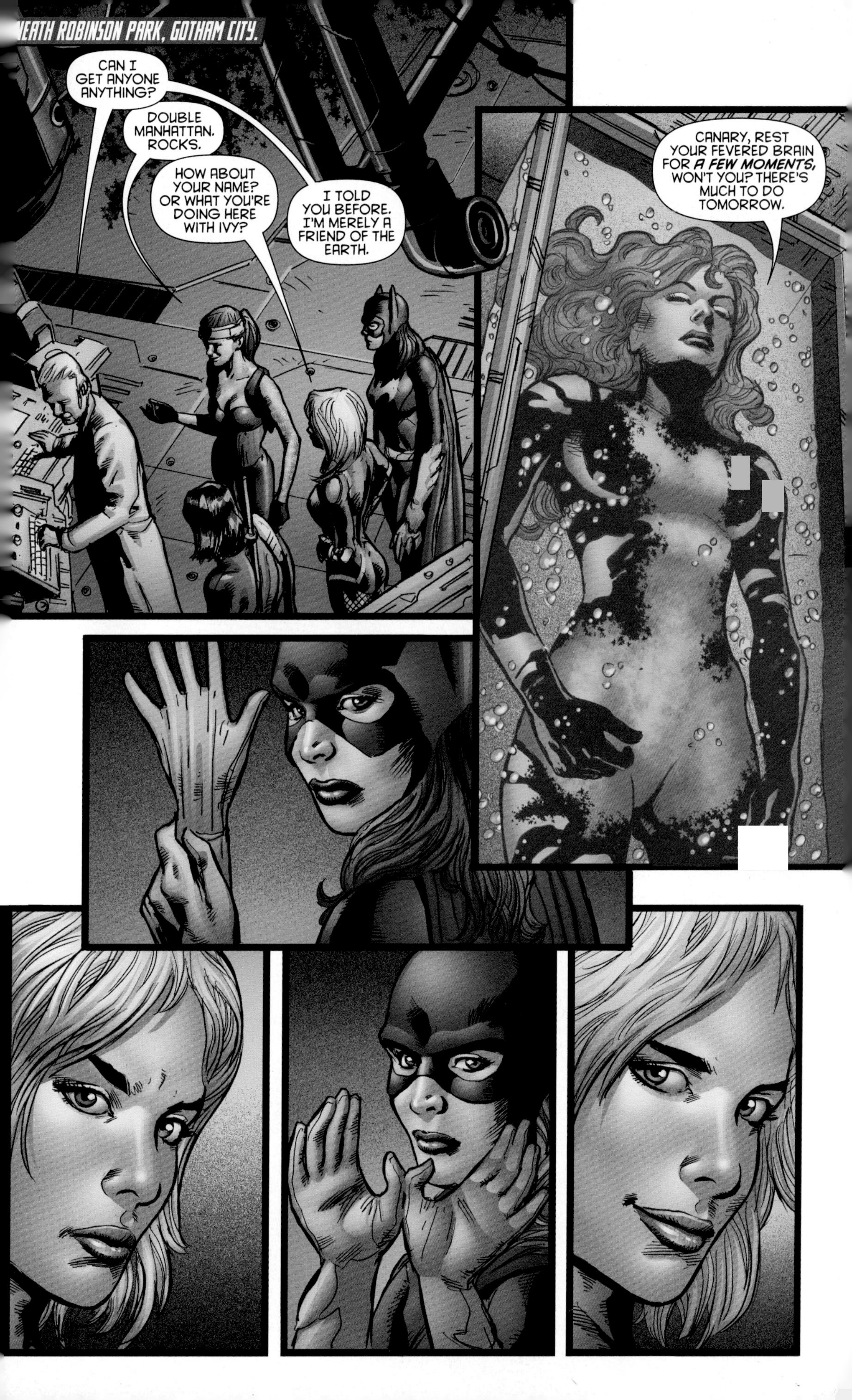
NEATH ROBINSON PARK, GOTHAM CITY.
CAN I GET ANYONE ANYTHING?
DOUBLE MANHATTAN. ROCKS.
HOW ABOUT YOUR NAME? OR WHAT YOU'RE DOING HERE WITH IVY?
I TOLD YOU BEFORE. I'M MERELY A FRIEND OF THE EARTH.
CANARY, REST YOUR FEVERED BRAIN FOR A FEW MOMENTS, WON'T YOU? THERE'S MUCH TO DO TOMORROW.

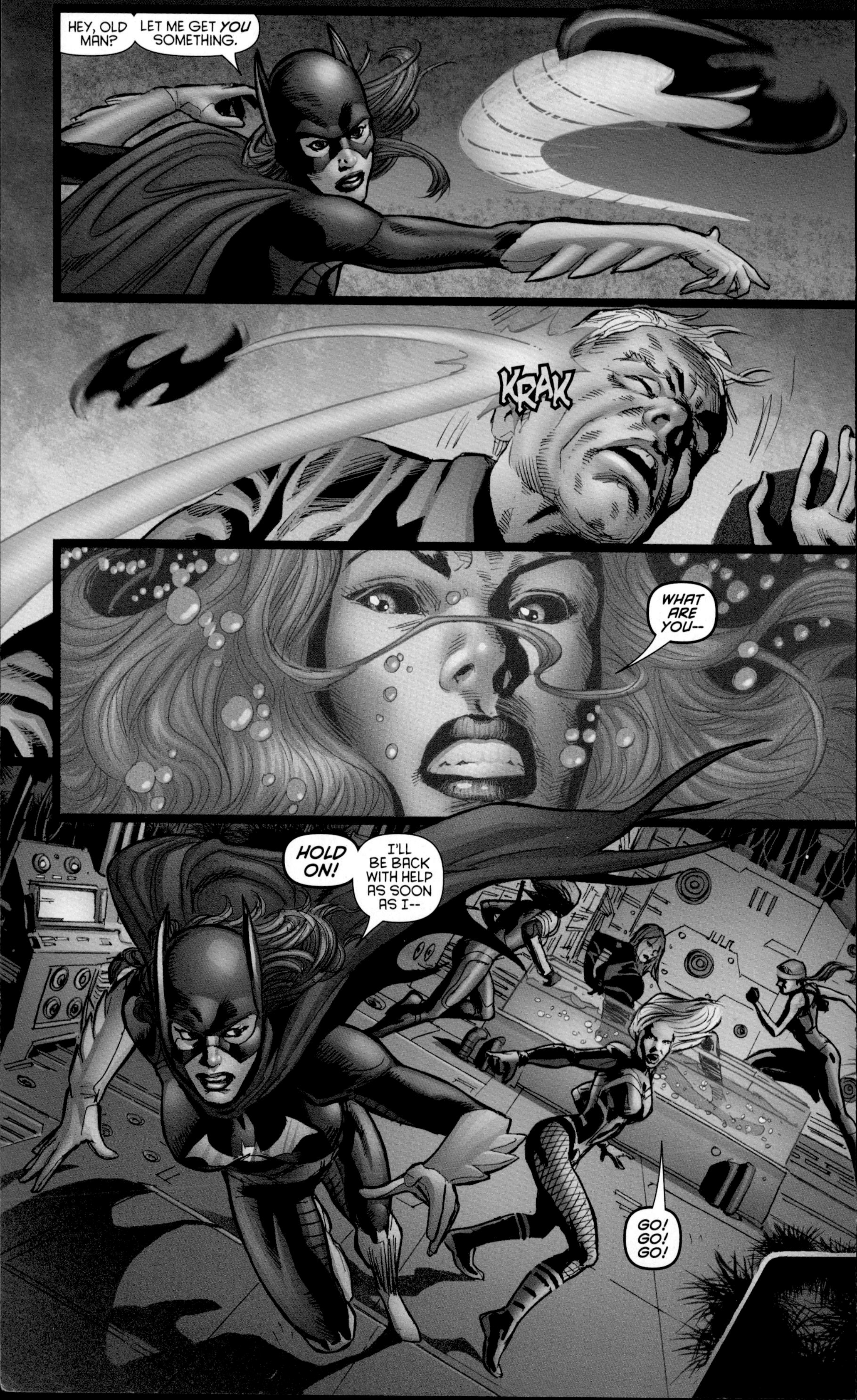
HEY, OLD MAN?
LET ME GET YOU SOMETHING.
KRAK
WHAT ARE YOU--
HOLD ON!
I'LL BE BACK WITH HELP AS SOON AS I--
GO! GO! GO!

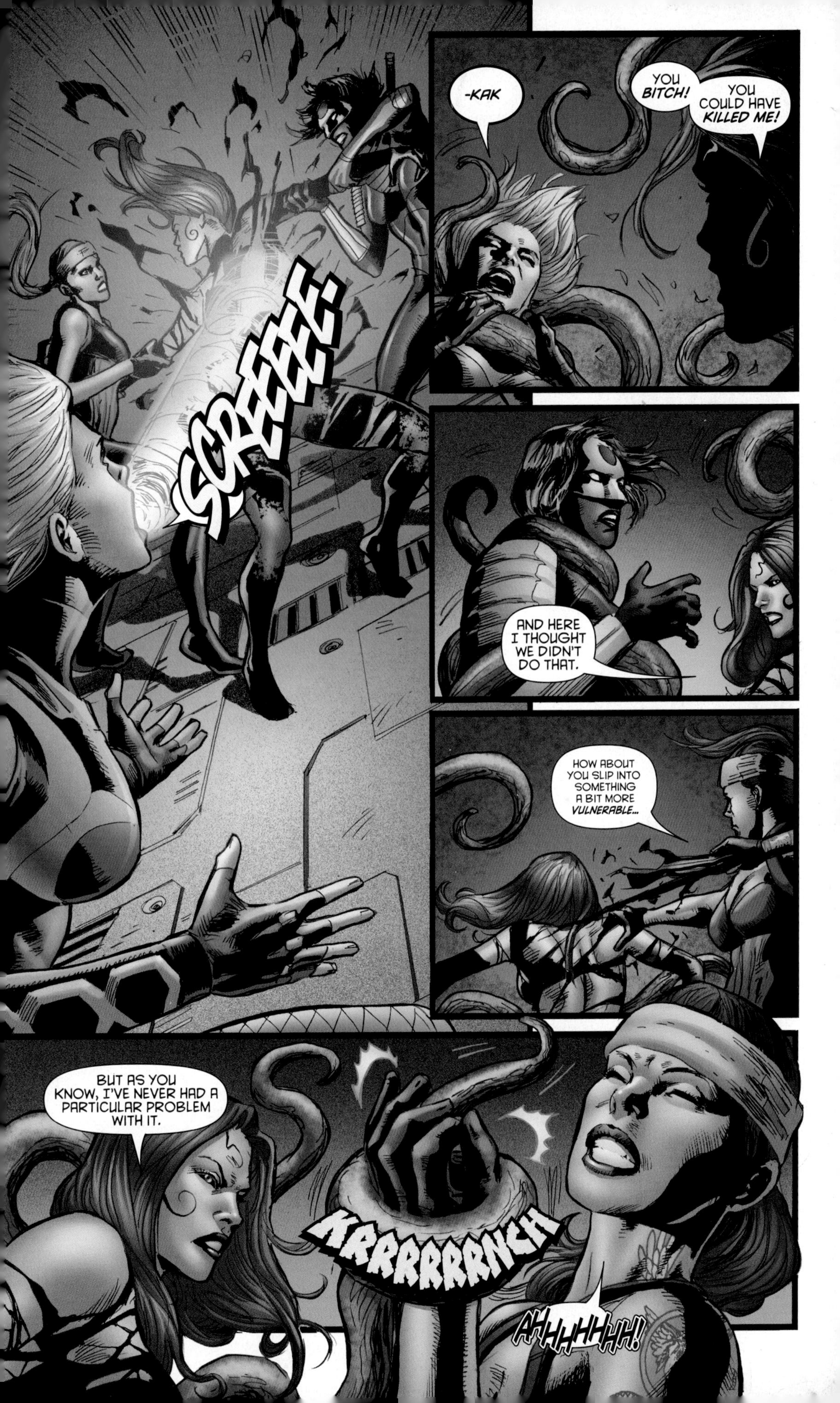
SCREEEEE!
-KAK
YOU BITCH!
YOU COULD HAVE KILLED ME!
AND HERE I THOUGHT WE DIDN'T DO THAT.
HOW ABOUT YOU SLIP INTO SOMETHING A BIT MORE VULNERABLE...
BUT AS YOU KNOW, I'VE NEVER HAD A PARTICULAR PROBLEM WITH IT.
KRRRRRRRNCH
AHHHHHH!

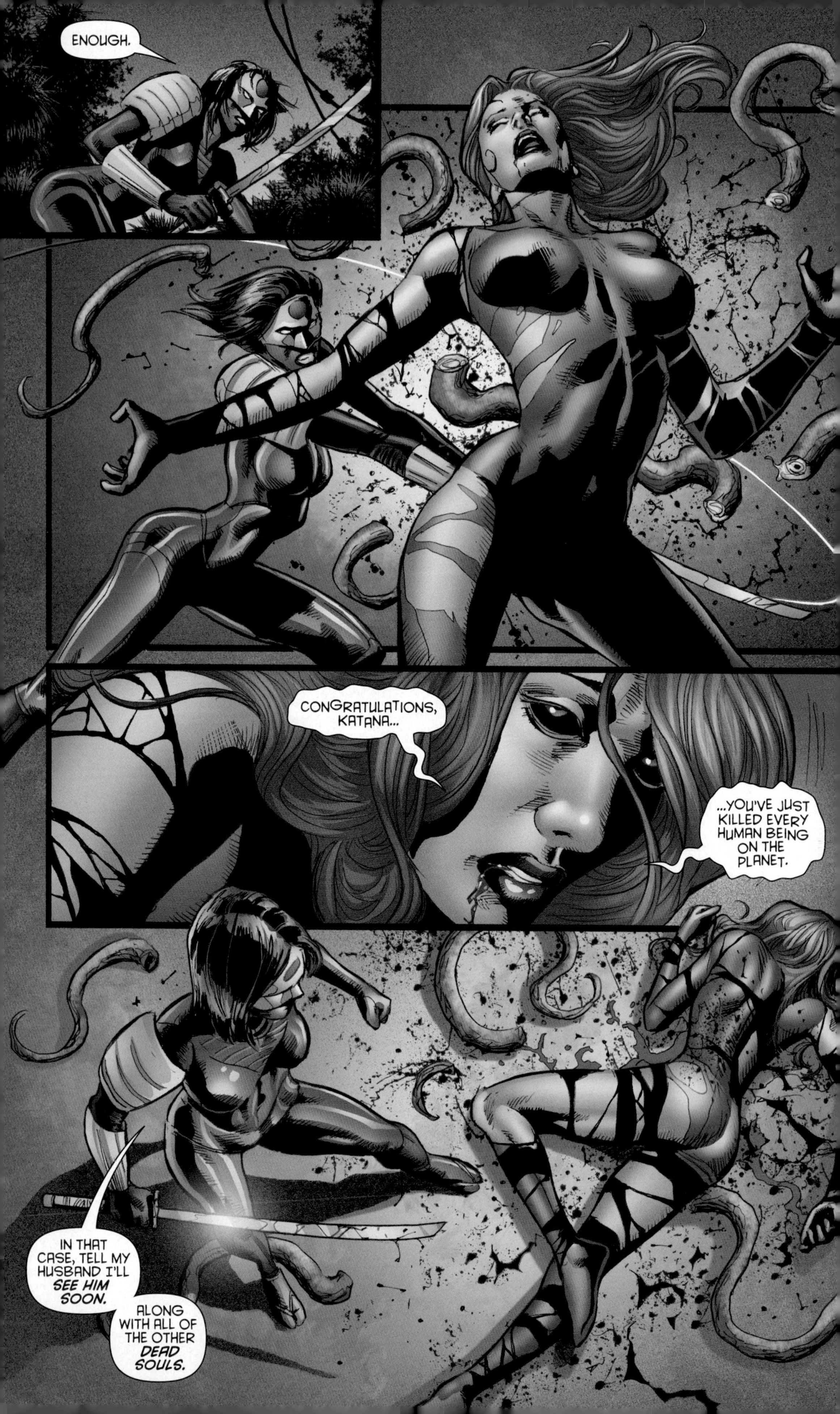
ENOUGH.
CONGRATULATIONS, KATANA...
...YOU'VE JUST KILLED EVERY HUMAN BEING ON THE PLANET.
IN THAT CASE, TELL MY HUSBAND I'LL *SEE HIM SOON.*
ALONG WITH ALL OF THE OTHER *DEAD SOULS.*

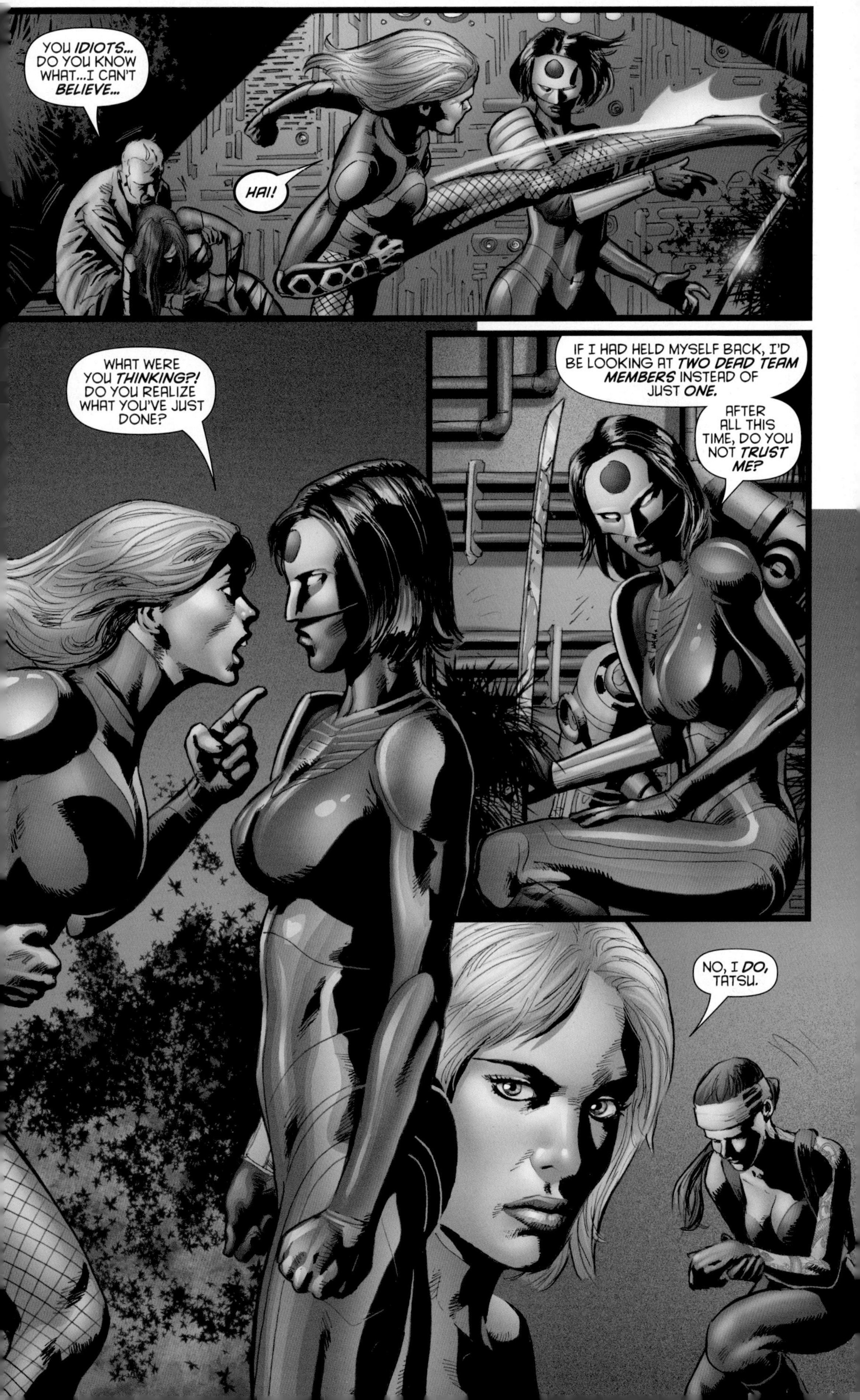
YOU *IDIOTS*... DO YOU KNOW WHAT...I CAN'T *BELIEVE*...
HAI!
WHAT WERE YOU *THINKING?!* DO YOU REALIZE WHAT YOU'VE JUST DONE?
IF I HAD HELD MYSELF BACK, I'D BE LOOKING AT *TWO DEAD TEAM MEMBERS* INSTEAD OF JUST *ONE.*
AFTER ALL THIS TIME, DO YOU NOT *TRUST ME?*
NO, I *DO*, TATSU.

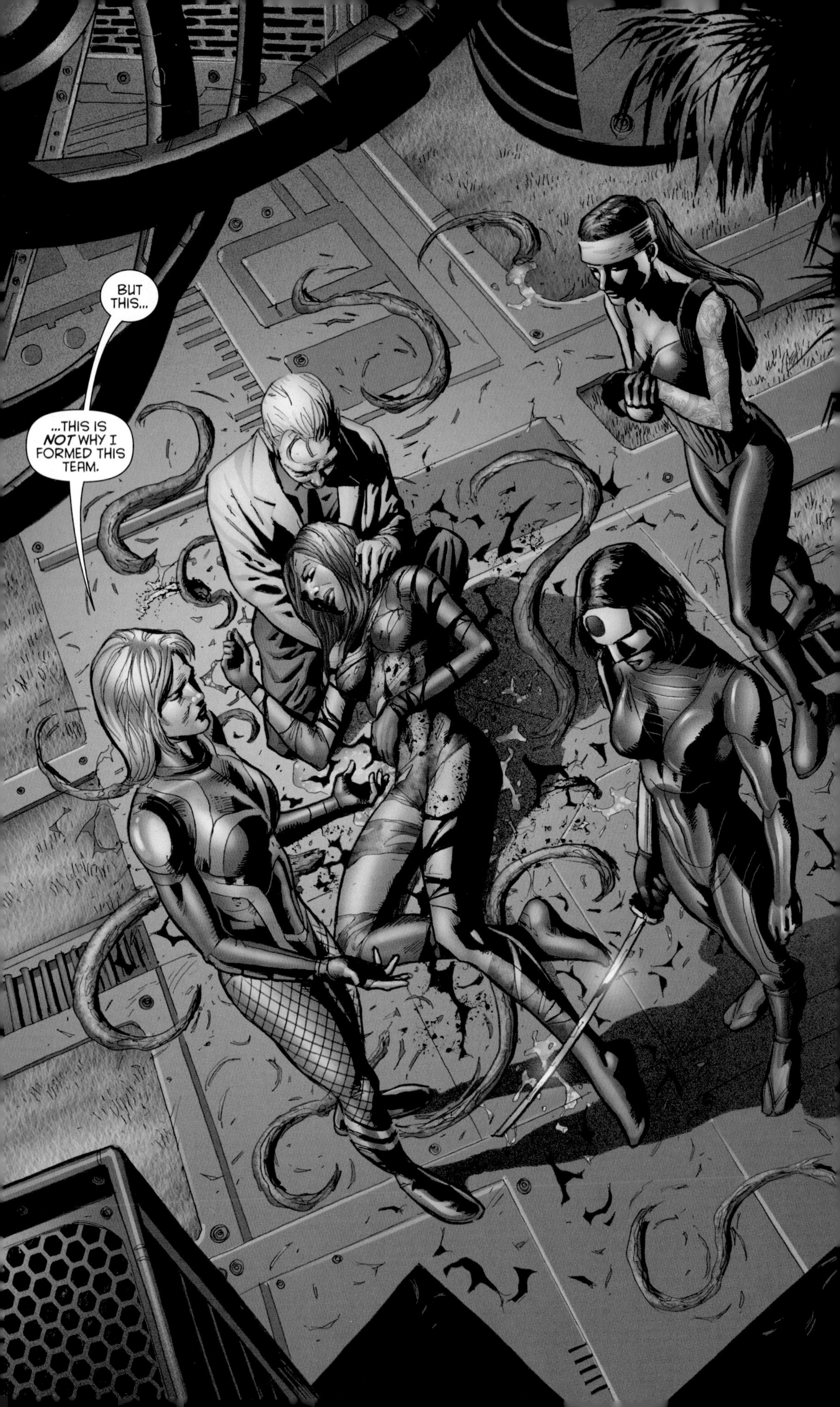
BUT THIS...
...THIS IS NOT WHY I FORMED THIS TEAM.

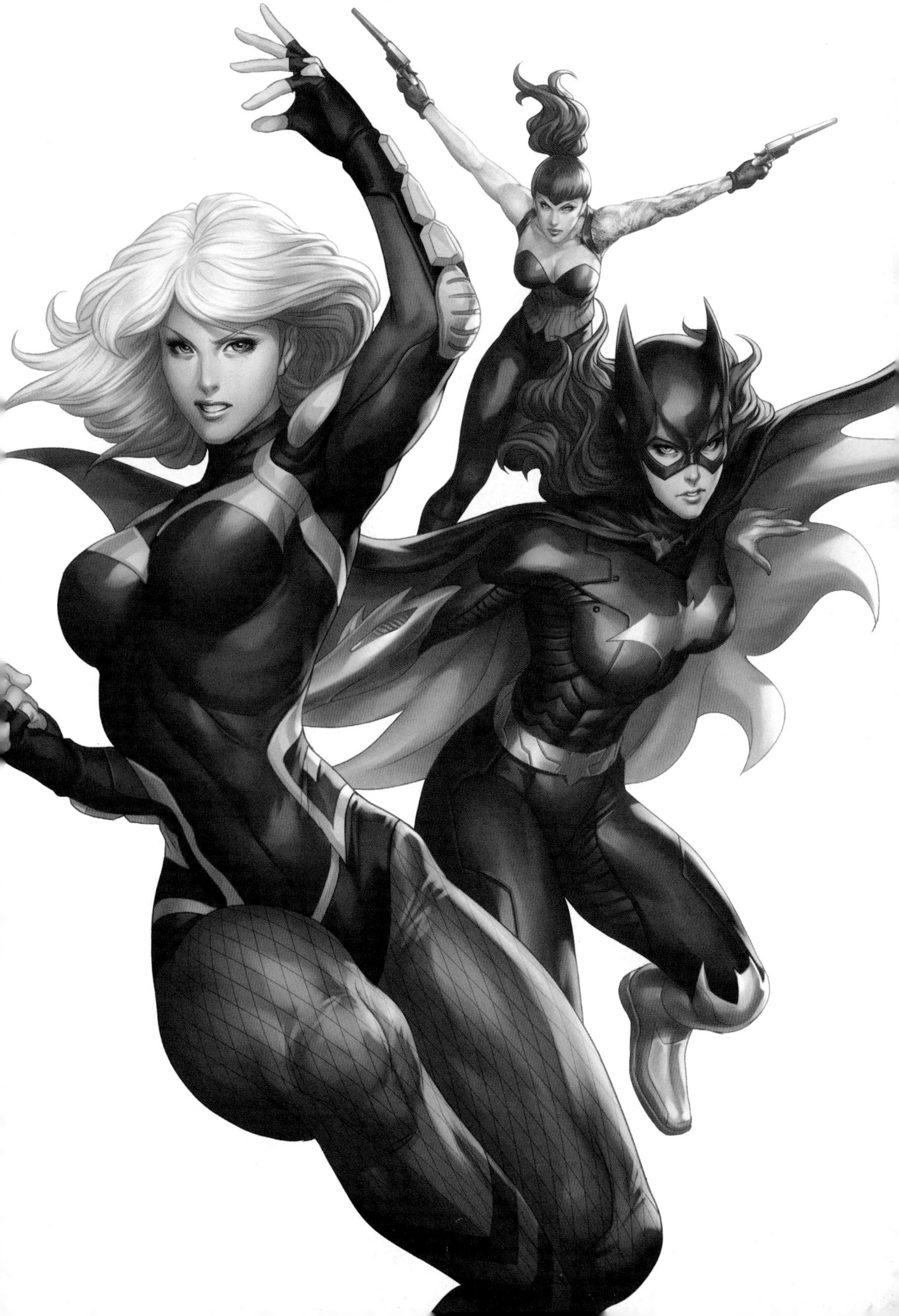

FIRST FLIGHT

DUANE SWIERCZYNSKI writer **ROMANO MOLENAAR** penciller **VICENTE CIFUENTES** inker cover art by **STANLEY "ARTGERM" LAU**

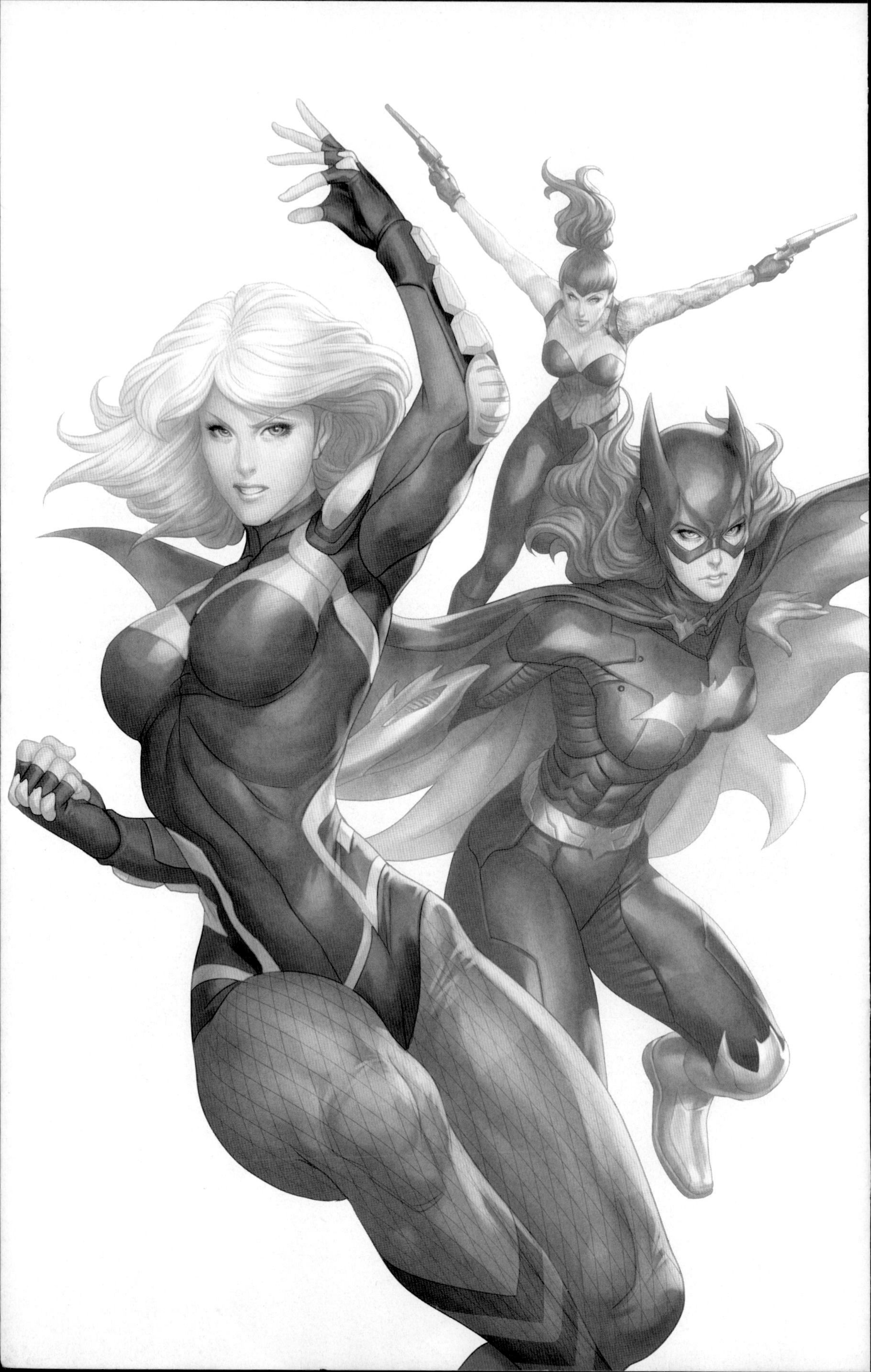

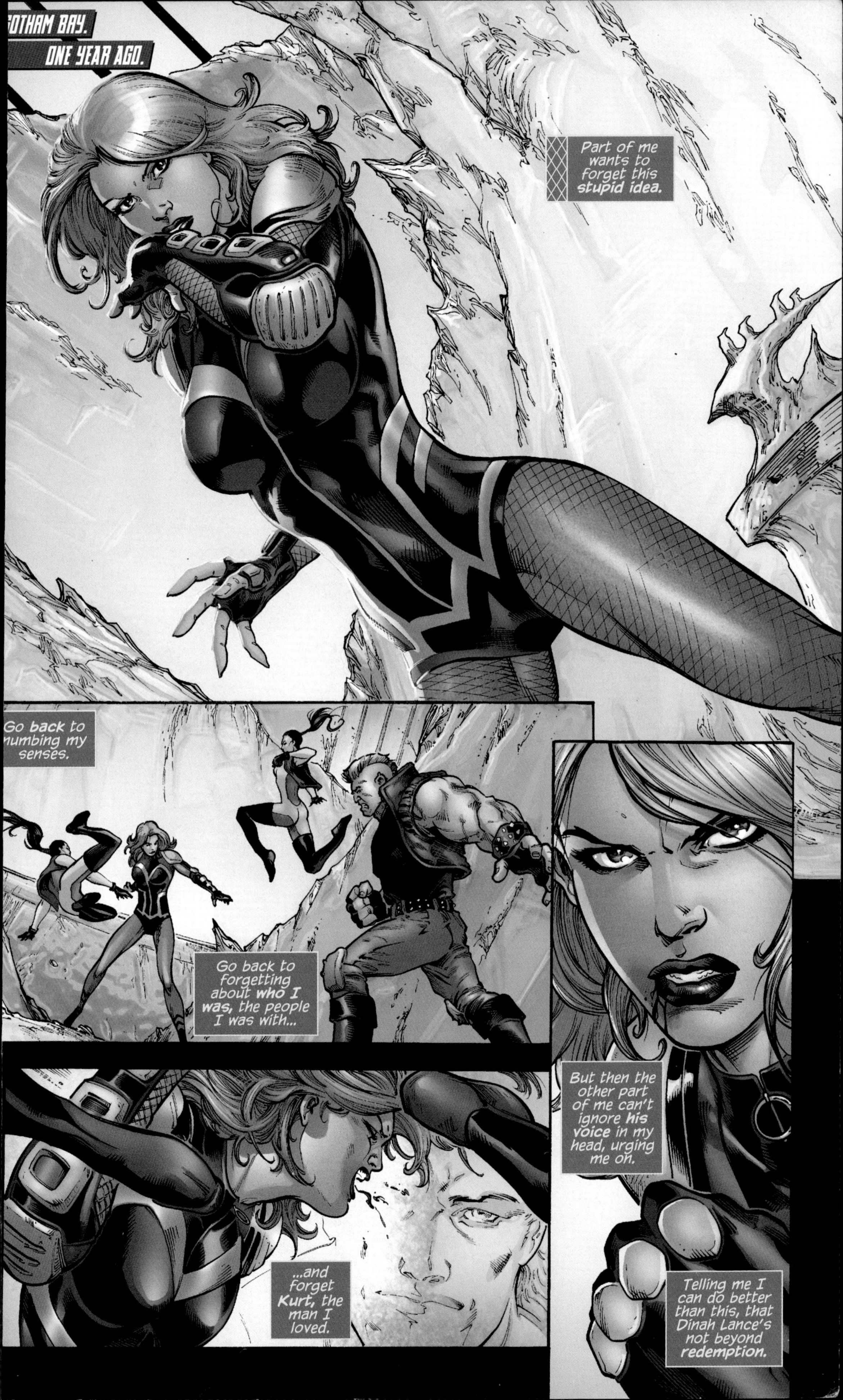
GOTHAM BAY.
ONE YEAR AGO.
Part of me wants to forget this stupid idea.
Go back to numbing my senses.
Go back to forgetting about who I was, the people I was with...
...and forget Kurt, the man I loved.
But then the other part of me can't ignore his voice in my head, urging me on.
Telling me I can do better than this, that Dinah Lance's not beyond redemption.

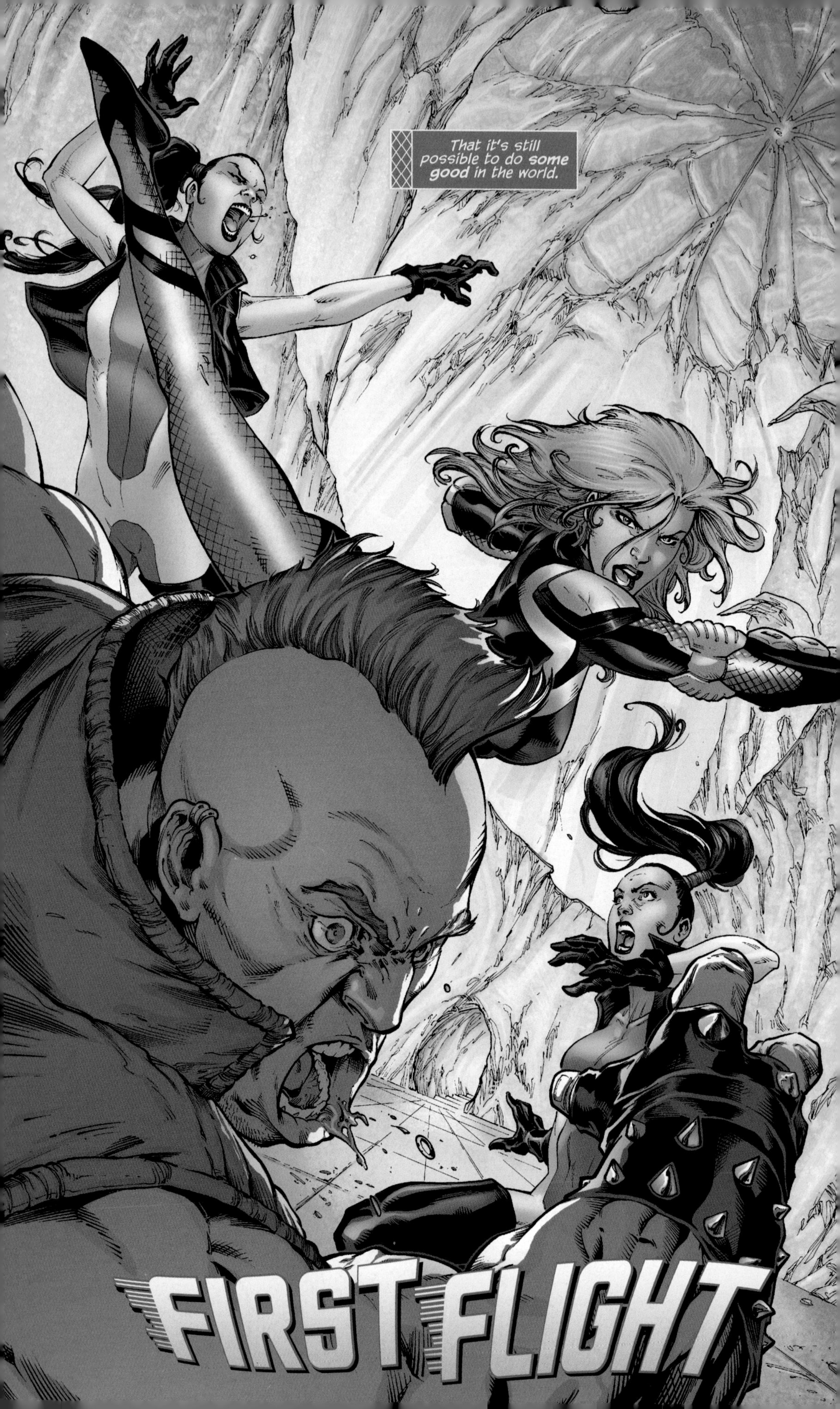

That it's still possible to do some good in the world.
FIRST FLIGHT

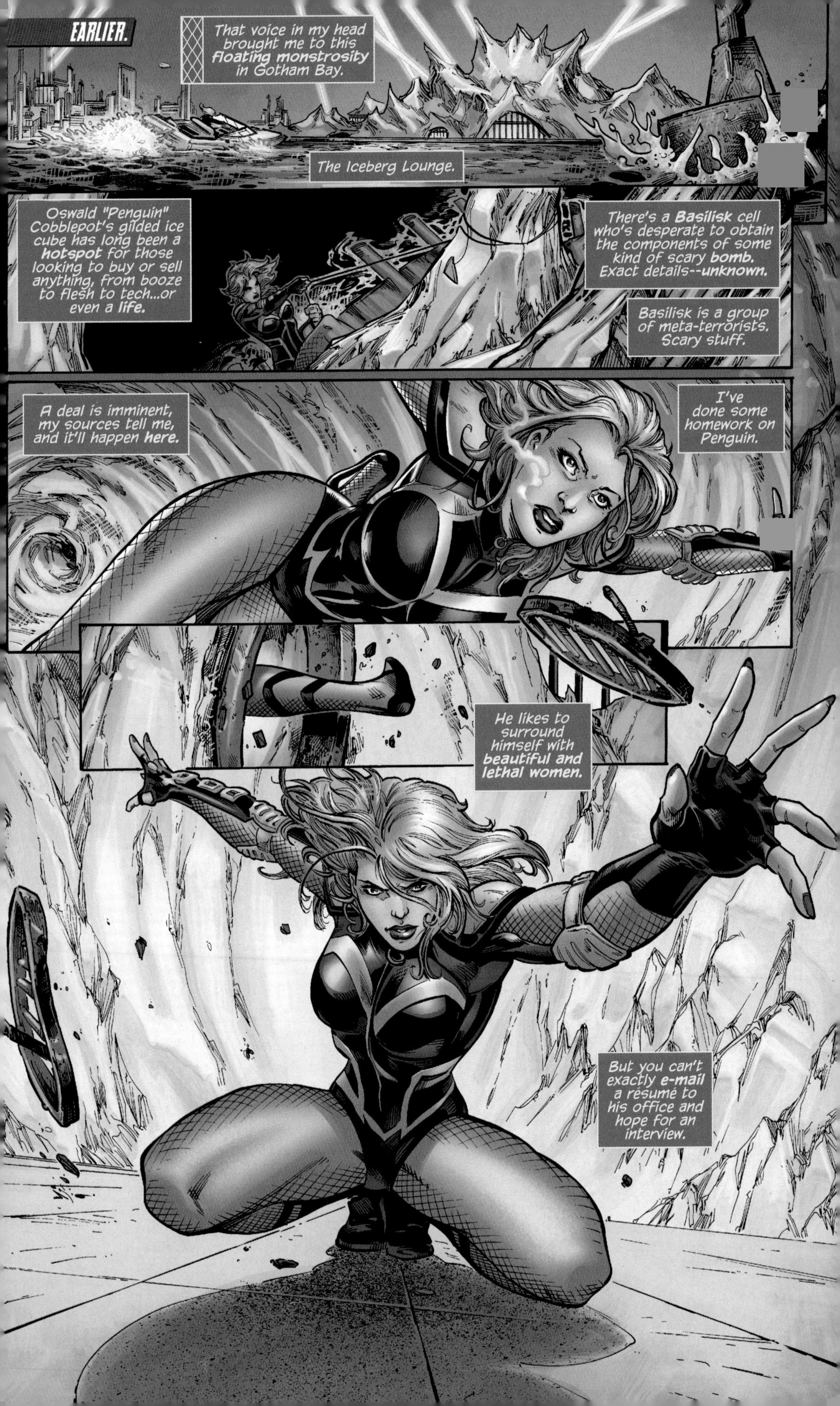
EARLIER.
That voice in my head brought me to this floating monstrosity in Gotham Bay.
The Iceberg Lounge.
Oswald "Penguin" Cobblepot's gilded ice cube has long been a hotspot for those looking to buy or sell anything, from booze to flesh to tech...or even a life.
There's a Basilisk cell who's desperate to obtain the components of some kind of scary bomb. Exact details--unknown.
Basilisk is a group of meta-terrorists. Scary stuff.
A deal is imminent, my sources tell me, and it'll happen here.
I've done some homework on Penguin.
He likes to surround himself with beautiful and lethal women.
But you can't exactly e-mail a résumé to his office and hope for an interview.

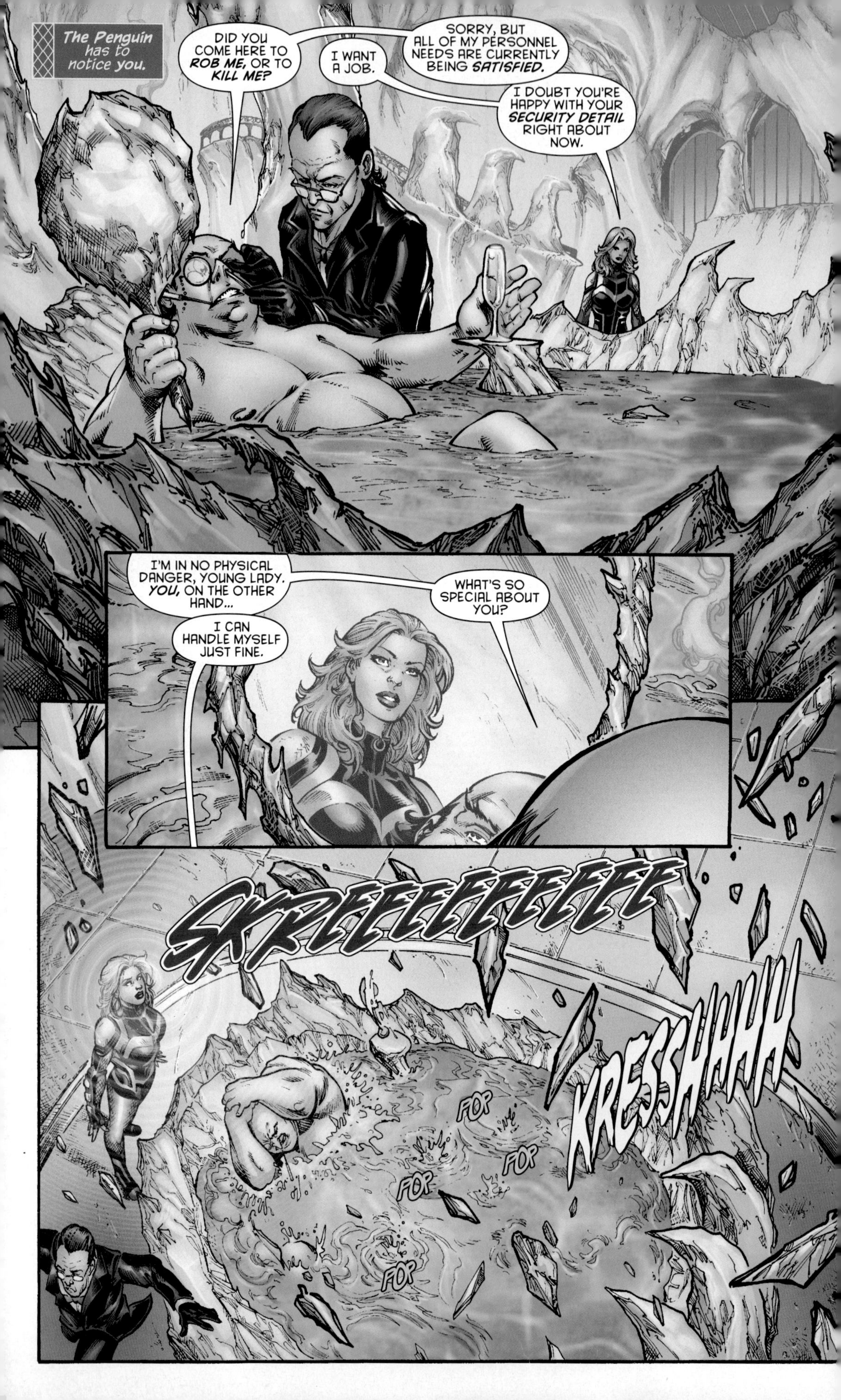

The Penguin has to notice you.
DID YOU COME HERE TO ROB ME, OR TO KILL ME?
I WANT A JOB.
SORRY, BUT ALL OF MY PERSONNEL NEEDS ARE CURRENTLY BEING SATISFIED.
I DOUBT YOU'RE HAPPY WITH YOUR SECURITY DETAIL RIGHT ABOUT NOW.
I'M IN NO PHYSICAL DANGER, YOUNG LADY. YOU, ON THE OTHER HAND...
I CAN HANDLE MYSELF JUST FINE.
WHAT'S SO SPECIAL ABOUT YOU?
SKREEEEEEEEEEE
KRESSHHHH
FOP
FOP
FOP
FOP

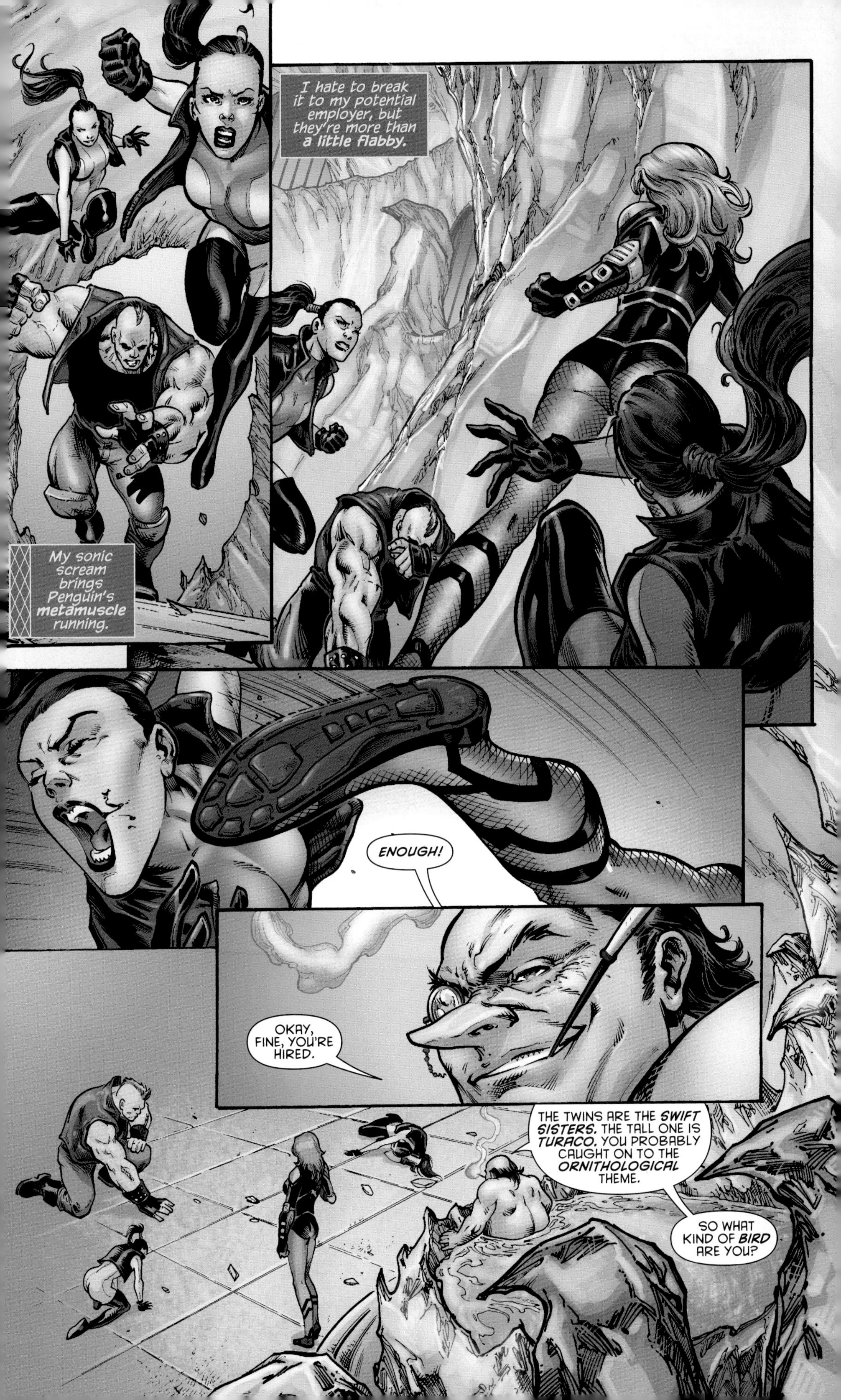
My sonic scream brings Penguin's metamuscle running.
I hate to break it to my potential employer, but they're more than a little flabby.
ENOUGH!
OKAY, FINE, YOU'RE HIRED.
THE TWINS ARE THE SWIFT SISTERS. THE TALL ONE IS TURACO. YOU PROBABLY CAUGHT ON TO THE ORNITHOLOGICAL THEME.
SO WHAT KIND OF BIRD ARE YOU?

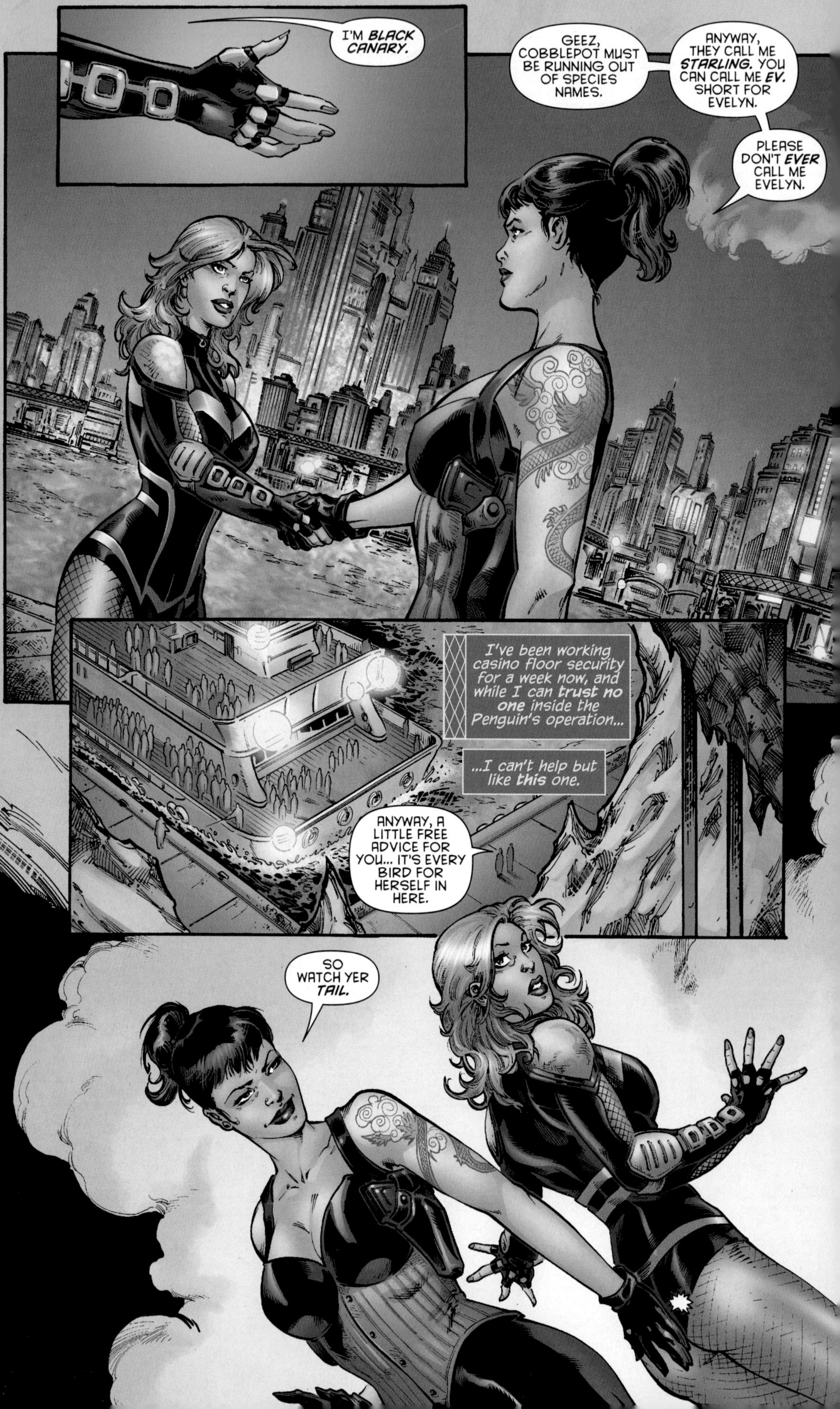
I'M BLACK CANARY.
GEEZ, COBBLEPOT MUST BE RUNNING OUT OF SPECIES NAMES.
ANYWAY, THEY CALL ME STARLING. YOU CAN CALL ME EV. SHORT FOR EVELYN.
PLEASE DON'T EVER CALL ME EVELYN.
I've been working casino floor security for a week now, and while I can trust no one inside the Penguin's operation...
...I can't help but like this one.
ANYWAY, A LITTLE FREE ADVICE FOR YOU... IT'S EVERY BIRD FOR HERSELF IN HERE.
SO WATCH YER TAIL.

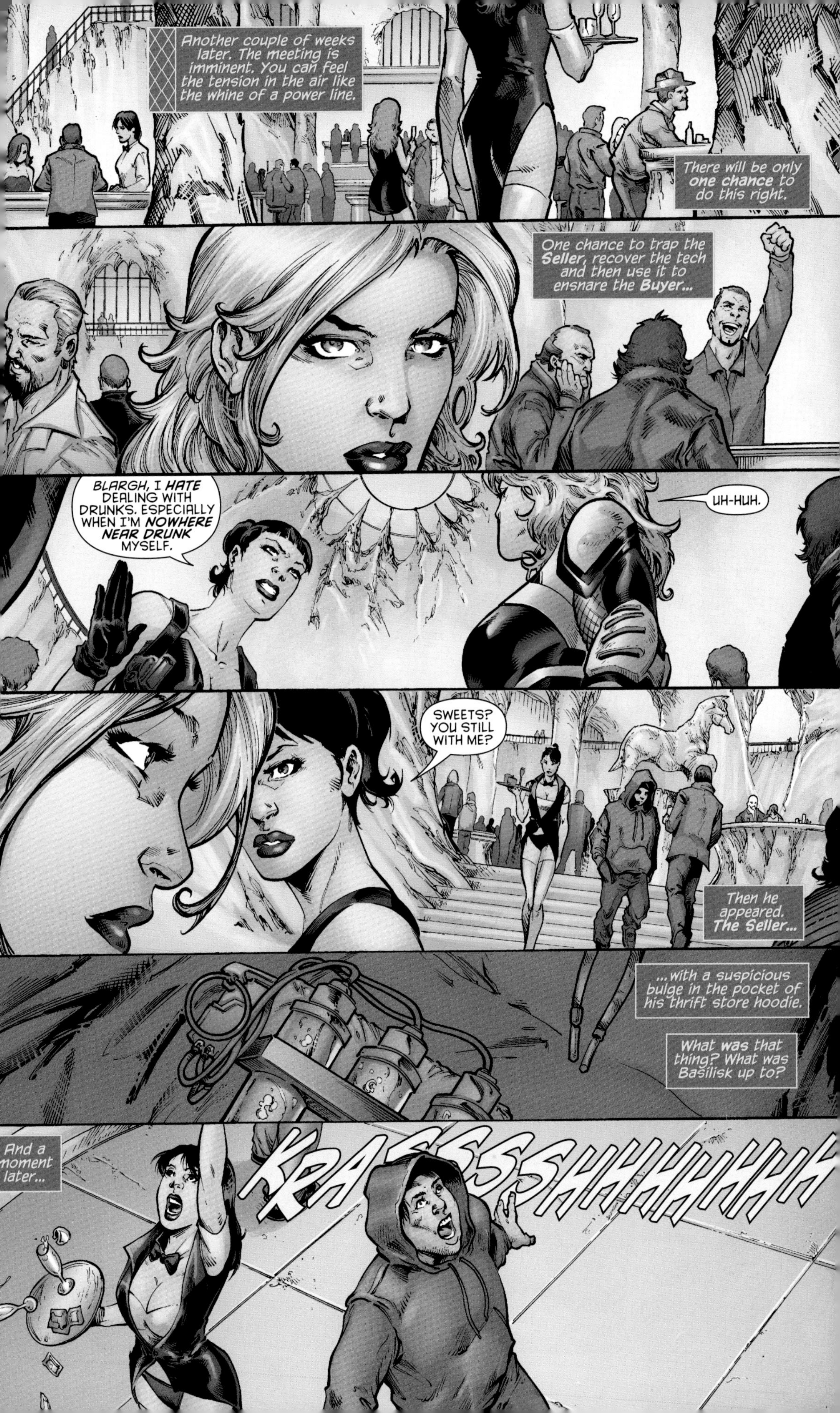

Another couple of weeks later. The meeting is imminent. You can feel the tension in the air like the whine of a power line.
There will be only one chance to do this right.
One chance to trap the Seller, recover the tech and then use it to ensnare the Buyer...
BLARGH, I HATE DEALING WITH DRUNKS. ESPECIALLY WHEN I'M NOWHERE NEAR DRUNK MYSELF.
UH-HUH.
SWEETS? YOU STILL WITH ME?
Then he appeared. The Seller...
...with a suspicious bulge in the pocket of his thrift store hoodie.
What was that thing? What was Basilisk up to?
And a moment later...
KRASSSSHHHHHHHK

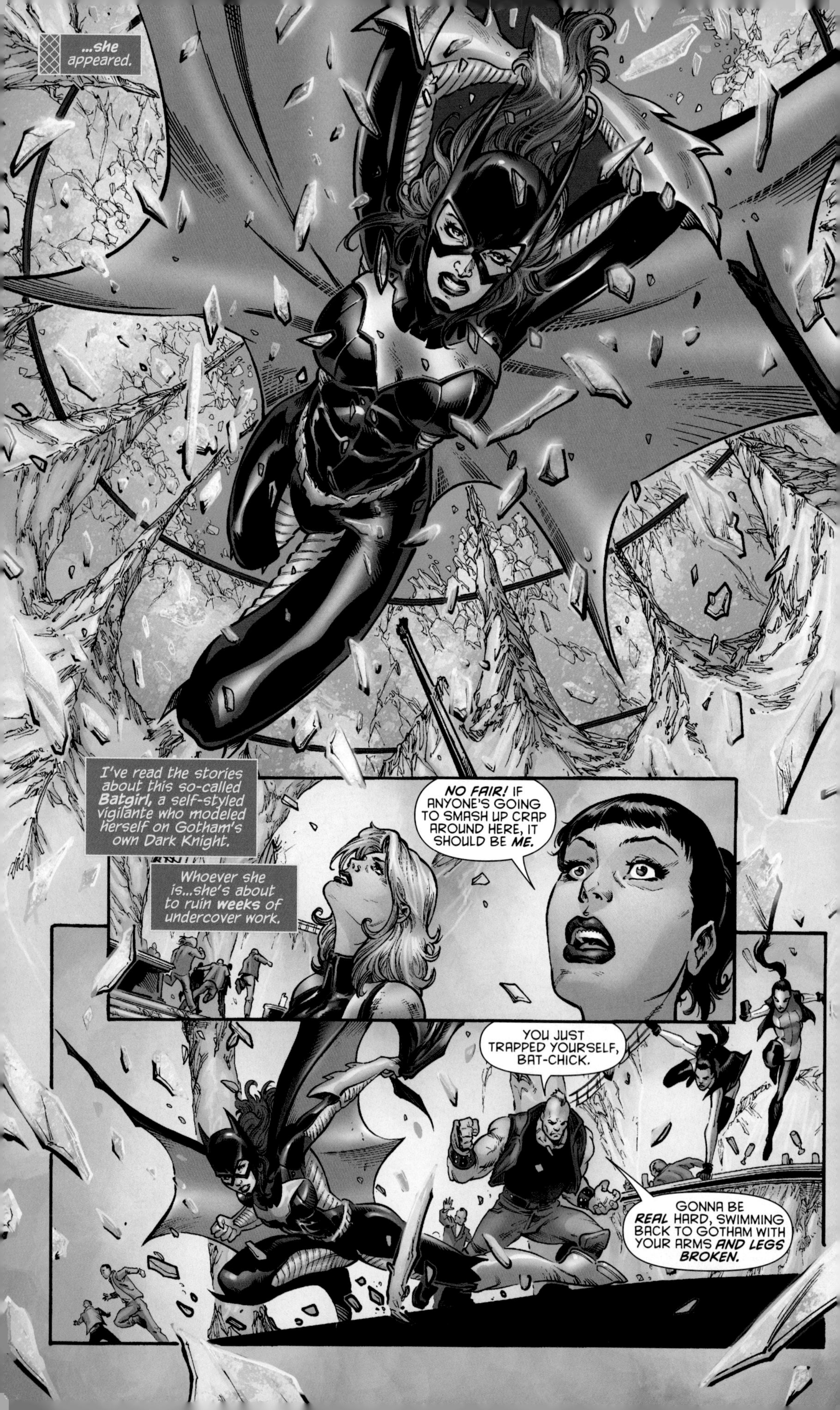

...she appeared.
I've read the stories about this so-called Batgirl, a self-styled vigilante who modeled herself on Gotham's own Dark Knight.
Whoever she is...she's about to ruin weeks of undercover work.
NO FAIR! IF ANYONE'S GOING TO SMASH UP CRAP AROUND HERE, IT SHOULD BE ME.
YOU JUST TRAPPED YOURSELF, BAT-CHICK.
GONNA BE REAL HARD, SWIMMING BACK TO GOTHAM WITH YOUR ARMS AND LEGS BROKEN.

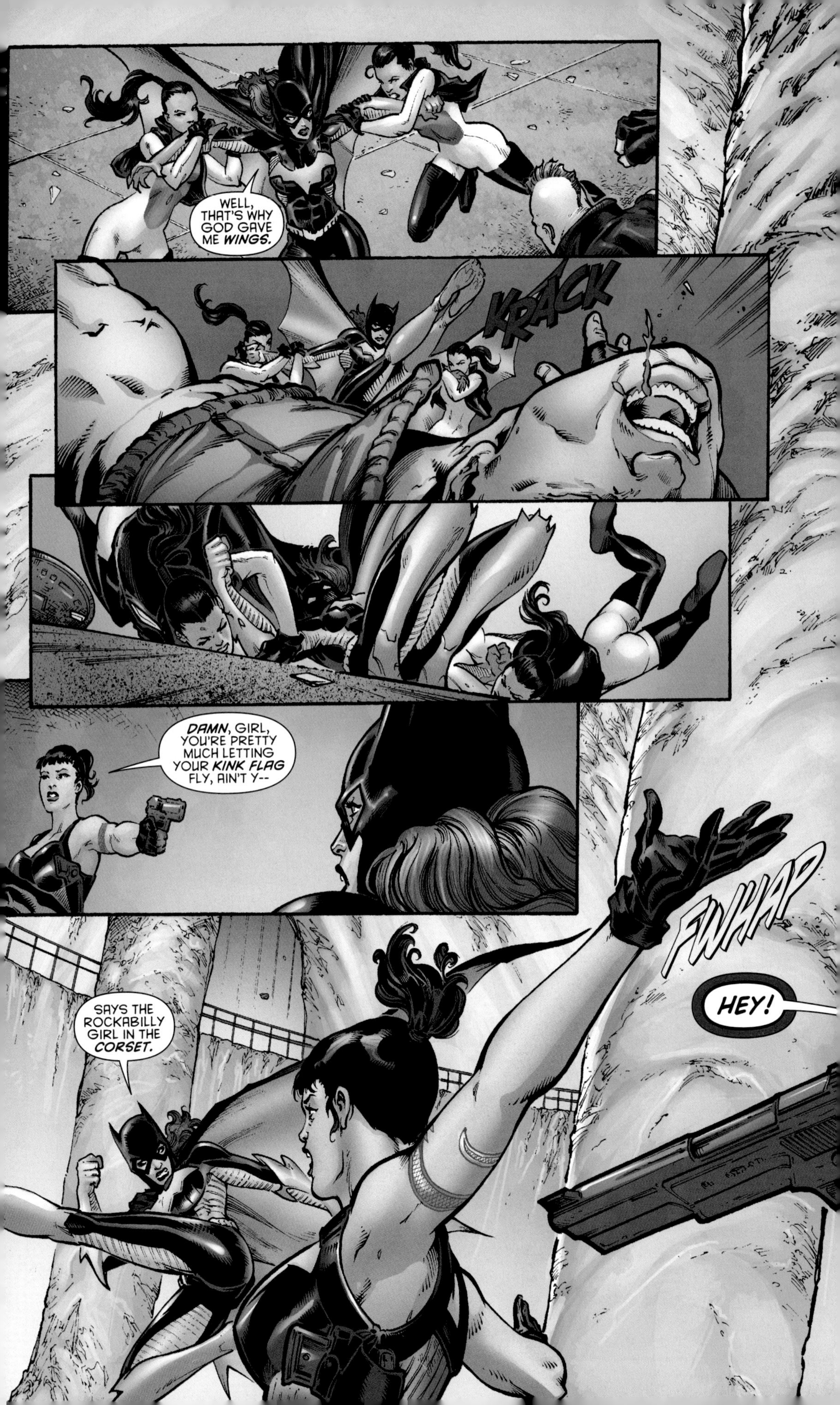
WELL, THAT'S WHY GOD GAVE ME WINGS.
KRACK
DAMN, GIRL, YOU'RE PRETTY MUCH LETTING YOUR KINK FLAG FLY, AIN'T Y--
FWHAP
HEY!
SAYS THE ROCKABILLY GIRL IN THE CORSET.

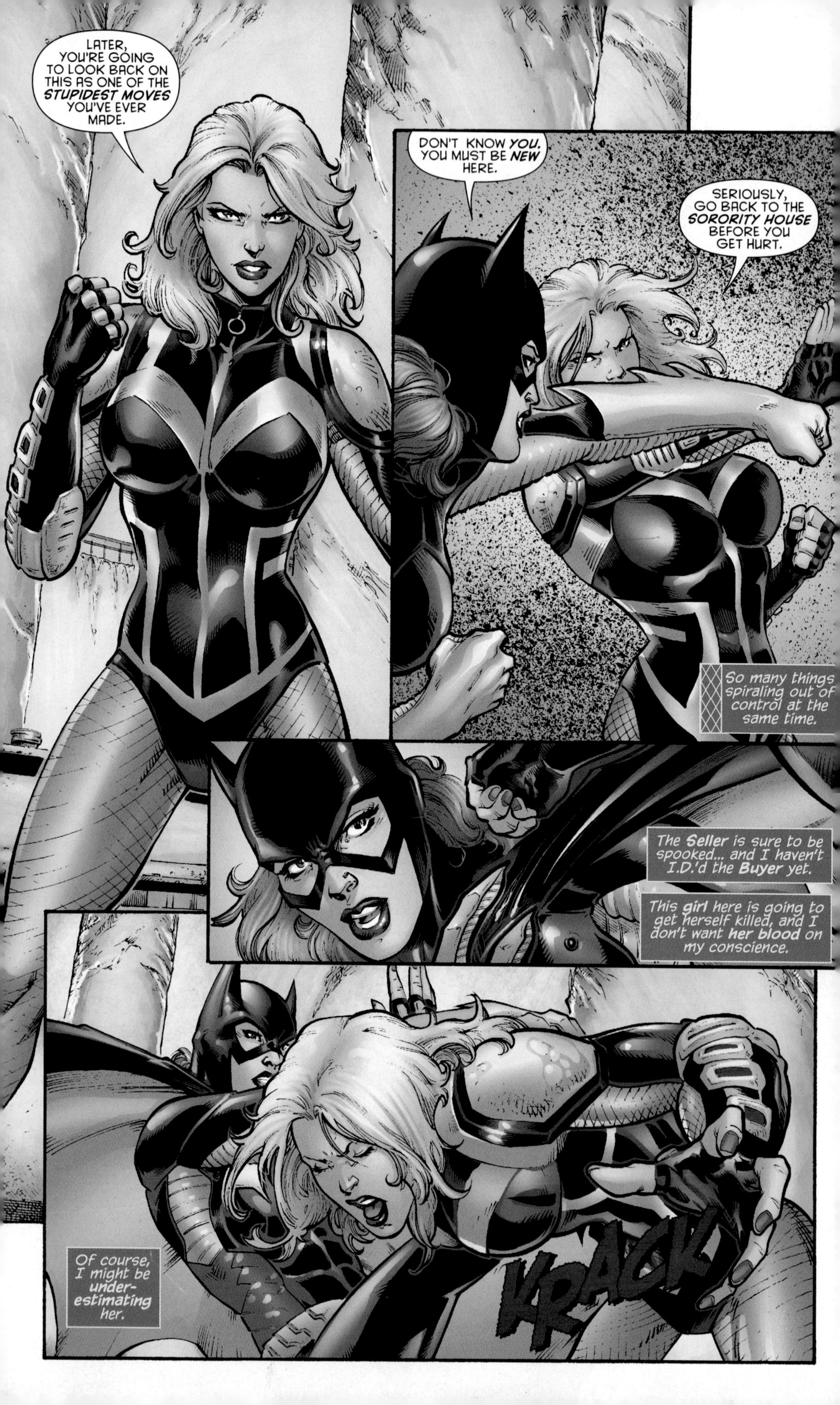
LATER, YOU'RE GOING TO LOOK BACK ON THIS AS ONE OF THE *STUPIDEST MOVES* YOU'VE EVER MADE.
DON'T KNOW *YOU.* YOU MUST BE *NEW* HERE.
SERIOUSLY, GO BACK TO THE *SORORITY HOUSE* BEFORE YOU GET HURT.
So many things spiraling out of control at the same time.
The **Seller** is sure to be spooked... and I haven't I.D.'d the **Buyer** yet.
This **girl** here is going to get herself killed, and I don't want **her blood** on my conscience.
Of course, I might be under-estimating her.
KRACK!

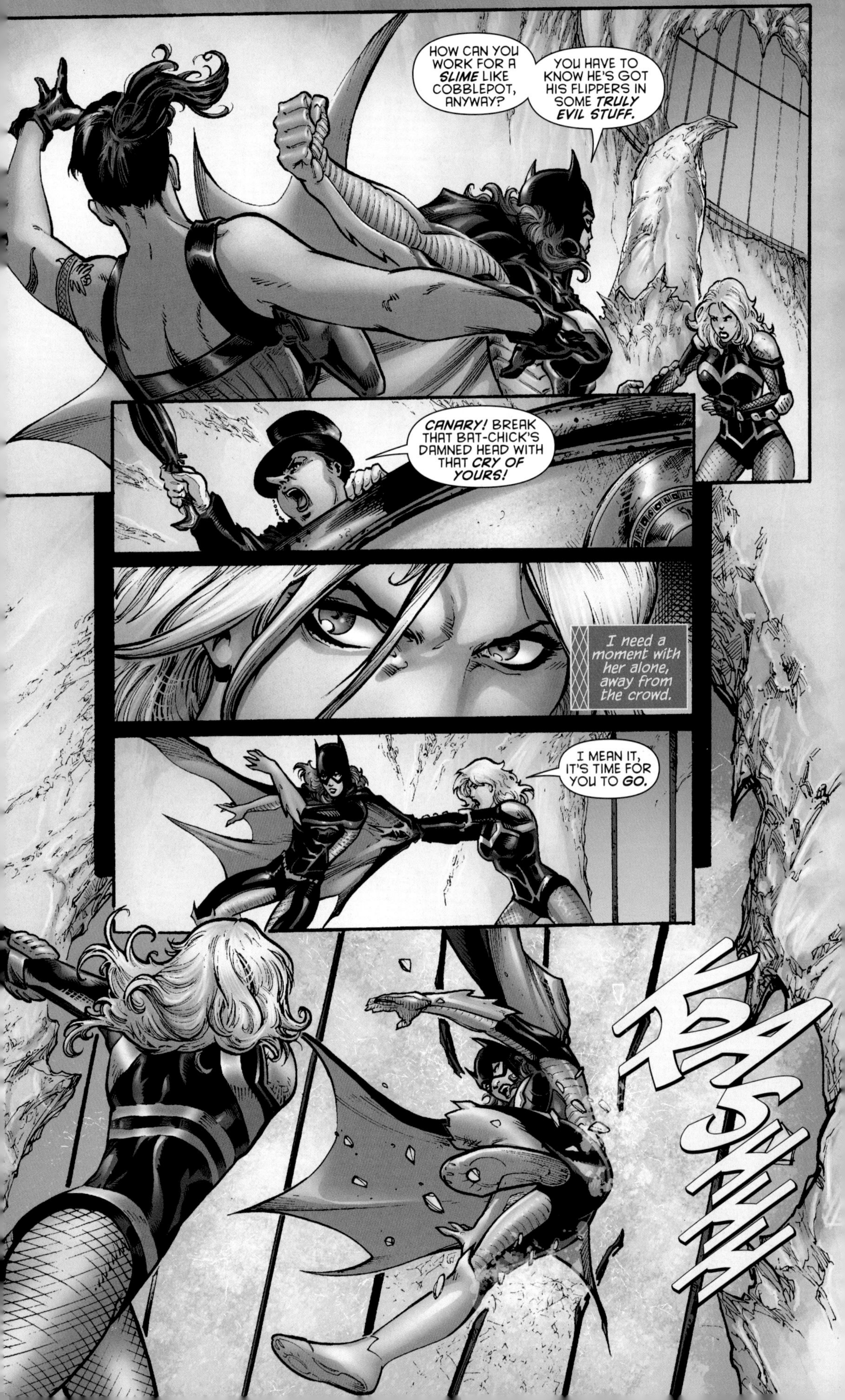

HOW CAN YOU WORK FOR A SLIME LIKE COBBLEPOT, ANYWAY?
YOU HAVE TO KNOW HE'S GOT HIS FLIPPERS IN SOME TRULY EVIL STUFF.
CANARY! BREAK THAT BAT-CHICK'S DAMNED HEAD WITH THAT CRY OF YOURS!
I need a moment with her alone, away from the crowd.
I MEAN IT, IT'S TIME FOR YOU TO GO.
KRASHHH

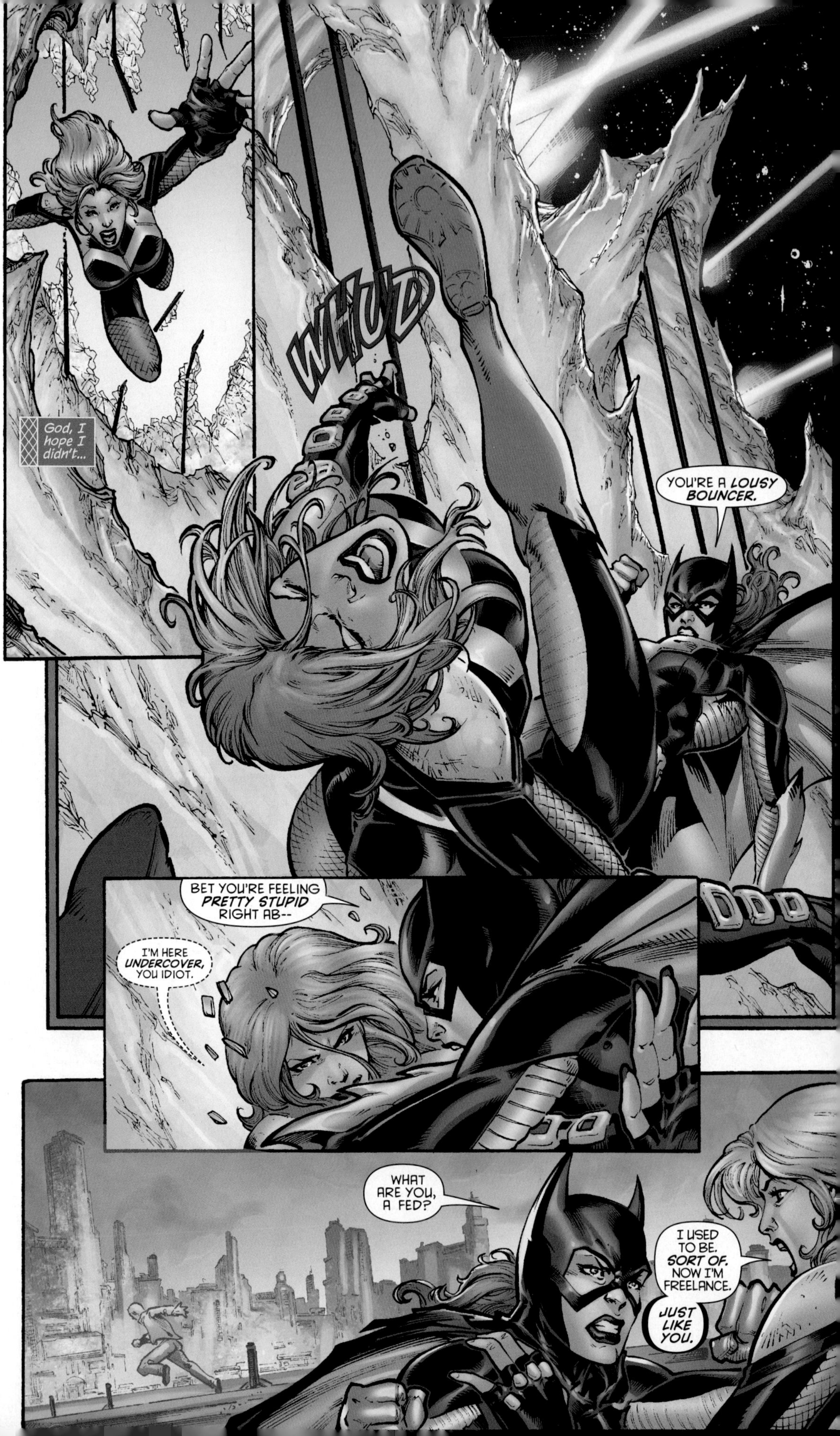
God, I hope I didn't...
WHUD
YOU'RE A LOUSY BOUNCER.
BET YOU'RE FEELING PRETTY STUPID RIGHT AB--
I'M HERE UNDERCOVER, YOU IDIOT.
WHAT ARE YOU, A FED?
I USED TO BE. SORT OF. NOW I'M FREELANCE.
JUST LIKE YOU.

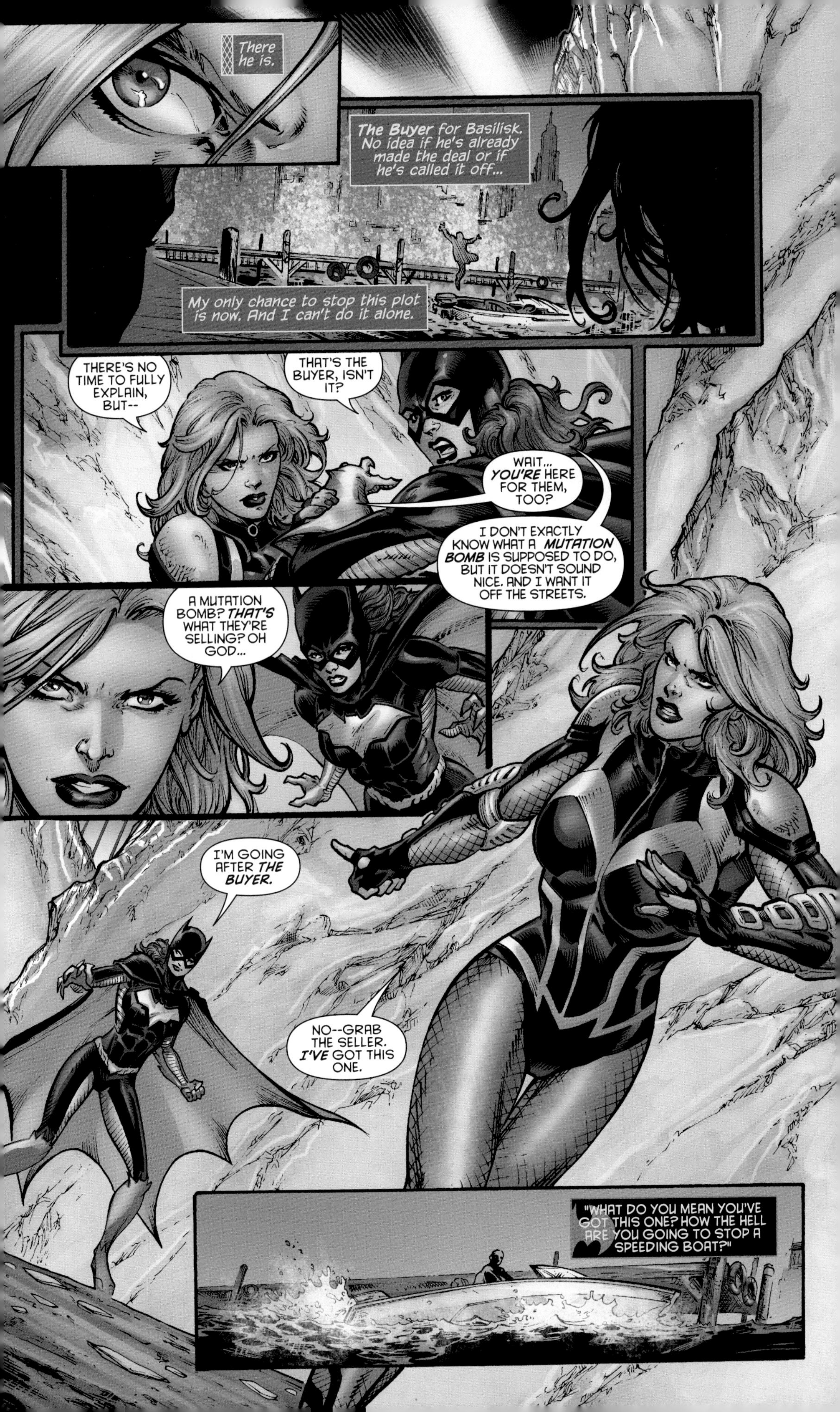

There he is.
The Buyer for Basilisk. No idea if he's already made the deal or if he's called it off...
My only chance to stop this plot is now. And I can't do it alone.
THERE'S NO TIME TO FULLY EXPLAIN, BUT--
THAT'S THE BUYER, ISN'T IT?
WAIT... YOU'RE HERE FOR THEM, TOO?
I DON'T EXACTLY KNOW WHAT A MUTATION BOMB IS SUPPOSED TO DO, BUT IT DOESN'T SOUND NICE. AND I WANT IT OFF THE STREETS.
A MUTATION BOMB? THAT'S WHAT THEY'RE SELLING? OH GOD...
I'M GOING AFTER THE BUYER.
NO--GRAB THE SELLER. I'VE GOT THIS ONE.
"WHAT DO YOU MEAN YOU'VE GOT THIS ONE? HOW THE HELL ARE YOU GOING TO STOP A SPEEDING BOAT?"

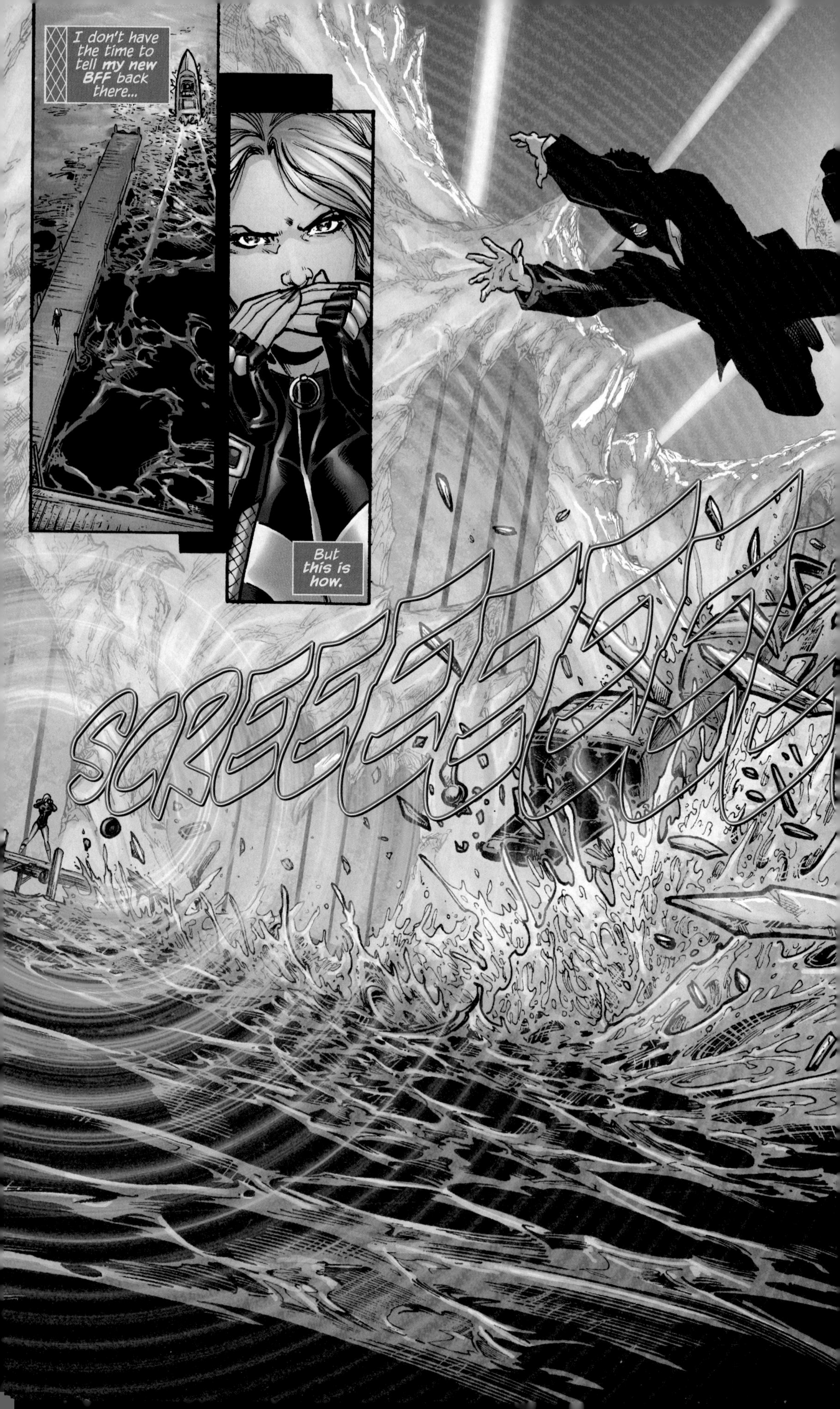
I don't have the time to tell my new BFF back there...
But this is how.
SCREEEEEEEEEEEEEEEEEEEEE

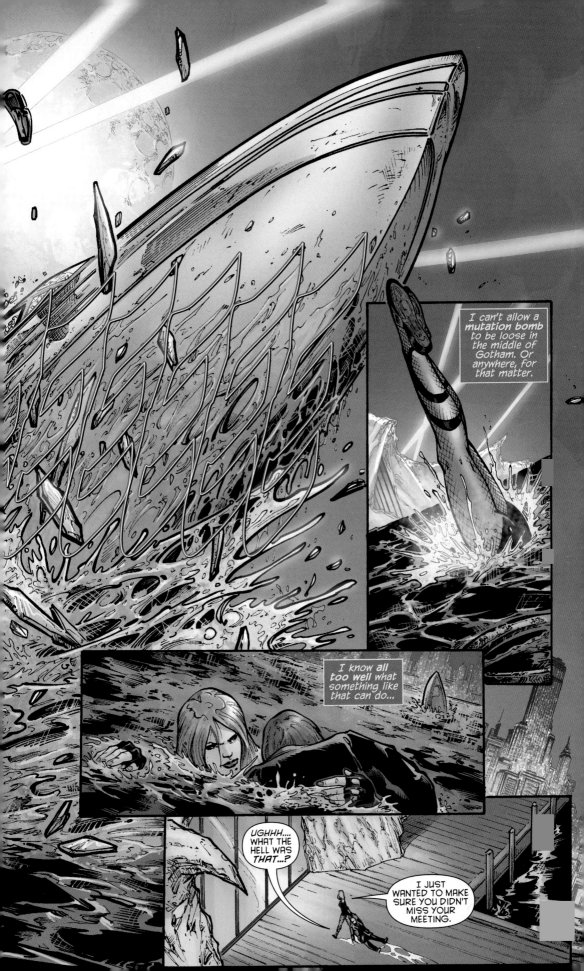

I can't allow a *mutation bomb* to be loose in the middle of *Gotham*. Or anywhere, for that matter.

I know *all too well* what something like that can do...

UGHHH.... WHAT THE HELL WAS *THAT*...?

I JUST WANTED TO MAKE SURE YOU DIDN'T MISS YOUR MEETING.

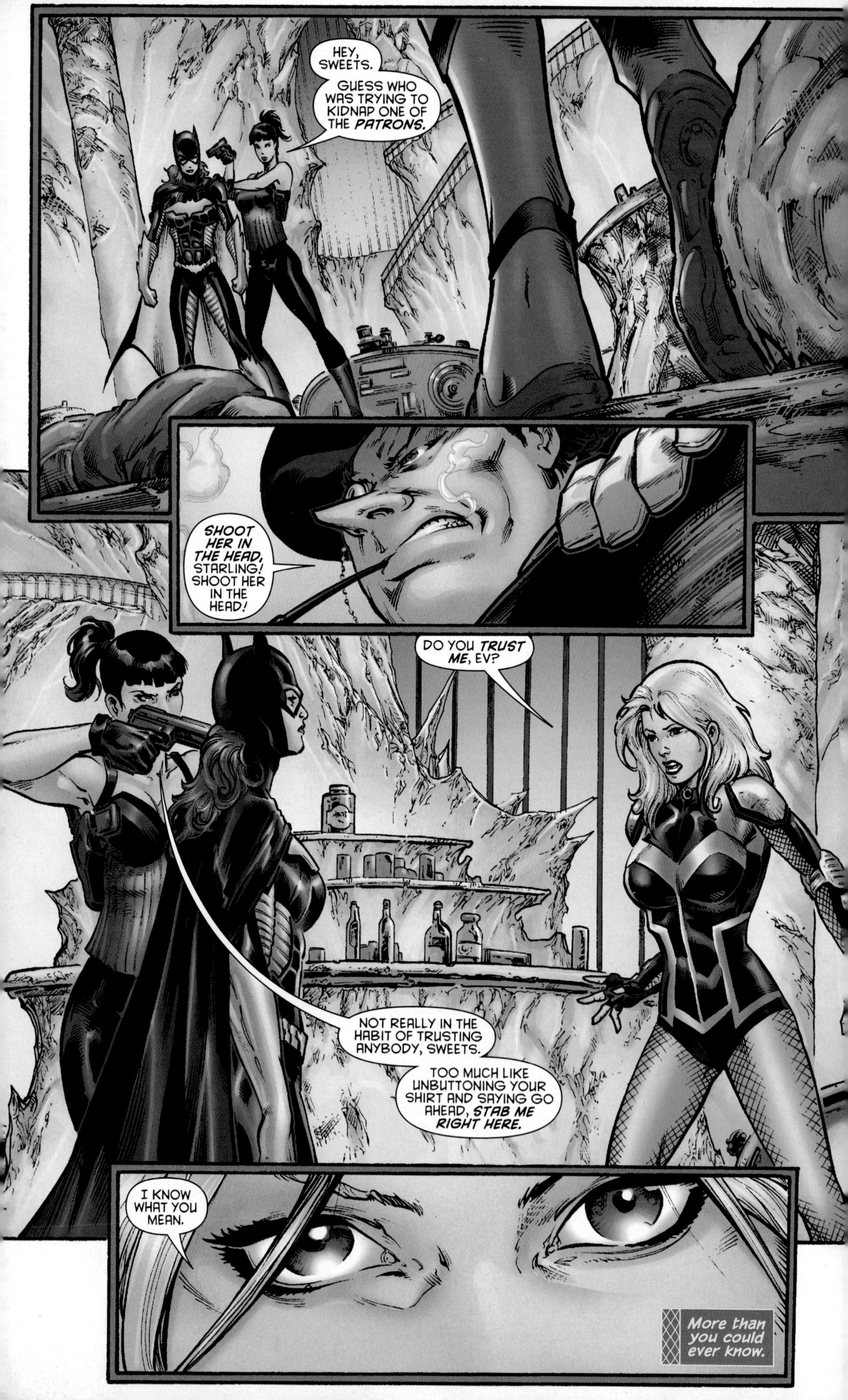
HEY, SWEETS.
GUESS WHO WAS TRYING TO KIDNAP ONE OF THE PATRONS.
SHOOT HER IN THE HEAD, STARLING! SHOOT HER IN THE HEAD!
DO YOU TRUST ME, EV?
NOT REALLY IN THE HABIT OF TRUSTING ANYBODY, SWEETS.
TOO MUCH LIKE UNBUTTONING YOUR SHIRT AND SAYING GO AHEAD, STAB ME RIGHT HERE.
I KNOW WHAT YOU MEAN.
More than you could ever know.

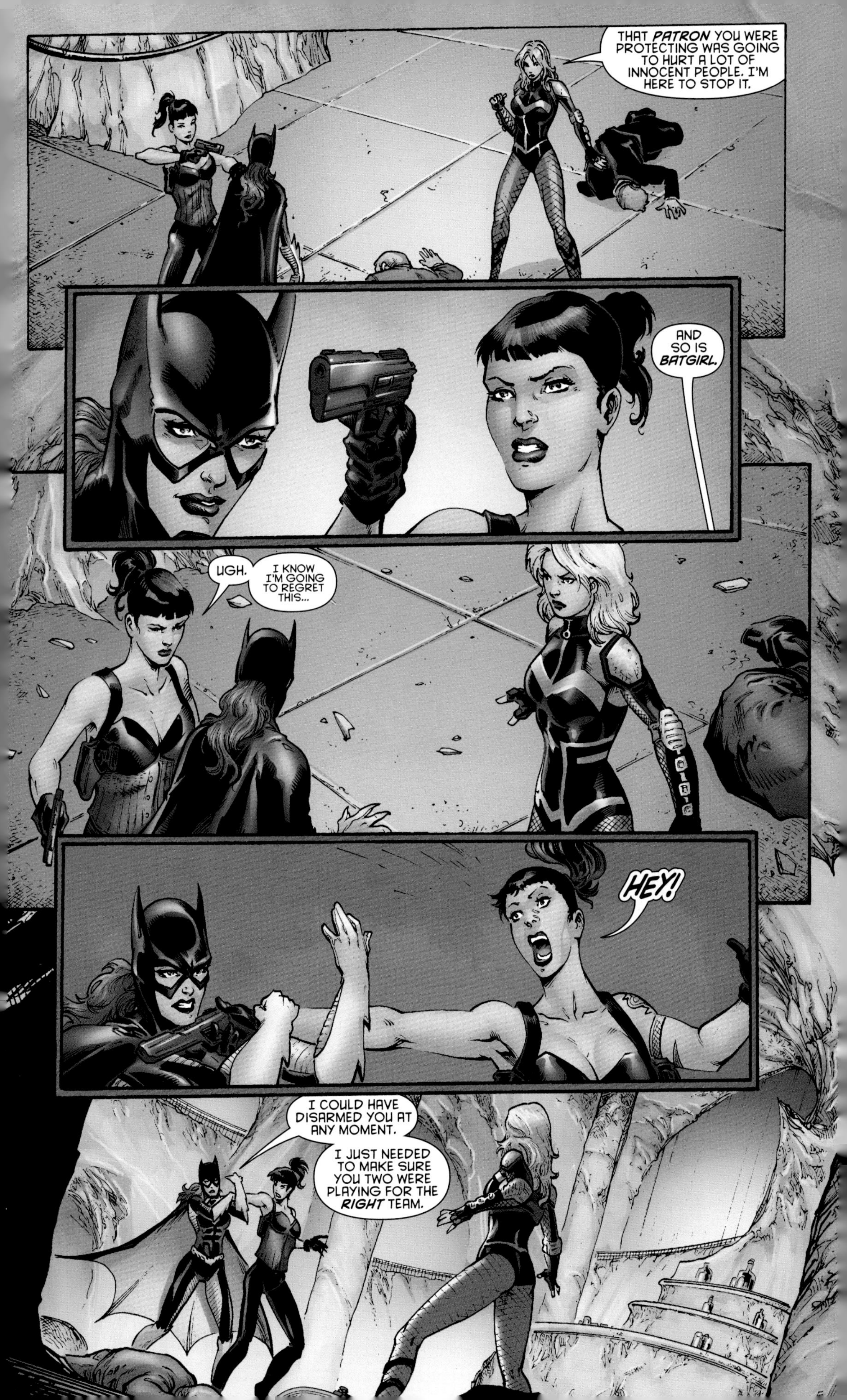

THAT PATRON YOU WERE PROTECTING WAS GOING TO HURT A LOT OF INNOCENT PEOPLE. I'M HERE TO STOP IT.
AND SO IS BATGIRL.
UGH.
I KNOW I'M GOING TO REGRET THIS...
HEY!
I COULD HAVE DISARMED YOU AT ANY MOMENT.
I JUST NEEDED TO MAKE SURE YOU TWO WERE PLAYING FOR THE RIGHT TEAM.

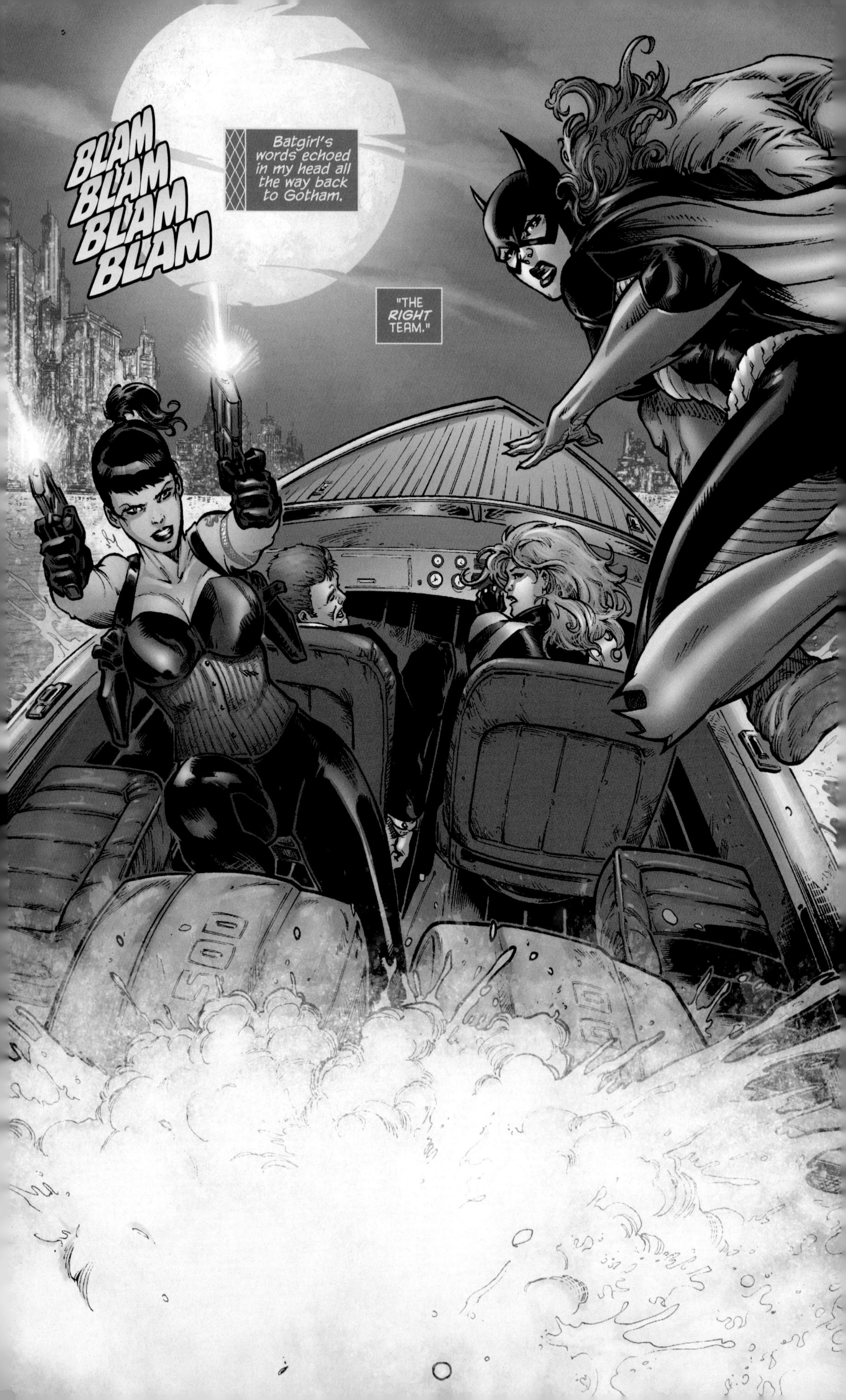
BLAM
BLAM
BLAM
BLAM
Batgirl's words echoed in my head all the way back to Gotham.
"THE RIGHT TEAM."

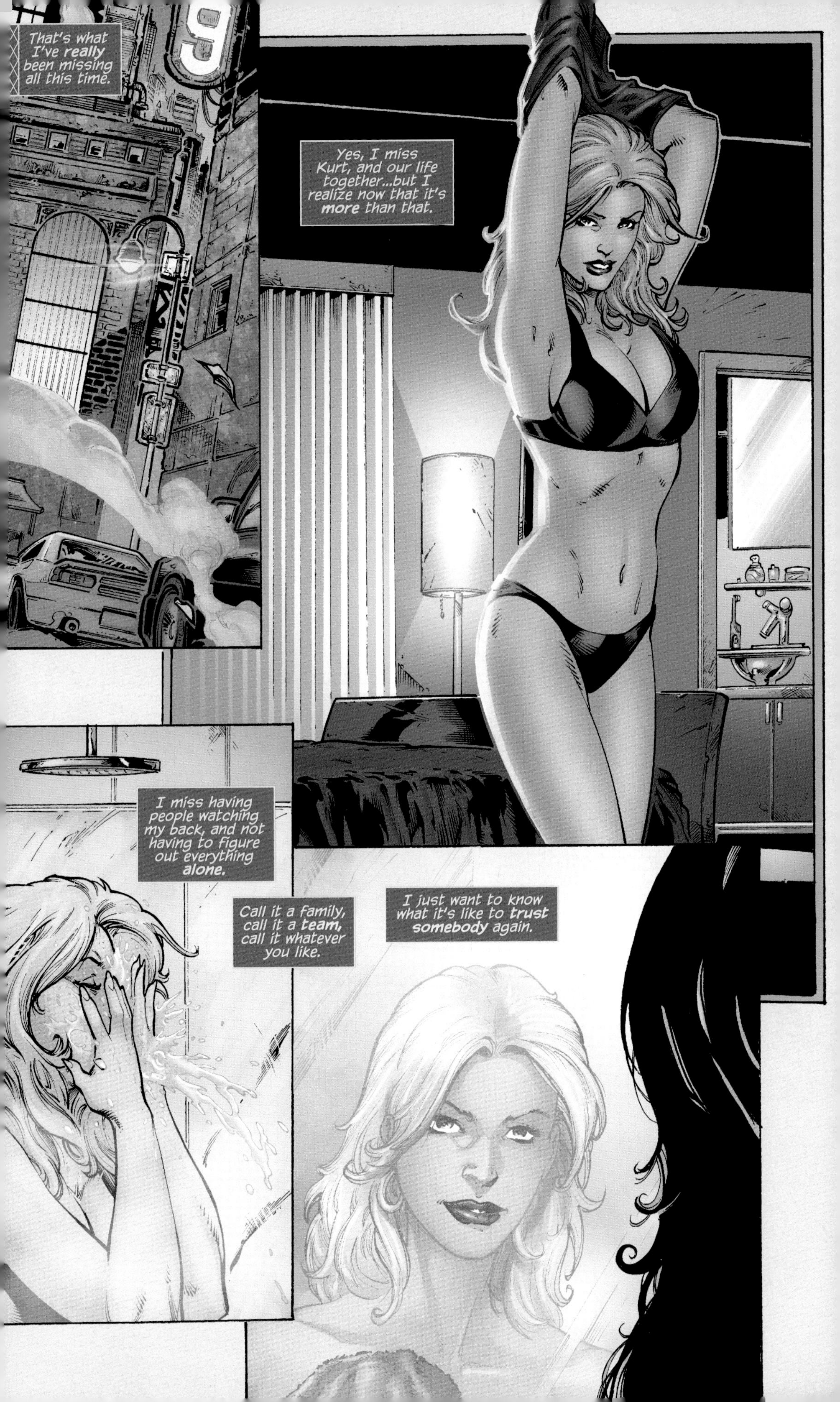

That's what I've really been missing all this time.
Yes, I miss Kurt, and our life together...but I realize now that it's more than that.
I miss having people watching my back, and not having to figure out everything alone.
Call it a family, call it a team, call it whatever you like.
I just want to know what it's like to trust somebody again.

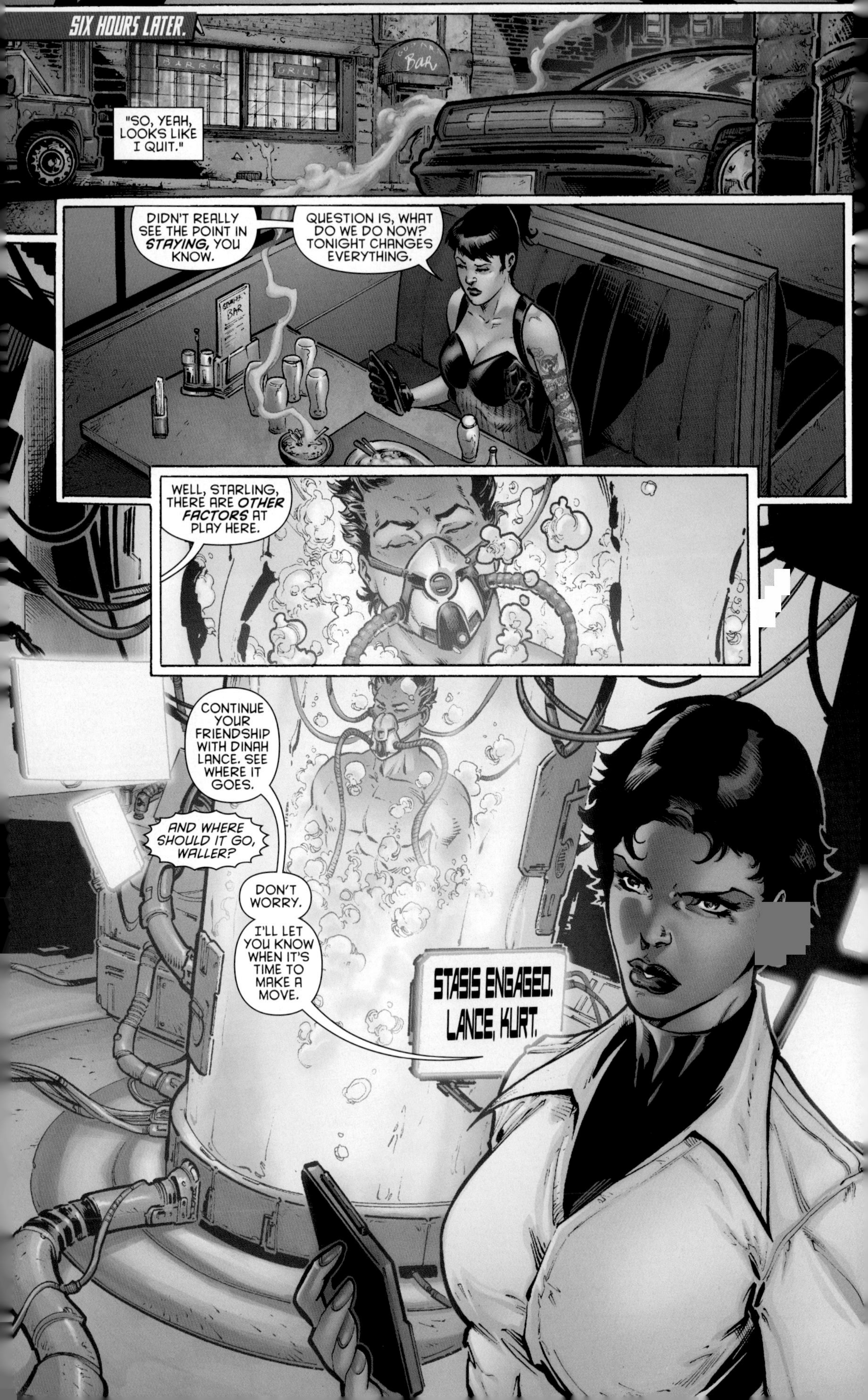
SIX HOURS LATER.
BAR
"SO, YEAH, LOOKS LIKE I QUIT."
DIDN'T REALLY SEE THE POINT IN STAYING, YOU KNOW.
QUESTION IS, WHAT DO WE DO NOW? TONIGHT CHANGES EVERYTHING.
WELL, STARLING, THERE ARE OTHER FACTORS AT PLAY HERE.
CONTINUE YOUR FRIENDSHIP WITH DINAH LANCE. SEE WHERE IT GOES.
AND WHERE SHOULD IT GO, WALLER?
DON'T WORRY.
I'LL LET YOU KNOW WHEN IT'S TIME TO MAKE A MOVE.
STASIS ENGAGED. LANCE, KURT.

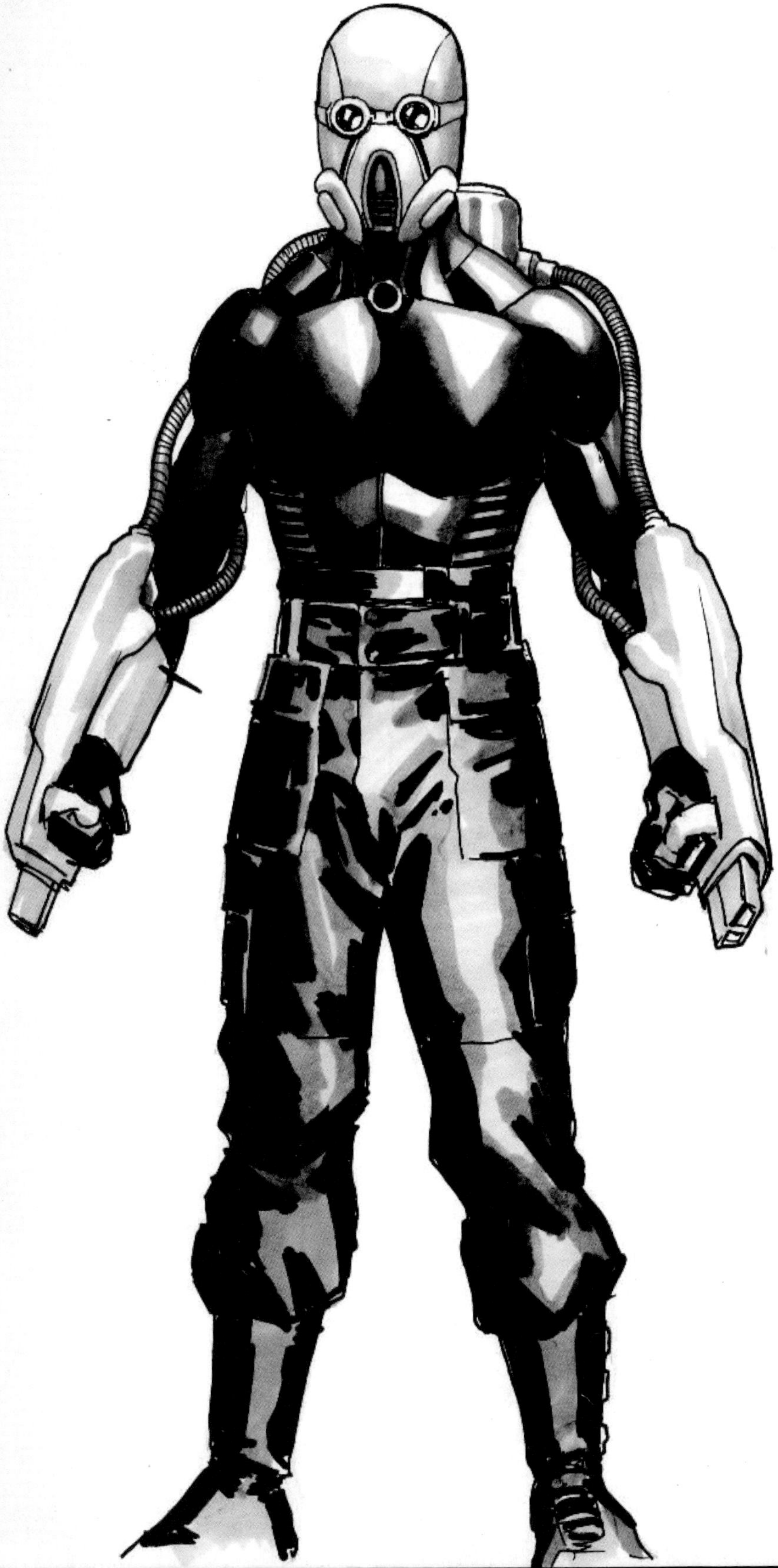

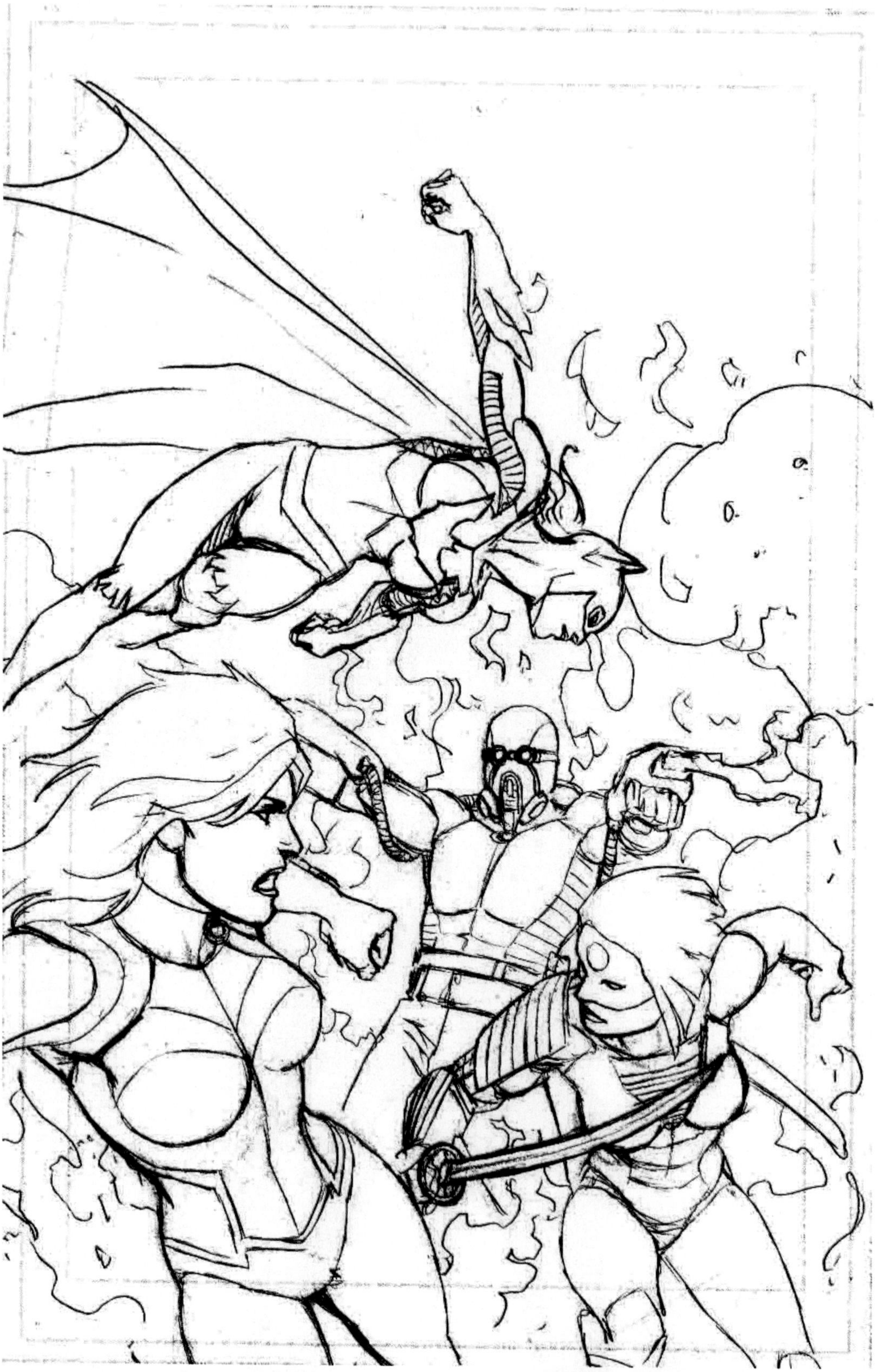

Cover issue #8 sketch by Jesus Saiz

Cover issue #9 sketches by Jesus Saiz

Cover issue #10 sketches by Travel Foreman

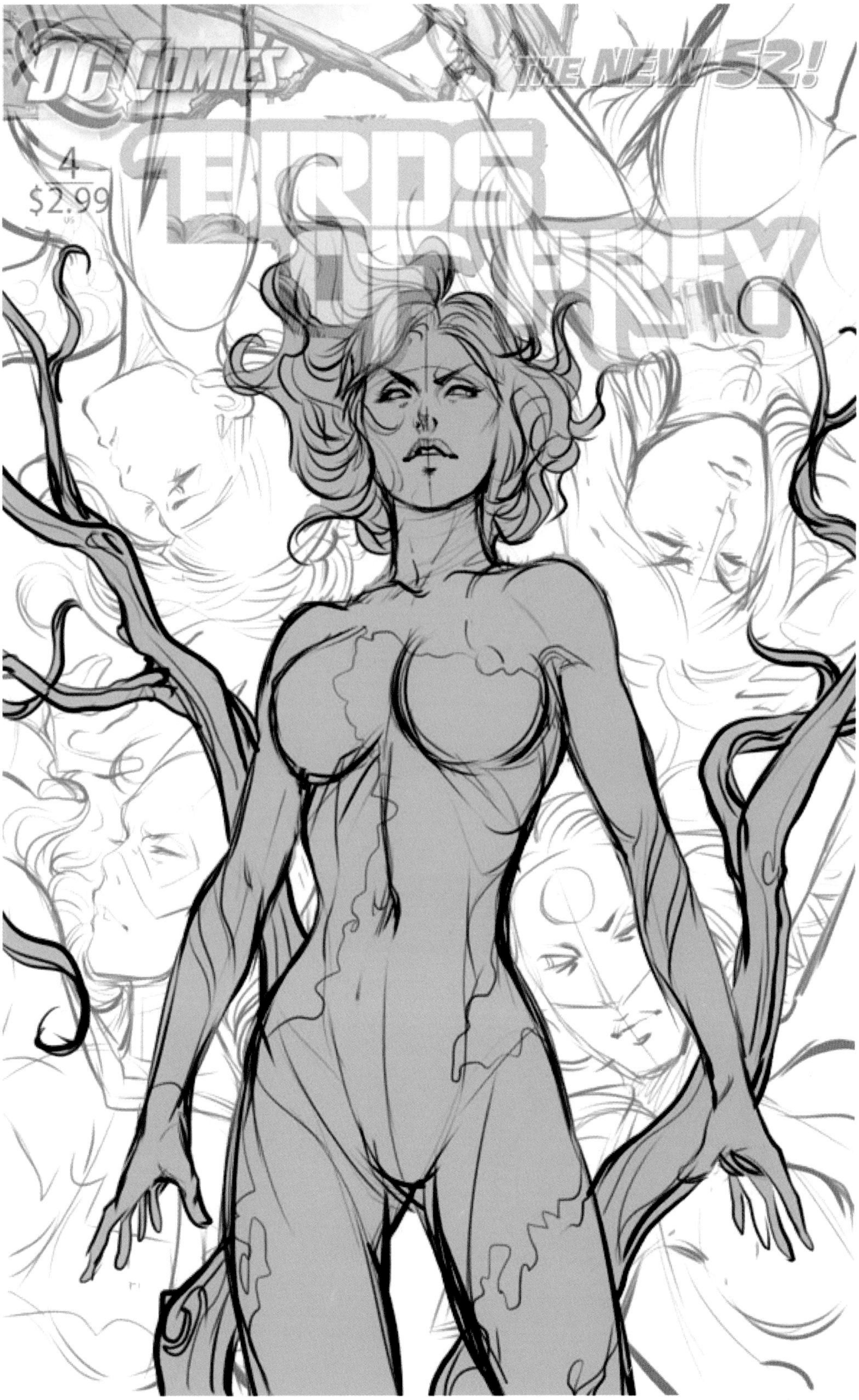
DC COMICS
THE NEW 52!
4
$2.99
US
BIRDS OF PREY

Cover issue #11 sketch by Stanley "Artgerm" Lau

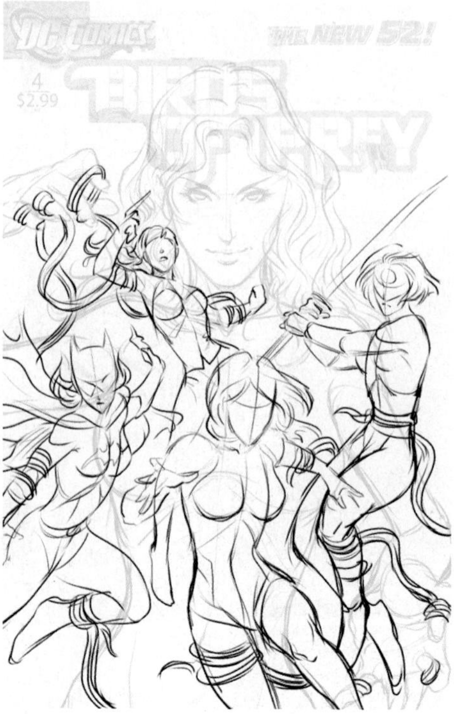
DC COMICS
THE NEW 52!
4
$2.99

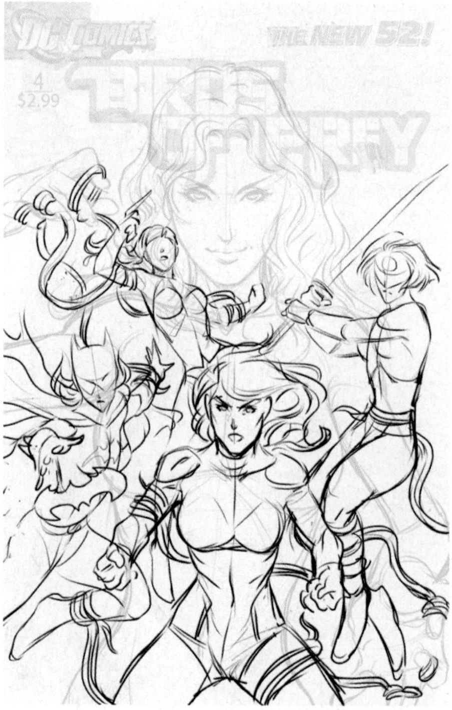
DC COMICS
THE NEW 52!
4
$2.99

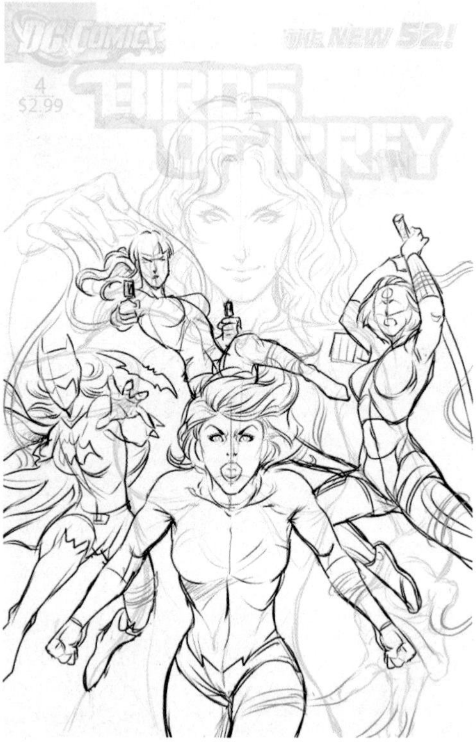
DC COMICS
THE NEW 52!
4
$2.99

Cover issue #12 sketches by Stanley "Artgerm" Lau

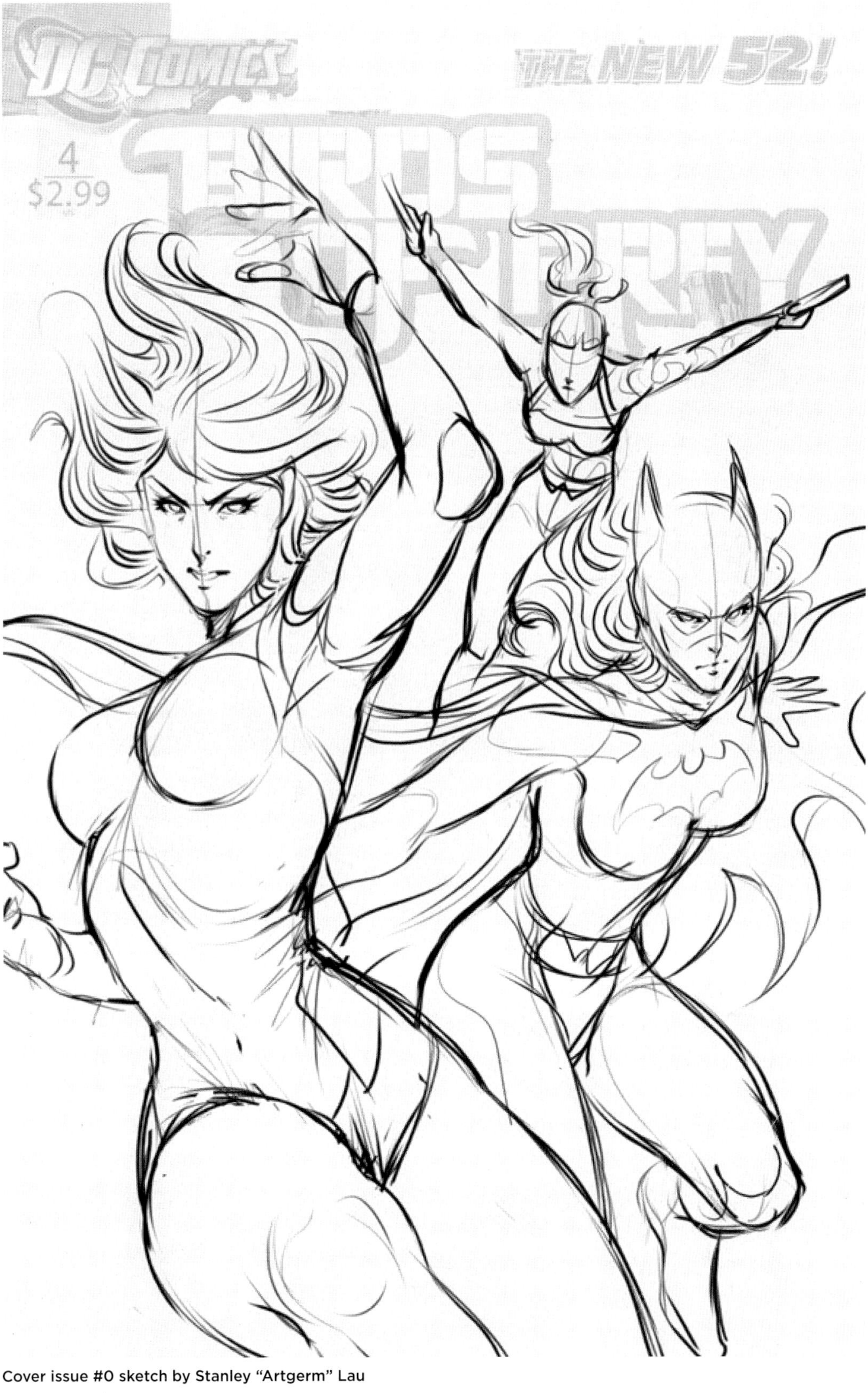
DC COMICS
THE NEW 52!
4
$2.99

Cover issue #0 sketch by Stanley "Artgerm" Lau

BIRDS OF PREY

EARLY SKETCHES BY TRAVEL FOREMAN

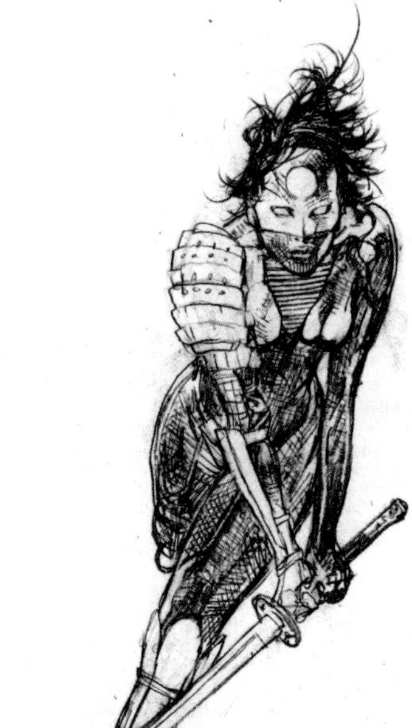

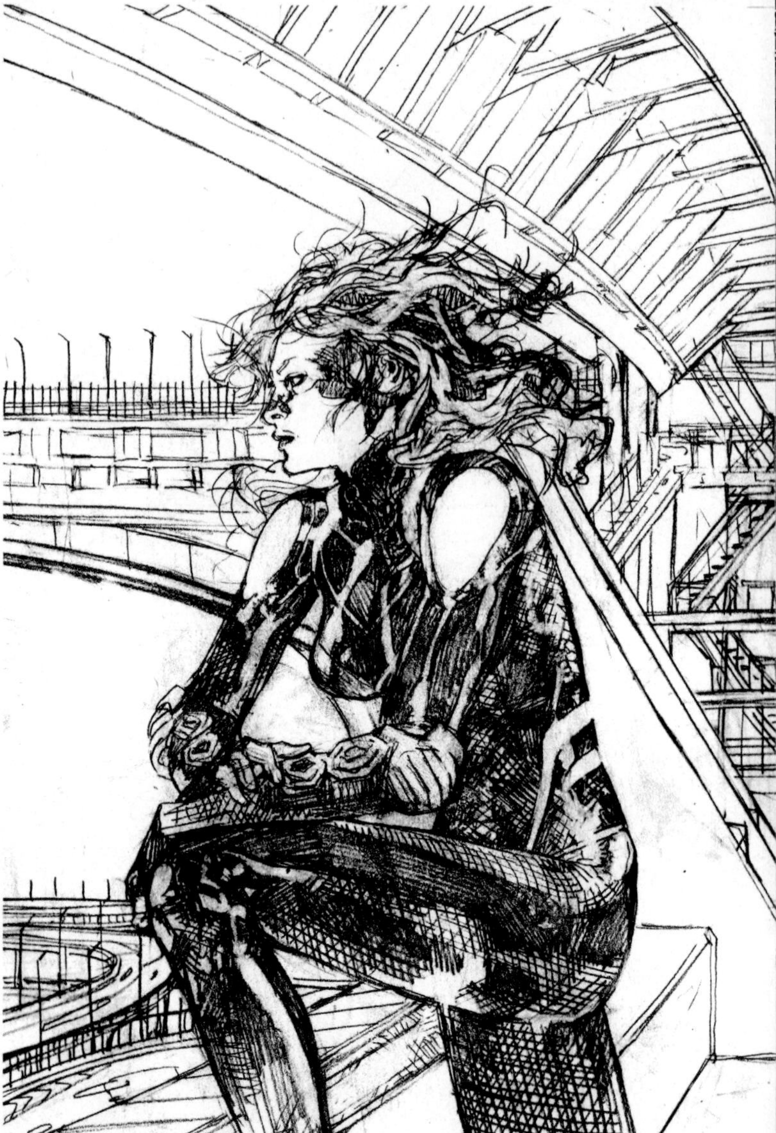

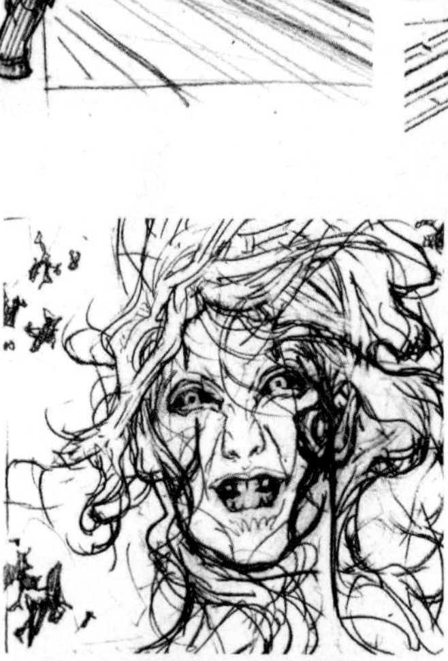

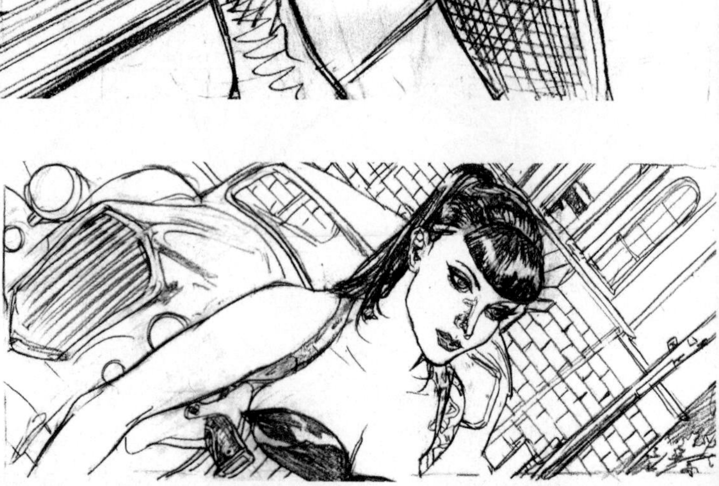

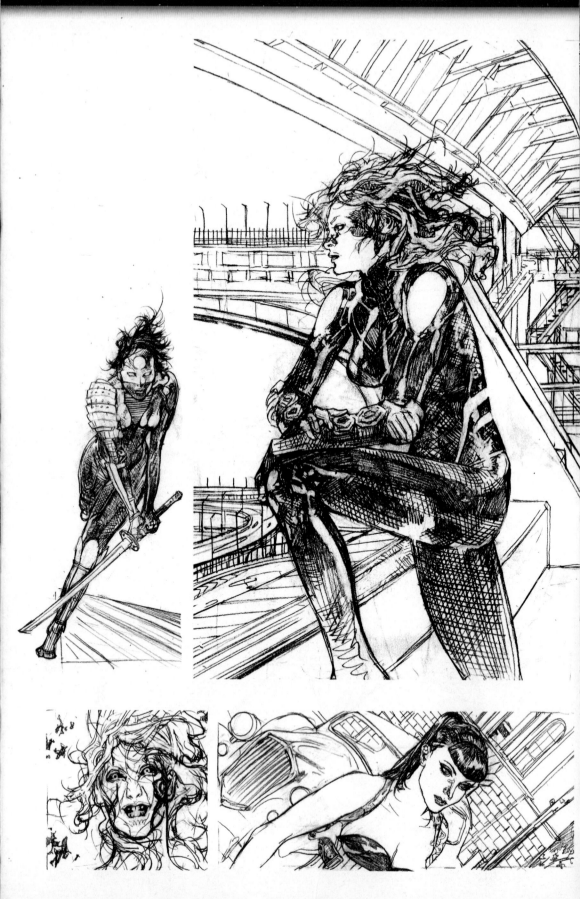